Advocacy for Paralegals

Arlene Blatt, LLB
JoAnn Kurtz, LLB

2009
Emond Montgomery Publications
Toronto, Canada

Emond Montgomery Publications Limited
60 Shaftesbury Avenue
Toronto ON M4T 1A3
http://www.emp.ca/highered

Printed in Canada.
Reprinted July 2013.

We acknowledge the financial support of the Government of Canada through the Canada Book Fund for our publishing activities.

The events and characters depicted in this book are fictitious. Any similarity to actual persons, living or dead, is purely coincidental.

Acquisitions and development editor: Bernard Sandler
Marketing manager: Christine Davidson
Director, sales and marketing, higher education: Kevin Smulan
Copy editor: Anita Levin
Proofreader: David Handelsman
Text designer and typesetter: Tara Wells
Indexer: Paula Pike
Cover designer: John Vegter

Library and Archives Canada Cataloguing in Publication

Blatt, Arlene
Advocacy for paralegals / Arlene Blatt, JoAnn Kurtz.

Includes index.
ISBN 978-1-55239-292-8

1. Trial practice—Canada. 2. Legal assistants—Canada. I. Title.

KE8422.B53 2009 347.71'075 C2008-907581-1
KF8915.B53 2009

To Leonard and Felicie Blatt

To Ely, Max, Jacob, and Danny Henry

Contents

PART V FINAL PREPARATION

PART VI ETHICAL ISSUES IN ADVOCACY

APPENDIXES

Acknowledgments

We would like to thank the following people for their help in writing this book: The Honourable M. Donald Godfrey of the Superior Court of Justice—Small Claims Court and His Worship Justice of the Peace Luigi Muraca of the Ontario Court of Justice, both of whom allowed us to observe them in court and then kindly took the time to meet with us and answer our questions; and Jodi Feldman, Deputy Judge of the Small Claims Court, Jason Lewis, licensed paralegal, and Linda Pasternak, Program Coordinator of Seneca College's Paralegal Diploma Program, each of whom met with us to answer questions.

Preface

This text is designed to help paralegals prepare and present a case before a court or tribunal. The text starts with a discussion of advocacy and an overview of the litigation process. It then takes students through the parts of a trial or hearing and tells them how to prepare for each of those parts. The text then moves on to a discussion of final preparation for the trial or hearing and concludes with an examination of ethical issues in advocacy. While the text makes specific reference to courts and tribunals in Ontario only and to Ontario rules of professional conduct, the general principles herein apply throughout Canada.

The Law Society of Upper Canada assumed responsibility for Ontario paralegal regulation and licensing in May 2007, and the first paralegal licences were issued in mid-2008.

Ontario law authorizes licensed paralegals to represent people

- in Small Claims Court,
- in the Ontario Court of Justice under the *Provincial Offences Act*,
- charged with summary conviction offences where the maximum penalty does not exceed six months' imprisonment, and
- before administrative tribunals, including the Financial Services Commission of Ontario.

All paralegals who apply for a paralegal licence after June 30, 2010 must have graduated from a legal services program accredited by the Law Society of Upper Canada.

This text covers the competencies required by the Law Society of Upper Canada in the Advocacy portion of an accredited paralegal education program, and deals with advocacy before the courts and tribunals before which licensed paralegals are permitted to appear.

Arlene Blatt, LLB
JoAnn Kurtz, LLB
January 2009

PART I

Introduction

CHAPTER 1

Advocacy and the Litigation Process

When you read a case report it is often hard to imagine that the case involves real people with a real dispute, whether civil or criminal, that ended up going to trial. A case report sets out the judge's decision, which he or she arrives at by applying the relevant law to the facts of the case. While this process may sound simple, it is not. The parties to the case—the plaintiff and the defendant in a civil case, and the Crown and the defence in a criminal case—typically disagree about the facts of the case. This disagreement results in a trial and, after hearing the conflicting evidence of both parties, the judge must determine which version to believe—in other words, what the facts of the case are. It is only after the judge makes his or her findings of fact that he or she can then apply the relevant law and come to a decision.

It is helpful to look at an example of a case in order to understand how the facts in an actual dispute are dealt with through the litigation process. See Box 1.1 for the facts of a civil dispute, which will be referred to as the Kitchen Renovation Case.

BOX 1.1

The Kitchen Renovation Case

Tina Fey and her husband, Tommy, hired Baldwin Brothers Construction to make some minor renovations to the kitchen in their home for a total contract price of $7,500. The work is now completed but the Feys and the Baldwins have a disagreement about payment for the installation of three pot lights. Tina and Tommy claim that the contract price included the installation of all necessary lights in the kitchen. Baldwin Brothers Construction, on the other hand, claims that the contract required them to install five pot lights only, and that the three additional pot lights were installed at the request of Tommy as an extra to be paid for separately. Tina and Tommy have paid the original contract price but refuse to pay any more. ◇

The parties cannot resolve this disagreement, so Baldwin Brothers Construction has started a Small Claims Court action claiming $750 for the cost of supplying and installing the three disputed pot lights.

At the trial of this case, the judge must decide whether to grant judgment to the plaintiff, Baldwin Brothers Construction (Alec Baldwin and Stephen Baldwin, carrying on business as Baldwin Brothers Construction), for the $750. The first part of the decision-making process is to determine what exactly the parties agreed to. Of course, the judge was not present when the contract was entered into, so he or she must make this decision based on the evidence presented by the parties in court.

As often happens, the parties in our case did not have a written contract. Tina Fey and Alec Baldwin were the only people present when the oral contract was made, and they each have a very different understanding of what they agreed to. The judge will listen to each party's retelling of the events and choose which version to believe. Sometimes the parties' versions of events differ because one of them is lying, but more often their versions differ simply because they remember the events differently. So, how does a judge choose between the different stories of two honest witnesses? The judge will believe the story that makes more sense to the judge—the one that is more likely to have happened. It is the role of the advocate to present the client's story in the more persuasive—more believable—way.

After determining the facts of the case, the judge will arrive at his or her decision by applying the relevant law to the facts. It is also the role of the advocate to advise the judge of the applicable law and to suggest to the judge how that law should be applied to the facts so that the advocate's client wins.

Advocacy is the term used to describe the process of presenting a case or defence at a trial or hearing before a civil court, a criminal court, or an administrative tribunal. An **advocate** is a person who pleads the cause of another before a court or tribunal. Advocates are often lawyers but, at tribunals and lower-level courts, paralegals may also act as advocates.

To appreciate the role of advocacy in the trial or hearing process, it is important to understand the relationship of advocacy to substantive law, procedural law, and the law of evidence.

Substantive law defines legal rights and obligations. Substantive law can be divided into a number of categories, such as contract law, tort law, family law, real estate law, and criminal law. It is substantive law that determines whether you have a civil cause of action or a defence to a civil action. It is also substantive law that defines the elements of a criminal offence and the defences available to that offence. Substantive law also determines what facts you must establish to constitute your claim or defence. The Kitchen Renovation Case involves the substantive law of contract.

Procedural law, both criminal and civil, deals with the way in which a dispute first comes to a court or tribunal, and is then brought forward to a final resolution at a trial or hearing. Procedural law is for the most part concerned with what occurs before the actual trial or hearing, and after. In our example, the case is governed by the procedural law of the Small Claims Court.

You will not be successful in asserting your claim or defence when you get to trial unless you can establish the facts that support your claim or defence. The law of evidence deals with how the facts (as required by substantive law) are to be proved.

Advocacy has been described as both a science and an art. The key to successful advocacy is preparation, which is the science of advocacy. The art of advocacy lies in the performance. Some people are naturally better than others at public speaking, but this art can be developed. However, no amount of art can take the place of thorough preparation. If you go to court prepared and organized, and are polite, you will be way ahead of most paralegals (and perhaps some lawyers) you will meet in opposition.

Good advocacy does not mean that you will win every trial or hearing. There are some cases that you cannot win, no matter how good an advocate you are. But you never want to lose a case that you should win—that is where good advocacy comes in.

This book is not about evidence or about civil or criminal procedure. It assumes that you already have a basic understanding of those areas and an understanding of substantive law. This book will teach you the skills necessary to become a good advocate. The book starts with an overview of the litigation process. It then takes you through the steps necessary to prepare and present a case at a trial or hearing, and concludes with a look at the ethical issues in advocacy.

Because this book is written for paralegals, it deals with advocacy before the courts and tribunals in which paralegals may lawfully appear. Trials can involve civil or criminal matters, and hearings can also take place before administrative tribunals. The advocacy skills involved in all of these trials and hearings are the same. While this book touches upon some specific aspects of criminal and administrative advocacy, its focus is primarily on civil cases.

REVIEW QUESTIONS

1. What is advocacy?
2. What is an advocate?
3. What is substantive law?
4. What is procedural law?
5. What is the law of evidence?
6. What is the key to successful advocacy?

PART II

Overview of the Litigation Process

CHAPTER 2

Steps in the Litigation Process

The focus of this book is advocacy at a trial or hearing, but the foundation for good advocacy starts at the earliest stages of the dispute. It is therefore necessary to understand the steps that take place in the litigation process, both before and during the actual trial or hearing.

This chapter provides an overview of the pre-trial procedures of the Small Claims Court, the Provincial Offences Court, and one administrative tribunal—the Landlord and Tenant Board.

THE CIVIL LITIGATION PROCESS: SMALL CLAIMS COURT

Paralegals may appear on civil trials before the Small Claims Court only. The Small Claims Court handles civil disputes involving money or personal property to a maximum of $10,000.* The forms and procedures of the Small Claims Court are simplified to allow parties to represent themselves, but parties often choose to retain a paralegal or lawyer, especially for more complicated disputes.

The parties to a Small Claims Court action are the **plaintiff** and the **defendant**. A Small Claims Court action is started when the plaintiff prepares and files a **plaintiff's claim** with the court, setting out the nature of the plaintiff's case against the defendant, together with any documents that support the claim, such as an invoice, a contract, or a letter. The plaintiff pays a filing fee to the court, and the court issues the plaintiff's claim by assigning a court file number and stamping the original claim form. The plaintiff must then **serve** the defendant with the claim and supporting documents by providing him or her with a copy. A defendant who wishes to dispute the plaintiff's claim has 20 days in which to serve the plaintiff with a **defence**, setting out the nature of the defendant's defence against the plaintiff's claim, together with any documents that support the defence, and file it with the court. The plaintiff's claim and the defence documents are referred to as the **pleadings** in the case. Pleadings are court documents that set out the facts on which each party relies in support of his or her claim or defence and are designed to provide the other side with notice of the claim or defence.

* The monetary jurisdiction of the Small Claims Court is being increased to $25,000, effective January 1, 2010.

A **settlement conference** is held in every defended action in the Small Claims Court before a judge (who will not be the judge at trial), a referee, or another court-appointed person. The settlement conference, which is scheduled by the court, is an informal and confidential meeting during which the parties try to resolve or simplify the issues that are in dispute. As stated in rule 13.03(1) of the Rules of the Small Claims Court, the purposes of a settlement conference are

- to resolve or narrow the issues in the action,
- to expedite the disposition of the action,
- to encourage settlement of the action,
- to assist the parties in effective preparation for trial, and
- to provide full disclosure between the parties of the relevant facts and evidence.

At the conference, the parties are required to disclose all the important facts and evidence about the case, and must therefore bring all relevant documents that relate to the case, such as receipts, estimates, contracts, letters, and photographs. At the conference, the judge or referee will comment on the strengths and weaknesses of each party's case and encourage the parties to consider settling all or some of the issues. The parties must attend the settlement conference, but the witnesses do not attend. If either of the parties is represented by a lawyer or agent, the lawyer or agent may also attend, but the parties must still be there. If the parties cannot resolve the dispute at the settlement conference, they should request that the court set a date for trial.

THE CRIMINAL LITIGATION PROCESS: PROVINCIAL OFFENCES COURT

The Provincial Offences Court deals with charges under the *Provincial Offences Act*. **Provincial offences** are non-criminal offences arising under provincial statutes, such as the *Highway Traffic Act*. The most common of these are driving-related offences, such as speeding, careless driving, driving without insurance, driving while suspended, and failing to stop at a red light. Provincial Offences Court is relatively informal and some defendants represent themselves. However, the penalties for traffic offences can include fines, demerit points, and licence suspension. In addition, a conviction can result in higher insurance premiums. For these reasons, many people choose to retain a lawyer or a paralegal to represent them.

The parties in a provincial offence matter are Her Majesty the Queen (or the Crown) and the defendant. The provincial offence process (for an offence under Part I of the *Provincial Offences Act*) starts with the issuance of an **offence notice** or **summons**, depending on the nature of the offence. A defendant who wishes to dispute the charge must schedule a trial. In some municipalities this can be done by mail; in others it is necessary to file a **notice of intention to appear** form with the appropriate provincial offences office.

The defendant is entitled to disclosure of the evidence that the Crown will be relying on at trial. The defendant requests disclosure by mail or fax to the Crown prosecutor handling the matter. The prosecutor should provide all relevant information, such as documents relied on, witness statements, and police officers' notes. It is possible to request additional disclosure from the prosecutor if important details are missing from the initial disclosure that are essential for the preparation of the defence.

ADMINISTRATIVE TRIBUNAL PROCESS: THE LANDLORD AND TENANT BOARD

An **administrative tribunal** is a quasi-judicial body created by statute law to deal with matters arising under specific statutes. For example, the Landlord and Tenant Board is created by the *Residential Tenancies Act, 2006* to administer the statute and to deal with disputes between residential landlords and tenants. Other administrative tribunals are the Social Benefits Tribunal, the Financial Services Commission of Ontario, the Assessment Review Board, and the Ontario Municipal Board. In this chapter and the next, the Landlord and Tenant Board is used to illustrate the pre-hearing and hearing process before an administrative tribunal.

At the Landlord and Tenant Board (the Board), either the landlord or the tenant may make an application to the Board, and a hearing will be scheduled before a member of the Board. In a proceeding before the Board, the party who files the application is called the **applicant** and the other party is called the **respondent**.

The applicant files an **application** with the Board. The Board will issue a **notice of hearing**, which must be served on the respondent together with the application. A respondent who wishes to defend an application may simply appear at the hearing and does not have to serve and file any form of dispute.

REVIEW QUESTIONS

1. What is the monetary jurisdiction of the Small Claims Court?
2. Who are the parties to a Small Claims Court action?
3. How is a Small Claims Court action started?
4. What must a defendant do to dispute the plaintiff's claim?
5. What are pleadings?
6. What is a Small Claims Court settlement conference, and what is its purpose?
7. What matters are dealt with by the Provincial Offences Court?
8. What are provincial offences? Provide some examples.
9. Who are the parties in a provincial offence matter?
10. How is the provincial offence process started for an offence under Part I of the *Provincial Offences Act*?
11. What must a defendant do if he or she wishes to dispute a charge under the *Provincial Offences Act*?

12. How does a defendant request disclosure of the evidence that the Crown will be relying on at trial?
13. What is an administrative tribunal?
14. Provide some examples of administrative tribunals.
15. Who are the parties to a proceeding before the Landlord and Tenant Board?
16. Briefly describe the process by which a matter is brought before the Landlord and Tenant Board.

CHAPTER 3

The Courtroom Experience

The trial or hearing is the last step in the litigation process. Appearing at a trial or hearing can be a frightening prospect for a new and inexperienced advocate. Even an experienced advocate may feel intimidated when appearing before a particular court or tribunal for the first time. It is very helpful to gain some familiarity with the courtroom procedure at the court or tribunal before your first appearance there. The best way to gain that familiarity is to go to the court or tribunal and watch.

This chapter discusses the structures of trials generally, and then focuses on the in-court procedure of the Small Claims Court, the Provincial Offences Court, and the Landlord and Tenant Board (as an example of an administrative tribunal).

THE STRUCTURE OF A TRIAL OR HEARING

A trial or hearing has three parts:

1. opening
2. evidence
3. closing.

At the opening of the trial or hearing, each party may be asked by the judge or other decision-maker to summarize what the case is about and what issues are in dispute.

The parties will then present evidence so that the decision-maker—a judge, justice of the peace, or other adjudicator—can determine the facts of the case; in other words, decide what actually happened between the parties. Evidence is presented by witnesses—the parties to the case and others with direct knowledge relevant to the case.

After all the evidence has been presented to the court, each party will have the opportunity to make a closing argument in which he or she summarizes the evidence that supports his or her case, the relevant law, and the reasons why the decision-maker should resolve the dispute in that party's favour.

SMALL CLAIMS COURT

As stated in Chapter 2, the Small Claims Court handles civil disputes involving money or personal property up to a maximum of $10,000.* Matters are dealt with by a judge, who is to be addressed as "Your Honour."

Arriving at Court

Small Claims Court trials usually start at 10:00 a.m. An Event Activity Report is posted on a bulletin board just outside the courtrooms. This report lists all matters scheduled for the day, and sets out the courtrooms in which each matter will take place. If you arrive early and the courtroom is locked, sit in the waiting area until the clerk announces that the courtroom is open.

As you enter the courtroom, the elevated judge's bench is usually directly ahead of you at the front of the courtroom. The court clerk sits at a table in front of the judge's desk facing the courtroom. Usually, the witness box is to the judge's left (on your right as you face the judge). There are also two counsel tables, one on each side, facing the judge. Usually, the table on the right as you face the judge is for the plaintiff, and the one on the left is for the defendant. See Figure 3.1.

After you enter the courtroom, go up to the clerk. He or she will ask you to identify yourself and the case on which you are appearing, how many witnesses you intend to call during the trial, and the estimated length of time your case will take. After speaking to the clerk you should sit in the gallery, the seating area at the back of the courtroom, until your case is called. If court is already in session when you arrive, enter the courtroom quietly and sit down in the gallery. If there is a break in the proceedings, you can identify yourself and your case to the clerk. Otherwise, wait until your case is called.

At 10:00, the clerk will leave the courtroom to go and get the judge. When the clerk returns, she or he will tell everyone to stand up, and the judge will then enter the courtroom. Once the judge sits, he or she will tell everyone to be seated. The judge will then go through the list of scheduled matters to determine who is present for each matter. Judges typically deal with consent matters, adjournments, and assessments or damages before dealing with trials. If a party to a case is not in the courtroom, the judge may hold the matter down for half an hour, after which time the judge will proceed with the trial in the party's absence.

When your case is called, walk to the counsel table at the front of the courtroom. As stated previously, the plaintiff's counsel table is usually on the right side of the courtroom (when facing the judge), and the defendant's counsel table is on the left. The tables usually have signs indicating where the plaintiff and the defendant should sit. Before your case begins, the judge or the clerk may ask you to state and spell your name. The judge may also ask you the capacity in which you are appearing—as counsel, agent, or student-at-law. Remember to stand whenever you speak to the judge and whenever he or she leaves the courtroom.

---

* Increasing to $25,000 on January 1, 2010.

The Trial

There is usually no formal opening statement in Small Claims Court. However, if the judge is unclear about the issues, he or she may ask you to summarize what your case is about and to identify the issues. For example, the judge may ask you, "What exactly is your claim/defence?" It is very helpful to prepare an opening statement so that you can respond to any questions the judge may have.

The parties then present their evidence by calling witnesses to testify as to the facts of the case. The clerk records the testimony of each witness. The plaintiff's advocate presents the plaintiff's evidence first. The judge asks the advocate to call his or her first witness, and the witness proceeds to the witness box. The clerk will ask the witness to state his or her name and spell it, and will ask the witness, "Do you know that it is a criminal offence to intentionally give false evidence in a judicial proceeding? Do you solemnly promise to tell the truth in this proceeding?" Once the witness is sworn in, the plaintiff's advocate conducts his or her **direct examination** of the witness by asking questions of that witness. The defendant's advocate then conducts his or her **cross-examination** of the witness. At the end of the cross-examination, the plaintiff's advocate is given an opportunity to conduct a **re-examination** of the witness—limited to questions about new issues raised in the cross-examination. The judge may then have some questions for the witness. At the end of the questioning, the witness is excused and may return to his or her seat in the courtroom. This process is repeated for each of the plaintiff's witnesses.

At the end of the plaintiff's evidence, the defendant's advocate presents the defendant's evidence. Each of the defendant's witnesses is sworn in, after which the defendant's advocate conducts his or her direct examination, followed by cross-examination by the plaintiff's advocate, re-examination by the defendant's advocate and, possibly, questioning by the judge.

At the end of the defendant's evidence, the plaintiff's advocate is given the opportunity to present **reply** evidence to respond to new matters raised by the defendant during his or her case.

At the end of the evidence, the judge will usually ask each party's advocate to make a **closing argument** summarizing his or her case and discussing the relevant law. The plaintiff's advocate gives his or her closing argument first, followed by the defendant. After the defendant's closing argument, the plaintiff is given an opportunity to reply.

Once the closing arguments are completed, it is up to the judge to make a decision and render judgment. The judge may deliver his or her judgment immediately or after a brief recess. Occasionally, the judge will reserve his or her decision until a later date. The judge will **endorse** the decision on the court record. If there is a photocopier in the courtroom, the clerk will make a copy of the judge's endorsement and give it to the parties to take with them.

PROVINCIAL OFFENCES COURT

As stated in Chapter 2, the Provincial Offences Court deals with charges under the *Provincial Offences Act*. Matters are dealt with by a justice of the peace (JP), not a judge, who is addressed as "Your Worship."

Arriving at Court

When you arrive at the court, you will be required to go through security screening by court personnel, so it is important not to bring any weapons into the court, including pocket or miniature knives.

There are lists posted outside the courtrooms setting out the matters scheduled for the day. There are four "tiers"—9:00 a.m., 10:30 a.m., 1:30 p.m., and 3:00 p.m. The notice of trial will state the time of your trial and the courtroom number.

Approximately 15 minutes before court opens, there will be an announcement advising people who have a matter in the courtroom to enter. When you enter the courtroom, the elevated bench for the justice of the peace will usually be directly ahead of you at the front of the courtroom. The court clerk will sit at a table in front of the JP's desk, facing the courtroom. Usually, the witness box will be to the JP's left (on your right as you face the JP). There will also be two counsel tables, one on each side, facing the JP. The Crown (prosecutor) sits at the table on the right as you face the JP. The table on the left is for the defendant. See Figure 3.2.

When you enter the courtroom, go up to the clerk. He or she will ask you to identify yourself and the case on which you are appearing. You may also wish to speak to the Crown about your case to negotiate or **plea bargain**. After speaking to the clerk and Crown, sit in the gallery, the seating area at the back of the courtroom, until your case is called. There is also a seating area outside the courtroom where you can wait. Your case will be paged when it is reached by the court.

Stand when the JP arrives in the courtroom. Once the JP sits, he or she will tell everyone to be seated. The JP will deal with unopposed matters first, and then hear the trials.

The Trial

When your case is called, approach the counsel table and identify yourself. The JP may ask you the capacity in which you are appearing—as counsel, agent, or student-at-law. The clerk will read the charge and ask how your client pleads. If your client pleads not guilty, the trial will begin.

The Crown presents his or her case first, by calling witnesses to give evidence. The clerk asks each witness to state and spell his or her full name and to either swear on the Bible or affirm that the evidence to be given will be the truth. Witnesses may sit while giving evidence. Once the witness is sworn in, the Crown conducts his or her direct examination of the witness by asking questions of that witness. The defendant's advocate then conducts a cross-examination of the witness. At the end of the cross-examination, the Crown is given an opportunity to conduct a re-examination of the witness—limited to questions about new issues raised in the cross-examination. The JP may then have some questions for the witness. At the end of the questioning, the witness is excused and may return to his or her seat in the courtroom. This process is repeated for each of the Crown's witnesses.

At the end of the Crown's evidence, the defendant's advocate presents the defendant's evidence, if any. Each of the defendant's witnesses is sworn in, after which the defendant's advocate conducts his or her direct examination, followed by cross-examination by the Crown, re-examination by the defendant's advocate and, possibly, questioning by the JP.

After all the evidence has been given, the JP will ask both the defence and the prosecution to make closing arguments summarizing their cases and discussing the relevant law. The defendant's advocate speaks first. After the closing arguments, the JP makes a decision to convict or acquit, and gives reasons for that decision.

If the defendant is acquitted, he or she is free to leave the court. If the defendant is convicted, the JP may ask for submissions regarding the appropriate sentence to be given to the defendant.

LANDLORD AND TENANT BOARD

As stated in Chapter 2, the Landlord and Tenant Board (the Board) deals with disputes between residential landlords and tenants. Matters are dealt with by a member of the Board sitting as an adjudicator, who is addressed as either Mr. or Madam Adjudicator, Mr. or Madam Member, or Mr. or Ms. (last name).

Arriving at the Board

Your hearing will be scheduled for either the morning or the afternoon. Many hearings are scheduled for the same day and time, and everyone is required to arrive at the same time. The Board member decides in which order to hear cases, and it is possible that your case may not be called until much later than the time listed on your notice of hearing.

When you arrive at the tribunal on the day of your hearing, sign in with the clerk and then proceed to the appropriate hearing room. The hearing room is less formal than a courtroom. The adjudicator sits at the front of the room, and there are two counsel tables in front of him or her. Usually, the applicant's advocate sits at the table on the right (when facing the adjudicator), and the respondent's advocate sits at the one on the left. There is no clerk. Witnesses sit to the adjudicator's left. See Figure 3.3. Sit in the body of the hearing room until your case is called.

The adjudicator will introduce himself or herself and explain the hearing process. He or she will also discuss the mediation services available and encourage parties to attempt to resolve their dispute with the assistance of a staff mediator.

The adjudicator calls cases by referring to the name of the parties and the street address of the residential property. Short matters, such as consents, withdrawals, and adjournments, are typically dealt with first. Matters that require a hearing are called next, usually in order of their position on the list. Sometimes, the adjudicator will ask the parties to give an estimate of the expected length of time their case will take (depending on such matters as the complexity of issues and the number of witnesses). The adjudicator may then proceed to deal first with the matters that are expected to take the least amount of time, saving the longest cases for last.

The Hearing

When your case is called, move up to the appropriate counsel table. The adjudicator will ask both advocates to identify themselves and the capacity in which they are representing their clients—as counsel, agent, or student-at-law. Adjudicators sometimes require paralegals to provide the client's written authorization for the paralegal to appear on behalf of the party.

The applicant's advocate speaks first and starts by explaining why the applicant has made the application. He or she will then call witnesses to give evidence in support of the applicant's case. Each witness is sworn in by the adjudicator. Once the witness is sworn in, the applicant's advocate conducts his or her direct examination of the witness by asking questions of that witness. The respondent's advocate then conducts his or her cross-examination of the witness. At the end of the cross-examination, the applicant's advocate may be given an opportunity to conduct a re-examination of the witness—limited to questions about new issues raised in the cross-examination. The adjudicator may then have some questions for the witness. At the end of the questioning, the witness is excused and may return to his or her seat in the hearing room. This process is repeated for each of the applicant's witnesses.

After the applicant's case is finished, the respondent's advocate will summarize the respondent's side of the story and will then call witnesses in support of the respondent's case. Each of the respondent's witnesses is sworn in, after which the respondent's advocate conducts his or her direct examination, followed by cross-examination by the applicant's advocate, re-examination by the respondent's advocate, and, possibly, questioning by the adjudicator.

After all the evidence has been presented, each party is given the opportunity to make a closing argument. The applicant speaks first. The adjudicator will usually make a decision, or order, immediately at the end of the hearing. Sometimes, he or she may need more time to make a decision, in which case the final order will be mailed to all the parties.

REVIEW QUESTIONS

1. State the three parts of a trial, and briefly describe what happens during each part.
2. Who decides matters in the Small Claims Court and how should you address that person?
3. What do you speak to the clerk about when you arrive at Small Claims Court?
4. What should you do when the judge enters the courtroom?
5. In what order are Small Claims Court matters generally dealt with?
6. What should you do when your case is called in Small Claims Court?
7. Is there an opening statement in Small Claims Court?
8. How do the parties present their evidence in Small Claims Court?
9. What happens after the evidence of both parties has been presented in Small Claims Court?
10. When and how does the judge make his or her decision in a Small Claims Court case?
11. Who decides matters in the Provincial Offences Court, and how should you address that person?

12. Who should you speak to when you arrive at Provincial Offences Court, and why?
13. What should you do when the justice of the peace enters the courtroom in Provincial Offences Court?
14. In what order are matters generally dealt with in Provincial Offences Court?
15. What should you do when your case is called in Provincial Offences Court?
16. How do the parties present their evidence in Provincial Offences Court?
17. What happens after the evidence of both parties has been presented in Provincial Offences Court?
18. When and how does the justice of the peace make his or her decision in a provincial offences case?
19. Who deals with matters at the Landlord and Tenant Board, and how should you address that person?
20. Who should you speak to when you arrive at the Landlord and Tenant Board, and why?
21. In what order are matters generally dealt with at the Landlord and Tenant Board?
22. How do the parties present their evidence at the Landlord and Tenant Board?
23. What happens after the evidence of both parties has been presented at the Landlord and Tenant Board?
24. When and how does the adjudicator make his or her decision at the Landlord and Tenant Board?

FIGURE 3.1 Standard Small Claims Court Courtroom Layout

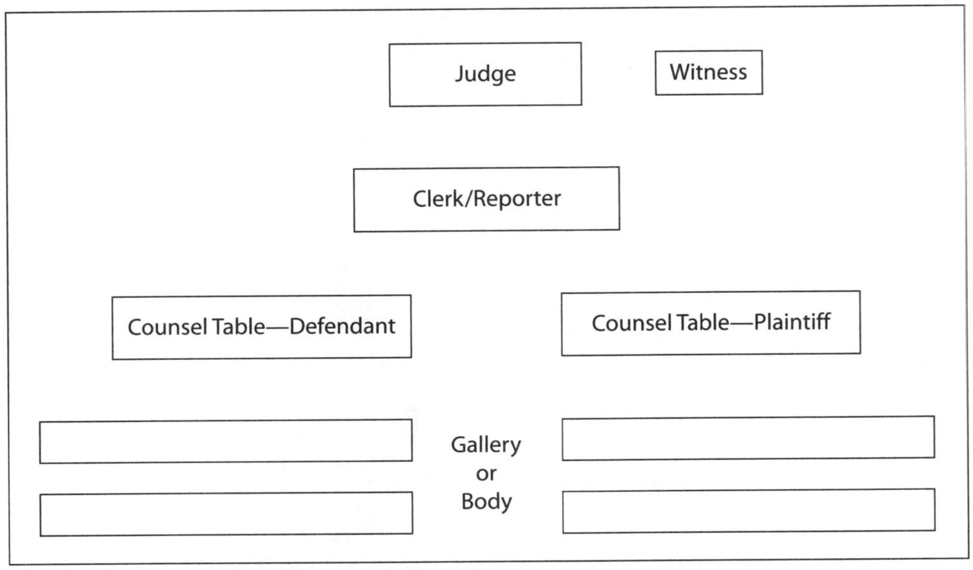

FIGURE 3.2 Standard Provincial Offences Courtroom Layout

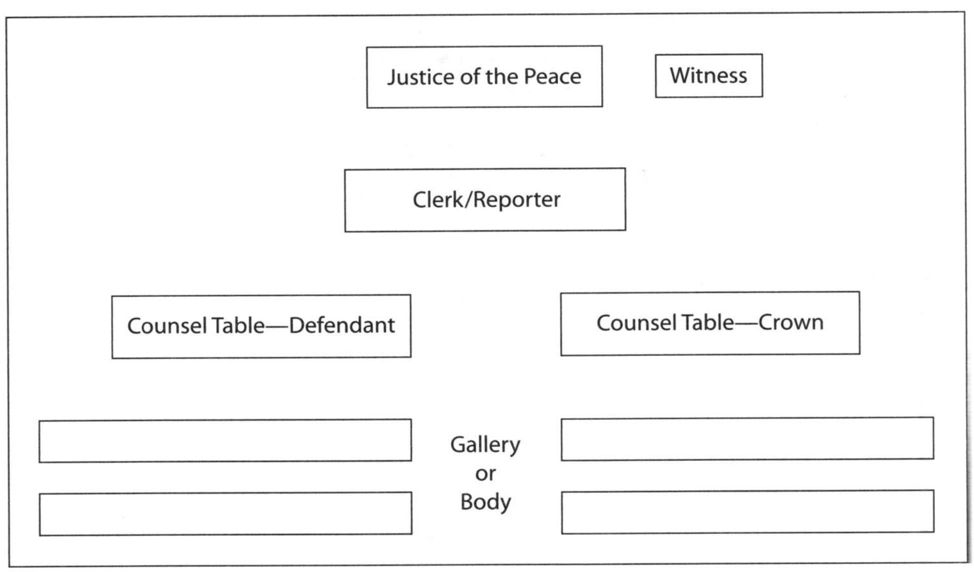

FIGURE 3.3 Standard Landlord and Tenant Board Hearing Room Layout

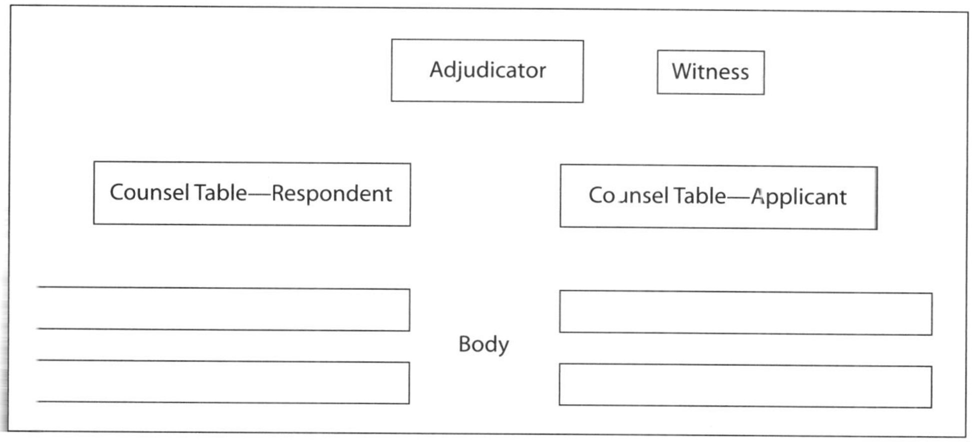

CHAPTER 4

Courtroom Etiquette

Courts and tribunals are formal settings steeped in years of legal tradition. An advocate is expected to behave in a polite and respectful manner, and to comply with rules of courtroom etiquette. Part of being prepared as an advocate is knowing those rules. This chapter discusses courtroom etiquette—how you and your client and witnesses should behave when appearing in court or before a tribunal—by answering questions commonly asked by paralegals.

WHAT DO I WEAR?

You should dress in a way that demonstrates respect for the court or tribunal, and that invites the participants in your trial or hearing to treat you with respect. Dress conservatively—it looks more professional. If your clothing is inappropriate, you will draw negative attention to yourself. Keep in mind that your credibility as an advocate is at stake, and your appearance influences the first impression you create on the judge, justice of the peace, or adjudicator.

Men should wear a suit and tie or dress pants and a sports jacket and tie. Women should wear a suit, or dress pants, or skirt with a jacket or sweater. Hats are not permitted to be worn in a courtroom or tribunal hearing room. An exception is made in the case of religious head coverings.

WHAT TIME SHOULD I ARRIVE AT THE COURT OR TRIBUNAL?

You should plan to arrive about 15 minutes before the time set for your trial or hearing. If your trial is set for 10:00 a.m., make sure you arrive by 9:45. It is always better to be early, just in case you need to call a witness, use the washroom, or review your case. Also, it gives you time to familiarize yourself with the courtroom or hearing room and to relax before your case starts. It can be very unnerving to arrive late and be expected to proceed right away.

WHERE DO I SIT?

This varies among the various courts and tribunals. Ideally, you should arrive at the court or tribunal early enough so that you can ask the court officers (if any) or other more experienced advocates where to sit. Make sure to speak to court officers and other advocates politely. Just because the judge is not present does not give you licence to be rude or disrespectful.

Usually, you will be required to sit in the gallery or body of the courtroom or tribunal room until your case is called. When your case is called, sit at the counsel table in front of the judge, justice of the peace, or adjudicator. The plaintiff, prosecutor, or applicant usually sits on the right side of the room as you are facing the bench, and the defendant or respondent sits on the left. The seating arrangement may be different at some tribunals. For example, advocates might instead sit opposite each other at a boardroom table.

WHERE DOES MY CLIENT SIT?

When your case is called, your client will sit beside you at the counsel table.

WHERE DO MY WITNESSES SIT?

Your witnesses will sit in the body of the court until they are required to give evidence. At that point they will proceed to the witness box located next to the judge, justice of the peace, or adjudicator (usually to his or her left). In some courts, the witness is permitted to sit while testifying; in others, the witness must stand. When the witness has finished giving evidence, he or she returns to the body of the court and sits down.

HOW DO I ADDRESS THE JUDGE, JUSTICE OF THE PEACE, OR ADJUDICATOR?

Always stand before you speak to the judge, justice of the peace, or adjudicator. In Small Claims Court, refer to the judge as "Your Honour." In Provincial Offences Court, refer to the justice of the peace as "Your Worship." At the tribunal, you may address the adjudicator as either Mr. or Madam Adjudicator, Mr. or Madam Member, or Mr. or Ms. (last name). The adjudicator may display his or her name on the desk and, in opening remarks, may state how he or she prefers to be called. For example, you may be asked to address the adjudicator as Mr. Smith, or Ms. Jones. If you are unsure about how to address the judge, justice of the peace, or adjudicator you should refer to him or her as Sir or Ma'am. Remember to always be respectful and polite when speaking to the judge, justice of the peace, or adjudicator.

HOW DO I ADDRESS THE LAWYER OR AGENT FOR THE OTHER SIDE?

You may use the term "my friend" to refer to counsel for the other side. However, it is preferable to refer to the other lawyer or agent as "counsel for the plaintiff/defendant" or "agent for the plaintiff/defendant." You may also refer to him or her by name—for example, Mr./Ms. Gentili. Never refer to opposing counsel by first name.

HOW DO I ADDRESS A PARTY TO THE CASE?

Refer to a party to the case by his or her legal status in the matter—the plaintiff or the defendant, or the applicant or the respondent. Alternatively, you may refer to a party by his or her status in the case—for example, the landlord or the tenant, or the homeowner or the contractor. You may also refer to a party simply by name—for example, Mr. Li. Again, never refer to a party by his or her first name.

HOW DO I ADDRESS A WITNESS?

Refer to witnesses by name—for example, Ms. Jones. Again, do not refer to or address a witness by his or her first name.

HOW DO I SPEAK TO THE OTHER SIDE'S AGENT OR LAWYER DURING THE TRIAL?

While it may be tempting to speak directly to the opposing side's agent or lawyer, you must never do so while your case is going on. You must always speak through the judge, justice of the peace, or adjudicator. Doing so shows that you recognize the authority of the judge, justice of the peace, or adjudicator to control proceedings in the courtroom or hearing room. Always use a respectful and civil tone whenever you speak to the opposing side. Never be rude.

HOW DO I SPEAK TO MY CLIENT DURING THE TRIAL OR HEARING?

If you must speak with your client during the trial or hearing, first ask permission of the judge, justice of the peace, or adjudicator. For example, in Small Claims Court, you should stand and say, "Excuse me, Your Honour. May I have a moment to confer with my client?" If the judge, justice of the peace, or adjudicator agrees, speak with your client as quietly and quickly as possible.

WHAT SHOULD I DO IF I NEED TO USE THE WASHROOM DURING THE CASE?

If at all possible, try to wait until the judge, justice of the peace, or adjudicator calls a recess. If you cannot wait, stand and politely ask the judge, justice of the peace, or adjudicator for a brief recess.

MISCELLANEOUS, BUT IMPORTANT!

- Turn off cellphones, pagers, and so on.
- Do not use cameras, video recorders, and so on.
- Do not eat, drink, chew gum, or read newspapers in the courtroom.
- Remove sunglasses and hats (except religious coverings).
- Stand whenever the judge or justice of the peace enters or leaves the courtroom.
- Do not make noise, or enter or leave while the judge or justice of the peace is speaking.
- If you arrive while court is in session, bow slightly to the judge or justice of the peace as you enter the courtroom.
- If you leave while court is in session, turn to face the judge or justice of the peace and bow slightly before exiting the courtroom.
- Do not drink water while speaking to the judge, justice of the peace, or adjudicator.

REVIEW QUESTIONS

1. What should you wear when appearing in a court or tribunal?
2. What time should you arrive at the court or tribunal?
3. Where should you sit in the court or tribunal?
4. Where should your client sit?
5. Where should your witnesses sit?
6. How should you address the judge, justice of the peace, or adjudicator?
7. How should you address the lawyer or agent for the other side?
8. How should you address a party to the case?
9. How should you address a witness?
10. How should you speak to the other side's agent or lawyer during the trial?
11. How do you speak to your client during the trial or hearing?
12. What should you do if you need to use the washroom during the case?

PART III

Preparing for the Trial or Hearing

CHAPTER 5
The Theory of the Case

When a judge, justice of the peace, or other adjudicator makes a decision in a case, he or she does so by applying the relevant law to the facts of the case. To win a trial or hearing you have to be successful on both the facts and the law—you have to present the judge or other decision-maker with a view of the facts and law that supports a decision in favour of your client. In other words, you need a theory of the case.

This chapter discusses the theory of the case—what it is, why it is important, and how to develop one.

THEORY OF THE CASE: WHAT IT IS AND WHY YOU NEED ONE

The **theory of the case**—your theory of your case—is a view of the facts and law that can justify a favourable decision for your client. As the saying goes, there are two sides to every story, and your theory of the case is your side of the story. It explains what happened in your case and why it happened. It also explains how the facts give rise to a valid cause of action, if you are the plaintiff or applicant, or a valid defence, if you are the defendant or respondent.

Your theory of the case should include all of the facts of the case that are not in dispute and your version of the facts that are in dispute. It must account for all of the facts of your case, both favourable and unfavourable, and should explain away as many of the unfavourable facts as possible.

Your opponent will have a theory of his or her case as well. You want your theory to be the more persuasive one. To be persuasive it must be understandable and not just plausible, but compelling. You want the judge or other decision-maker to think not only that the facts might have happened as your theory suggests, but that it makes sense for them to have happened just that way.

You will not succeed at trial or hearing with merely a compelling and convincing story. The story must also satisfy the requirements of substantive law. In other words, the facts must constitute either a valid cause of action or a valid defence. Your theory of the case must apply the relevant law to the facts of your case.

Developing a theory of your case will help you understand and develop your case. It will help you to separate relevant facts from irrelevant ones, and to distinguish between favourable facts and unfavourable ones. At the trial or hearing, your theory of the case will provide a context for the judge or other decision-maker to understand your case as well.

Do not wait until you start to prepare for a trial or hearing to develop your theory of the case. It should be your first step in a case, starting with your very first client interview as you sort through the facts of your client's story and make preliminary decisions about potential causes of action or defences. Your theory will govern how you draft your pleadings, the additional information you seek, the legal research you do, and the way in which you conduct the trial or hearing.

HOW TO DEVELOP YOUR THEORY OF THE CASE

There are six steps to follow in developing your theory of the case:

1. Gather the facts of the case.
2. Identify the legal issues raised by the facts.
3. Research and find the relevant law.
4. Determine how you will put the relevant facts into evidence.
5. Assess your own case.
6. Assess your opponent's case.

1. Gather the Facts of the Case

The facts are the foundation of your case. They are at the source of your client's legal problem and determine the legal issues involved.

The first step in the fact-gathering process is to conduct a detailed interview of your client. Start by letting the client tell his or her story in his or her own words. If your client is a plaintiff or applicant, find out why he or she wants to start proceedings. If your client is a defendant or respondent, find out why he or she has been sued or what offence he or she has been charged with. As you develop a sense of the area of law involved, you can start to focus on the relevant facts and weed out irrelevant facts. Ask your client for any documentary evidence, such as letters, contracts, or photographs, making sure to protect and preserve any physical evidence you obtain.

Depending on the complexity of the case, consider interviewing potential witnesses and obtaining documents from third parties. Memories fade over time, so contact witnesses sooner rather than later. Prepare a summary of each witness's statement and, if possible, have the witness sign it. There is a more complete discussion of witness interviews at the end of this chapter.

Objective facts are the most valuable—for example, the fact that the tenant signed a written lease, or the fact that it was snowing at the time of a motor vehicle accident. The more objective facts you have, the stronger your case will be. Conversely, the more objective facts you face, the more difficult your case will be.

2. Identify the Legal Issues Raised by the Facts

Identify the client's problem, why he or she is retaining you, and then the legal issues raised by the facts.

Start with what the client wants. For example, the client may want to terminate a lease or may want to avoid having to pay damages for breach of contract.

Next, determine the area of law involved. Start by identifying the problem by general area—for example, landlord and tenant law, contract law, tort law, or highway traffic law. Then, identify the specific area of law involved: if the general area of law is landlord and tenant law, is the specific area assignment of tenancy or termination of tenancy? Narrow the area of law as much as possible: if the specific area of law is termination of tenancy, is the narrower area non-payment of rent or damage to the premises? The more specific the area of law that you investigate, the more quickly and easily you will find answers. You may have to do some preliminary research to educate yourself on a particular area of law before you can narrow the area of law.

Finally, formulate the issues. Write down each issue you identify, starting with the word "whether"—for example, "whether a landlord has the right to terminate a tenancy because of damage caused by the tenant."

3. Research and Find the Relevant Law

Substantive law defines the elements of a civil cause of action or a defence to a civil action, and defines the elements of a criminal offence and the defences available to that offence. Substantive law also determines the facts you must establish to constitute your claim or defence. In other words, the law provides a context for the facts you have gathered. Your research helps you to determine which facts are relevant and often requires you to find additional facts.

Start your legal research with secondary sources, such as textbooks, encyclopedias, and digests that provide a general overview of the subject area, and use these to find the primary sources of law (cases, statutes, and regulations) that are relevant to your issues. Once you have looked at the law, you may find that the issues you identified on a preliminary basis are not correct; you may also find that you need more information from your client. If your preliminary identification of the issues was faulty, or if you receive new information, you may have to do further research on the subject.

4. Determine How You Will Put the Relevant Facts into Evidence

The substantive law tells you which facts you need to prove. You must then consider *how* you will prove these facts.

Make a list of each fact you must prove. For each fact, ask yourself what evidence is required to prove that fact and how that evidence will be produced at a trial or hearing. Will a particular fact be proved by the testimony of a witness, and if so, which witness? Do you have documentary evidence to support a particular fact, and if so, which witness can prove and explain the particular document?

5. Assess Your Own Case

Once you have completed steps 1–4, you must take a critical look at your theory to identify the strengths and weaknesses of your own case. Your theory should have a firm foundation in strong facts, and the inferences drawn from those facts must be reasonable. Your theory should also explain away, in a plausible manner, as many unfavourable facts as possible. Finally, your theory must make sense—it cannot be based on wishful thinking!

6. Assess Your Opponent's Case

Developing your theory of the case involves not only preparation of *your* case but also preparation for *your opponent's* case. Your opponent will also have a theory of the case. You must anticipate what his or her theory of the case is and prepare for it. Your opponent will most likely know about any facts that are unfavourable to your case. Consider whether there is some point of law that can defend you against that fact. If not, consider a way to explain the fact away in a reasonable fashion. It is far better to admit an unfavourable fact and explain it away on your own terms than to allow the fact to be drawn out by your opponent. For example, your client may have signed the contract, but you can argue that it was signed under duress or as a result of undue influence.

Be honest in your assessment of the relative strengths and weaknesses of your case and your opponent's case. It may be in your client's best interests to settle rather than to proceed to a trial or hearing.

INTERVIEWING WITNESSES

As part of the development of your theory of your case, you will have to meet with and interview your witnesses. The goal of a witness interview is to gather facts within a limited amount of time. To be effective as an interviewer, you have to be organized, knowledgeable, patient, a good listener, and a good note-taker.

The five stages to an effective witness interview are

1. preparing
2. listening
3. questioning
4. concluding
5. creating a witness statement/note-taking.

These five stages are broken down into 11 steps in Table 5.1, below.

1. Preparing

Before you meet with the witness, you must prepare for the interview. Review all of the pleadings in the case, and familiarize yourself with the legal issues involved. Read over any statements or interview notes from your client and any other witnesses.

2. Listening

Most people think that an interview involves the asking of questions, and indeed that is true. However, at the start of a witness interview, your major role is that of a listener, after encouraging the witness to tell his or her story.

Start by greeting the witness, introducing yourself, and making the witness feel comfortable. Ask a few general, opening questions to elicit the witness's story. Let the witness tell the story in his or her own words. Do not worry if the witness's story is overly detailed—you will not know which details are relevant until you hear the entire story—or disorganized—you can organize the story later.

Your goal is to listen in such a way that you

- *show you are paying attention* in order to encourage the witness to speak—for example, by nodding and by saying, "tell me more," "uh huh," and "I see"; and
- *show understanding* by
  - paraphrasing feelings—for example, "I can see that upset you very much"; and

- ◇ paraphrasing or summarizing content—for example, "So if I can just summarize what you've said, it seems that … Is that correct?"; and
- ◇ clarifying—asking a question to clear up any ambiguity.

3. Questioning

After the witness has completed his or her story, go back and ask questions to

- fill in gaps in the story,
- obtain further details,
- obtain background information or explanations,
- clarify ambiguities or contradictions in the story, and
- determine the relevance of aspects of the story.

You should also ask questions to confirm the witness's qualifications to give evidence by testing the witness's

- *competence to testify*—as a lay witness, that he or she actually saw or heard the events in some way; as an expert witness, that he or she possesses special knowledge, skill, experience, training, or education;
- *credibility*—about any matters that would tend to show whether the witness is honest; and
- *bias*—by determining whether the witness has an interest in the matter in question that would tend to prejudice his or her testimony.

Use different types of questions at various points during the interview. Consider the following types of questions and their uses:

- *Open-ended questions* allow the witness to choose the information the witness thinks is relevant to a particular subject—for example, "What do you know about the facts of this case?" or "Is there anything else about this matter I should know?" Use this type of question at Step 2 and Step 8 in Table 5.1.
- *Narrow questions* allow you to focus on both the subject matter and the specific aspect that the witness should address in the answer—for example, "What can you tell me about the condition of the apartment?" Use this type of question at Step 2 and Step 4.
- *Yes/no questions* are very specific about subject matter and allow the interview subject to answer only "yes" or "no." For example, "Did you pay a last month's rent deposit?" Use this type of question at Step 4.
- *Leading questions* make a statement that asserts what is relevant, and by their form suggest that the witness agrees with the statement—for example, "You didn't give notice to terminate in writing, did you?" Use this type of question at Step 7 when confirming information with the interview subject or when dealing with a difficult interview subject or with an interview subject who is hard to understand.

Once you are fairly satisfied that you have the witness's entire story, tell the witness your understanding of the facts, and ask whether the witness agrees with it. If the witness disagrees with your understanding of the facts, ask for and make any necessary corrections. Before you conclude the interview, ask the witness whether there is anything else he or she has not told you that the witness thinks you should know.

4. Concluding

Conclude the interview by getting the witness's complete address, telephone number, and other contact information and by thanking the witness for participating in the interview.

5. Creating a Witness Statement/Note-Taking

You must make notes of what the witness says as you conduct the interview. When the interview is finished, do not just put your notes into a file. Instead, take the time to organize the witness's story, and set it out in a witness statement.

TABLE 5.1 Witness Interview

Preparing	◆ Review the pleadings. ◆ Familiarize yourself with the legal issues. ◆ Review statements/interview notes from your client and any other witnesses.	
Listening	1. Greet the witness and introduce yourself. 2. Elicit the story with opening questions. 3. Let the witness set out his or her story in the witness's own words.	Note-taking
Questioning	4. Question on the facts for gaps, depth, background, ambiguities, and relevance. 5. Confirm the witness's qualifications as to competence, credibility, and bias. 6. Restate your view of the facts. 7. Ask whether the witness agrees with your view of the facts; if he or she does not, ask for and make the necessary corrections. 8. Ask whether there is anything else the witness has not told you that the witness thinks you should know.	
Concluding	9. Get the witness's complete address, telephone number, and other contact information. 10. End the interview.	
Creating a witness statement	11. Create a witness statement from the notes you have taken throughout the interview.	

BOX 5.1

Baldwin Brothers Witness Statements in the Kitchen Renovation Case

Alec Baldwin's Witness Statement

My brother Stephen and I are the owners of a contracting company called Baldwin Brothers Construction. We're licensed contractors and have been in business for ten years, and do general contracting work, specializing in small renovation projects. Six months ago, Tina Fey called me to discuss a renovation of her kitchen. She found out about my company because we were doing some work in the neighbourhood. I went to her house to discuss the work she wanted to have done. She told me that she wanted to have her kitchen cabinets painted white and to have new hardware installed on the doors. She also wanted a new countertop, and to replace the existing lighting with pot lights. She also wanted to have the walls and ceiling painted.

We talked about how many pot lights she would need to make her kitchen bright. I told her that pot lights normally cost $250 each installed, and that five would be the right number for her kitchen. She asked what would happen if she wanted more light, and I said, "Then we can install more" even though I was sure five would be enough.

Based on our discussions I gave her a price of $7,500 for all the work and she agreed. My brother Stephen and I came a week later to start the work, and Tina paid me a deposit of $2,500. After the kitchen counter was installed, I left to work on another job, and my brother Stephen did the rest of the work himself.

The job was finished within a week. We did a good job and the Feys seemed happy with our work. Everything was fine until Stephen gave Tommy Fey the bill for the work. The bill was for $8,250—the original contract price of $7,500 plus $750 for supplying and installing the three additional pot lights.

Stephen Baldwin's Witness Statement

My brother Alec and I are owners of a contracting company called Baldwin Brothers Construction. Six months ago, we were hired by Tommy and Tina Fey to renovate their kitchen. We were hired to paint the kitchen and the cabinets, install a new countertop, and install pot lights. My brother Alec negotiated the contract with the Feys.

My brother and I came a week later to start the work. Tommy Fey was at home during the renovation. When it was time to install the pot lights, I checked with Tommy about the location of the five lights I was planning to install. Tommy told me he didn't think that five lights would provide enough light. I told him to tell me how many he wanted and that I could install more. He told me he wanted three more, and I said fine. He never asked me what it would cost, so we never discussed money.

The job was finished within a week. We did a good job and the Feys seemed happy with our work. Everything was fine until I gave Tommy the bill for the work. The bill was for $8,250—the original contract price of $7,500 plus $750 for supplying and installing three additional pot lights. He asked what the extra $750 was for, and I said it was for three extra pot lights at $250 each, over and above the five lights that were included in the contract. He said the contract included "all necessary lights" and he wouldn't pay any more than the $7,500 originally agreed to. He gave me a cheque for $5,000. ◇

DEVELOPING THE THEORY OF THE KITCHEN RENOVATION CASE

In Chapter 1, Box 1.1 set out the basic facts of a dispute involving a kitchen renovation contract. In the sections below, we apply the six steps for constructing a theory of the case to the Kitchen Renovation Case, for both the plaintiff and the defendants.

Theory of the Plaintiff's Case

STEP 1: GATHER THE FACTS OF THE CASE

Box 5.1 contains the interview notes of Alec Baldwin and Stephen Baldwin, the principals of the plaintiff corporation Baldwin Brothers Construction in the Kitchen Renovation Case.

After completing the interviews, the plaintiff's advocate will prepare a summary of the facts, as follows:

- The defendants hired the plaintiff to do some renovations to their kitchen.
- The plaintiff agreed to install a new countertop, paint the kitchen cabinets and install new hardware on the doors, paint the walls and ceiling, and install five pot lights.
- The contract price was $7,500.
- The defendants gave the plaintiff a deposit in the amount of $2,500.
- At the request of the defendants, the plaintiff installed three additional pot lights at a cost of $250 each.
- The plaintiff completed all the work required and gave the defendants an invoice for $8,250 (the original contract price of $7,500 plus $750 for the installation of three additional pot lights).
- The defendants paid $5,000.
- The defendants owe $750.

STEP 2: IDENTIFY THE LEGAL ISSUES RAISED BY THE FACTS

The primary legal issue in this case is whether the Feys breached the contract by failing to pay the entire amount billed. The issue turns on a determination of the terms of the agreement between the parties, specifically whether the contract price included the installation of only five pot lights or of all necessary lights, and, if the latter, what the meaning of "all necessary lights" is.

The area of law involved is contract law, and in particular contract interpretation.

STEP 3: RESEARCH AND FIND THE RELEVANT LAW

Common-law principles of contract law apply to this case. There is clearly a contract between the parties. The only issue is one of interpretation. In interpreting contracts, the courts try to give effect to the intention of the parties on the basis of the clear meaning of the words they use. Each party must persuade the court that his or her interpretation of the contract is the correct one.

STEP 4: DETERMINE HOW YOU WILL PUT THE RELEVANT FACTS INTO EVIDENCE

There are no documents in this case because the contract was oral.

Alec will testify about the negotiation of the original contract, including the number and cost of the pot lights, and the payment of the deposit. He can also testify that only five pot lights were needed to make the kitchen bright.

Stephen will testify about the completion of the work, Tommy Fey's request for additional pot lights, and the fact that full payment was not received upon completion.

STEP 5: ASSESS YOUR OWN CASE

Alec will give evidence that the contract provided for five pot lights only, not for "all necessary lights." A judge should be willing to accept Alec's version of the facts because it is not likely that a contractor would agree to provide an undefined number of lights. Even if the judge agrees that the contract was for "all necessary lights," the plaintiff maintains that five pot lights were all that was necessary.

STEP 6: ASSESS YOUR OPPONENT'S CASE

It is possible that the defendants will persuade the judge to accept their version of the terms of the contract, and that eight pot lights were necessary to make the kitchen bright.

Theory of the Defendants' Case

STEP 1: GATHER THE FACTS OF THE CASE

Box 5.2 contains the witness statements prepared from the interview notes of the defendants, Tina Fey and Tommy Fey, in the Kitchen Renovation Case.

BOX 5.2

Tina and Tommy Fey's Witness Statements in the Kitchen Renovation Case

Tina Fey's Witness Statement

Six months ago, I met with Alec Baldwin of Baldwin Brothers Construction about renovating my kitchen. I found out about the company because they had done some work in the neighbourhood. Alec came to my house to discuss with me the work I wanted to have done. I told him that I wanted to have my kitchen cabinets painted white and to have new hardware installed on the doors. I also wanted a new countertop, and to replace the existing lighting with pot lights. I also wanted to have the walls and ceiling painted.

When we talked about the pot lights, he mentioned that pot lights cost about $250 each. I told him that I wanted the kitchen to be bright, and he assured me that he would install the necessary number of pot lights as part of the contract price. I asked him how many that would be, and he said five. I asked what would happen if I needed more lights, and he said, "Then we can install more."

Alec and his brother Stephen came a week later to start the work, and I gave him a deposit of $2,500. My husband took some time off work so that he could be home to supervise. The job was finished within a week. The work was excellent, and everything looked great. Everything was fine until Stephen gave my husband the bill for the work. Instead of $7,500, as we had agreed, the bill was for $8,250. My husband dealt with the bill.

Tommy Fey's Witness Statement

Six months ago, my wife and I hired Baldwin Brothers Construction to renovate our kitchen. They were going to paint the kitchen and the cabinets, install a new countertop, and install pot lights. My wife negotiated the contract with the company.

Alec and his brother Stephen came a week later to start the work. I took some time off work to stay home to supervise. When it was time to install the pot lights, Stephen checked with me about the number and location of the lights. He said he was planning to install five lights and showed me where. I told him I didn't think that would provide enough light. Stephen said, "Tell me what you want. I can install more." I told him three more, and he said fine. We never discussed money.

The job was finished within a week. The work was excellent, and everything looked great. Everything was fine until Stephen gave me the bill for the work. Instead of $7,500, as we had agreed, the bill was for $8,250. I asked what the extra $750 was for, and Stephen said it was for three extra pot lights. I told him that all lighting was included in the original price and that I wouldn't pay any more than $7,500. I gave him a cheque for $5,000. ◇

After completing the interviews, the defendants' advocate will prepare a summary of the facts, as follows:

- The defendants hired the plaintiff to make some renovations in their kitchen.
- The plaintiff agreed to install a new countertop, paint the kitchen cabinets and install new hardware on the doors, paint the walls and ceiling, and install all necessary pot lights to make the kitchen bright.
- The contract price was $7,500.
- The defendants gave the plaintiff a deposit in the amount of $2,500.
- While the work was being done, Tommy Fey and Stephen Baldwin discussed the number and placement of the pot lights and settled on eight lights.
- The plaintiff completed all the work required and gave the defendants an invoice for $8,250 ($750 more than the contract price).
- The defendants paid $5,000, which covered the contract in full. The plaintiff is not entitled to any additional payment.

STEP 2: IDENTIFY THE LEGAL ISSUES RAISED BY THE FACTS

The primary legal issue in this case is whether the defendants are contractually obligated to pay $750 above the original contract price. The issue turns on a determination of the terms of the agreement between the parties, specifically whether the contract price included the installation of only five pot lights or of all necessary lights, and, if the latter, what the meaning of "all necessary lights" is.

The area of law involved is contract law, and in particular contract interpretation.

STEP 3: RESEARCH AND FIND THE RELEVANT LAW

Common-law principles of contract law apply to this case. There is clearly a contract between the parties. The only issue is one of interpretation. In interpreting contracts, the courts try to give effect to the intention of the parties on the basis of the clear meaning of the words they use. Each party must persuade the court that his or her interpretation of the contract is the correct one.

STEP 4: DETERMINE HOW YOU WILL PUT THE RELEVANT FACTS INTO EVIDENCE

There are no documents in this case because the contract was oral.

Tina will testify about the negotiation of the original contract, including the number and cost of the pot lights, and the payment of the deposit. She will testify that Baldwin Brothers agreed to provide all necessary pot lights as part of the contract price. She can also testify that eight pot lights were needed to make the kitchen bright.

Tommy will testify about the completion of the work and his discussion with Stephen about the number and location of the pot lights. He will testify that eight pot lights were needed to make the kitchen bright. He will also testify that he paid the contract price in full.

STEP 5: ASSESS YOUR OWN CASE

Tina will give evidence that the contract provided for "all necessary lights" and that Alec merely suggested that five lights would be enough. Both Tina and Tommy will testify that eight lights were necessary to make the kitchen bright. Tina's evidence will make it clear that her main concern was the brightness of the kitchen, not the actual number of lights.

STEP 6: ASSESS YOUR OPPONENT'S CASE

A judge may be willing to accept Alec's version of the facts because it is not likely that a contractor would agree to provide an undefined number of lights. Even if the judge agrees that the contract was for "all necessary lights," the judge may not be persuaded that eight lights were in fact necessary.

REVIEW QUESTIONS

1. What is the theory of the case?
2. What must your theory of your case include?
3. How do you make your theory of your case persuasive?
4. When should you start to develop your theory of your case, and why?
5. What are the six steps to follow in developing a theory of the case?
6. What is the goal of a witness interview?
7. What are the five stages of an effective witness interview? Briefly summarize each stage.

8. What are open-ended questions, and at what steps of a witness interview should you use them? Provide an example.
9. What are narrow questions, and at what steps of a witness interview should you use them? Provide an example.
10. What are yes/no questions, and at what step of a witness interview should you use them? Provide an example.
11. What are leading questions, and at what step of a witness interview should you use them? Provide an example.

PART IV

The Trial or Hearing

CHAPTER 6

Opening Statement

There is a basic rule in public speaking: start by telling your audience what you are going to tell them; tell them; then tell them what you have told them. If a trial or hearing were a speech, the opening statement is the advocate's way of telling the audience (the judge or other decision-maker) what the advocate is going to tell him or her.

The purpose of the opening statement is to inform the judge or other decision-maker about the case he or she is about to hear. The judge may have already read the pleadings and may therefore have some idea about what the case is about. However, it is still helpful for him or her to hear an overview of the case from the perspective of each side, including the result each desires. An opening statement puts the legal and factual issues in context for the judge. It is like a map, telling the judge where you intend to go in the case.

This chapter discusses the opening statement—why it is important, how to prepare one, and how to present it.

WHY PREPARE AN OPENING STATEMENT?

At the Superior Court level, the Crown, plaintiff, or applicant is always entitled to make an opening statement, in both jury and non-jury trials, before presenting his or her evidence. Counsel for the accused, defendant, or respondent will usually then make his or her opening statement after the completion of the Crown's, plaintiff's or applicant's case and just before calling his or her evidence. In a non-jury trial, the accused, defendant, or respondent may be permitted to give the opening statement directly after that of the Crown, plaintiff, or applicant.

In practice, counsel appearing at the Superior Court level rarely make an opening statement in non-jury trials, and there are generally no opening statements in Small Claims Court or Provincial Offences Court trials, or in administrative tribunal hearings.

However, it is still a good idea to prepare an opening statement. Preparing an opening statement helps you focus your thinking about your case, and is an excellent way to prepare for a trial or hearing. Although the judge, justice of the peace, or adjudicator may not ask you to deliver a formal opening statement, he or she may, at the outset of the trial or hearing, ask you to summarize what your case is about or ask you other questions about your case. If you have prepared an opening statement, you will be able to respond in a clear and concise manner. This is the first opportunity you have to speak to the judge or other decision-maker, and you want to create a positive first impression.

PREPARING YOUR OPENING STATEMENT

When preparing your opening statement, ask yourself, "If I were the judge, what would I want to know to help me understand the case and the evidence?" Your opening statement should set out the facts that you intend to prove at trial, and why those facts are significant. Your opening statement is the "blueprint" of your case; it essentially outlines your theory of your case for the judge or other decision-maker. It provides the framework of your case, without going into a lot of detail. When preparing an opening statement, the goal is to include all the necessary information that the judge or other decision-maker needs to be able to understand what the case is about (from your perspective), both factually and legally. Having said that, an opening statement does not give a detailed legal argument, but simply sets out the legal issues to be decided in the case. The actual law and how it is applied are saved for the closing argument.

FORMAT OF OPENING STATEMENT

There is no prescribed format or structure of an opening statement, but the following format will help you accomplish your goals.

1. State the theme of your case.
2. Identify the parties.
3. State the cause of action (plaintiff or applicant) or defence (defendant).
4. State the facts of the case consistent with your theory.
5. State the legal issues.
6. State the outcome you desire.

1. State the Theme of Your Case

Start your opening statement by telling the judge or other decision-maker the theme of your case. The theme of your case is derived from the theory of your case: it is your theory reduced to one or two sentences—just enough so that the judge or decision-maker gets a sense of the general area of law involved and your take on the matter. It should be the answer you would give to a friend who asks you, "What is your case about?" For example, "This is a case about a homeowner who did not pay for the supply of materials by the contractor" or "This is a case about a tenant who did not terminate a tenancy properly."

2. Identify the Parties

Briefly explain who the parties are and how they fit into the overall picture. For example, "The plaintiff is a contractor who agreed to provide materials and services to the defendant homeowner." Such a statement helps the judge better understand each party's role in the case. Because the plaintiff presents his or her opening statement first, only the plaintiff needs to identify the parties. There is no need for the defendant to restate this information during his or her opening statement.

3. State the Cause of Action or Defence

The plaintiff states the cause of action of the case. For example, "This case involves the tort of battery." The cause of action provides the structure for the facts and the law. The defendant states his or her defence. For example, "The defendant's defence is that the plaintiff consented to the contact."

4. State the Facts of the Case Consistent with Your Theory

This is the main part of your opening statement—it sets out your version of the facts of the case and will help the judge to follow the testimony of your witnesses and to understand the importance of what they say. Highlight only the main facts, being careful not to present any evidence at this point. State your version of the facts in a way that is understandable, believable, and makes sense. You may also state whom you will be calling as witnesses.

5. State the Legal Issues

Identify the legal issues raised by the facts of the case. Issues are usually introduced by the word "whether." For example, "The legal issue in this case is whether the tenancy was properly terminated," or "The legal issue in this case is whether the homeowner breached the contract." In some cases there may be only one issue; in other cases there may be several. Set out all of the legal issues and identify the issues only. Do not argue the issues by referring to the relevant law or state how they should be resolved.

6. State the Outcome You Desire

Conclude your opening statement with a brief statement of the outcome you desire in the case. If you are claiming an amount of money in damages, this is not the time to go into detail about the dollar amounts you are seeking. For example, you should simply say, "The plaintiff is claiming one month's rent" and omit the dollar amount at this point. Defendants will usually be requesting that the plaintiff's case be dismissed.

ADJUST YOUR LANGUAGE FOR ORAL PRESENTATION

Keep in mind that you will be delivering your opening statement orally; the judge or other decision-maker will not be reading what you have written. Accordingly, after you prepare your opening statement using the above format, read through it and adjust your language so that it is appropriate for an oral presentation. The following pointers may be helpful:

- *Keep your sentence structure simple and your sentences short.* Complex sentences that may be simple to read are difficult for a listener to understand.

- *Use introductory sentences to take the place of headings.* State what you will be talking about at the start of each part of the opening statement. For example, "There are three issues in this case. The first issue is … The second issue is … The third issue is …"
- *Use words you know how to pronounce.* Make sure you will be able to deliver your opening statement without tripping over any of your words.

Box 6.1 contains a sample opening statement for the plaintiffs in the Kitchen Renovation Case.

BOX 6.1

Plaintiff's Opening Statement in the Kitchen Renovation Case

Good morning, Your Honour. My name is Smith, initial A, and I am the licensed paralegal for the plaintiff in this case.

This is a case about homeowners who did not pay the full contract amount for a kitchen renovation completed by the contractor.

The plaintiff is a small contracting company. The defendants hired the plaintiff to make some minor renovations to the kitchen in their home.

The plaintiff's claim is for damages for breach of contract.

The facts are as follows:

About six months ago, the plaintiff entered into a contract with the defendants. The parties agreed that the plaintiff would perform the following work in the defendants' kitchen: install a new countertop, paint the cabinets and install new hardware on the cabinet doors, paint the walls and ceiling, and install five pot lights. It was also agreed that additional pot lights could be installed at a cost of $250 each. The contract price was $7,500, and the defendants gave the plaintiff a deposit in the amount of $2,500. At the request of the defendants, the plaintiff installed three additional pot lights. The plaintiff completed the job and gave the defendants an invoice for $8,250 (the original contract price of $7,500 plus $750 for the supply and installation of the three additional pot lights). The defendant paid $5,000 but refused to pay the balance owing in the amount of $750.

The legal issue in this case is whether the defendants breached the contract in failing to pay the cost of the additional three pot lights.

The plaintiff claims damages for the unpaid balance of the contract price. ◇

PRACTISE YOUR OPENING STATEMENT

Practise delivering your opening statement so that your delivery will add to, and not detract from, your statement's effectiveness.

You should be familiar enough with your opening statement so that you do not have to read it. Instead, try to talk to the judge or other decision-maker and tell him or her about your case. You do not have to memorize your opening statement. You may look to your notes, read a passage, pause, and look at the judge. Sometimes working from memory may cause your delivery to be stilted. Instead, use your notes to help you with your pacing. Block your argument out; use large print so that you will be forced to read only small bits at a time and will not lose your place. Leave lots of white space between ideas to remind yourself to pause.

Practise speaking slowly so that the decision-maker will be able to follow and absorb what you have to say. Speak a lot more slowly than you think you need to.

Use pacing to reinforce the organization and meaning of your opening statement. Pause between sentences; pause longer between paragraphs. Your pacing takes the place of commas, periods, and paragraphs.

Practise using the appropriate honorific: Your Honour, Your Worship, Ms. Adjudicator, as the case may be.

Practise speaking loudly. The decision-maker must be able to hear you if he or she is to understand you.

Finally, practise speaking with expression. If you speak in a monotone, you will bore the decision-maker and lose his or her attention. Make a special effort to avoid "up-talk," the tendency, especially among young people, to make statements sound like questions. "Up-talk" makes a speaker sound nervous and tentative, rather than confident and persuasive.

REVIEW QUESTIONS

1. What is the purpose of the opening statement?
2. What is the recommended format for an opening statement? Briefly describe what should be included in each step.
3. How and why should you adjust the language of your opening statement so that it is appropriate for an oral presentation?
4. Why is it important to practise delivering your opening statement?
5. How should you practise your opening statement?

DISCUSSION QUESTION

Prepare an opening statement for the defendants in the Kitchen Renovation Case.

CHAPTER 7

Direct Examination of Witnesses

Judges, justices of the peace, and adjudicators make decisions in cases by applying the law to the facts of the particular case. Before a judge or other decision-maker can make a decision in a case, he or she must first determine what happened in the case. Usually, the two sides in a case have different versions of what happened in the case—sometimes slightly different, other times vastly different. The judge or other decision-maker has to choose between the two versions. You tell the judge or other decision-maker your version of what happened (your theory of the case) through the direct examination (also known as examination-in-chief) of your witnesses. This chapter discusses the purpose of and the preparation for the direct examination of your witnesses.

MEANING AND PURPOSE OF DIRECT EXAMINATION

Direct examination is the questioning of your own witness(es) under oath. The purpose of direct examination is to elicit from your witnesses the evidence you need to satisfy all of the elements of your claim or defence. Your goal in direct examination is to have your witness(es) present the more persuasive version of the facts. To achieve this goal, you must design your questions in such a way that, when answered, a logical, complete, believable, and understandable story unfolds. There should be no factual gaps in the story. You must also anticipate where your version of the story will differ from that of the other side and then focus your direct examination on these points—and convince the court that your story is more believable. Through direct examination, you have the opportunity to put forward your client's version of the disputed facts in a controlled and persuasive manner. The purpose of direct examination is to establish the facts only. It is not the time to argue the law or draw conclusions from the evidence.

PREPARING YOURSELF FOR DIRECT EXAMINATION

You cannot achieve the objectives of direct examination without extensive preparation. To prepare yourself for direct examination, start by asking yourself the following questions.

What Facts Do You Need to Prove?

You address this question when you develop your theory of the case. As discussed in Chapter 5, you review the law to determine the facts you must prove to establish your cause of action or defence.

How Will You Prove Each Fact?

You also address this question when you develop your theory of the case. Again, as discussed in Chapter 5, make a list of each fact you must prove and, for each fact, ask yourself what evidence is required to prove that fact and how that evidence will be produced at trial: What witness will you call? Do you have documentary evidence to support the fact?

Who Are Your Witnesses?

Who has direct knowledge of the facts of your case? Make a list of all of your potential witnesses and the aspect of your case on which each can testify. For example, Witness A can testify to the fact that the contract was signed, and Witness B can testify to the fact that the contract price was paid.

In What Order Will You Call Your Witnesses?

Consider how best to tell the story so that it makes sense and will be understood and remembered by someone with no familiarity with the facts. Ideally, the witness who knows most of the story and can provide an overall context should give evidence first. Usually, this will be a party to the case (plaintiff, applicant, defendant, or respondent).

What Do You Want the Witness to Say and in What Sequence? Are There Any Documents to Be Introduced?

Go back through your list of facts and your witness statements. Take all of the facts about which the witness can testify and put them in a logical order. Make a note of any supporting documents that the witness can identify.

Eliminate Any Unnecessary Repetition of Evidence

You may have two or more witnesses who can give evidence on the same fact. In that case, you must consider whether you need more than one witness to testify about that fact—in other words, to **corroborate** evidence of that fact already given by another witness. You do not need to corroborate evidence about a fact that is not in dispute. Corroboration is also generally not required to prove an objective fact—for example, the fact that a contract was signed. In such cases, the corroborating evidence will be unnecessarily repetitive and may bore the judge or other decision-maker. However, corroboration is recommended if you are trying to prove a fact that is in dispute or a subjective fact—for example, that a tenant's behaviour was disturbing other tenants. If two witnesses testify about the tenant's behaviour, this fact becomes more believable and convincing than if only one witness testifies.

Develop the Witness's Story

Now that you have finalized the facts to be covered in the witness's testimony and the sequencing of those facts, write out the facts as a narrative so that it flows naturally. Ask yourself, "If the witness told a perfect story, what would it sound like?" Write out that story. You should end up with a detailed, logical, understandable, and persuasive story.

Pay particular attention to those areas in which your version of the facts differs from that of the other side. Do not omit unfavourable facts: include them and try to explain them away in a plausible manner. Your witness will be more convincing if he or she does not appear to be hiding anything. Focus on the areas that are in dispute. Anticipate the other side's theory, and develop the aspects on which your witness is likely to be cross-examined.

Avoid hearsay—for example, "The landlord told me that other tenants also complained." Also avoid irrelevant detail.

Prepare Your Questions

Only now, after having developed the story, are you ready to write out your questions. The most common mistake of novice advocates is to start with their questions instead of starting with the story. The result is a stilted direct examination in which there are too many questions, and the focus is on the questioner and his or her questions rather than on the witness and his or her story. When preparing your questions, focus on the story you want told, and not on your questions. In other words, the questions are driven by the story. Write out the story first, and then insert questions designed to elicit each part of that story. It is your job to design your questions so that when answered, a complete story unfolds. This will keep the focus on the witness, not you, and will result in a story that flows naturally.

Start your direct examination with questions about the witness's background. Questions such as "What do you do for a living?" and "Where do you live?" help to personalize or humanize the witness, and will help to put the witness at ease.

Your final notes should then set out each question you intend to ask, followed by the answer you want to that question. See the heading "Formulating Your Questions" below for more guidance.

PREPARING YOUR WITNESSES FOR DIRECT EXAMINATION

It is not enough to prepare yourself for direct examination. You will not accomplish very much if you are prepared but your witnesses are not, because it is the witnesses, not you, who will be presenting the evidence at the hearing. You will need to prepare each witness in the following areas:

- what the witness will say,
- how the witness will say it,
- where the witness will say it, and
- what the other side will ask the witness in cross-examination.

What the Witness Will Say

Start by explaining to the witness why his or her evidence is important and how it fits into the entire case. Review your questions with the witness in advance of the trial so that the witness is familiar with you and your questions. The witness should know what information you are looking for when you ask a particular question. If you will be introducing any exhibits through the witness, make sure the witness has seen them and knows how to identify them.

You may also want to explain some basic rules of evidence so that the witness understands the nature of your questions. Your witness should know that generally you cannot ask leading questions during direct examination, and what a leading question is. That way, he or she may be able to help you out when it is difficult for you to ask a non-leading question. You should also explain to the witness that the decision-maker is not interested in the witness's opinion, unless, of course, the witness is being called as an expert witness. Finally, the witness should be reminded that he or she may testify only about the facts of which he or she has direct knowledge. Hearsay is not admissible and the witness should therefore know not to repeat what someone else has told him or her.

How the Witness Will Say It

You want your witness to tell the truth, and you want your witness to be believed, so it is a good idea to "coach" the witness on how to present his or her testimony so that he or she does not appear to be lying. Tell your witness to be polite, to speak clearly and in a loud enough voice, and to maintain eye contact with you when answering questions. Remind your witness to dress in a conservative and respectable manner.

Where the Witness Will Say It

Witnesses are usually very nervous about having to be in court—they are scared of courtrooms and judges, and they are especially nervous about being cross-examined! You can help your witness feel more comfortable by preparing him or her for the courtroom experience.

Go over the trial or hearing process with your witness and the order in which things will happen. It may also be helpful to show your witness the courtroom before the trial and to explain who the various people are and what they do. Show the witness where he or she will testify, and explain the process of being sworn in or affirmed.

What the Other Side Will Ask the Witness in Cross-Examination

For most witnesses, cross-examination is the scariest part of the trial or hearing, and for good reason. Cross-examination is the part of the trial or hearing that cannot be rehearsed or scripted. Unlike direct examination, where the witness knows you and is familiar with your questions, the witness does not know the other side's advocate, nor does the witness know what questions he or she will ask.

Cross-examination involves the unknown, which makes witnesses very nervous. You must counter the unknown by preparing your witness extremely well for the cross-examination. The best way to do this is to conduct a mock cross-examination of the witness. Pretend that you are the opposing side's advocate, and ask the questions that you anticipate will be asked of this witness. This preparation will give the witness a good sense of what he or she can expect during cross-examination at the trial or hearing. Tell your witness to listen to the questions very carefully and to answer only the question asked—the witness should never volunteer any additional information. Your witness should know that he or she is entitled to say, "I don't know" or "I don't remember" or "I don't understand the question" if any of these is the case. If your witness cannot respond to a question with only a "yes" or "no," he or she is entitled to explain. Advise your witness to remain calm and polite throughout and to always tell the truth. Finally, remind your witness to stop speaking if you make an **objection**. See Chapter 13 for more about objections. See Chapter 8 for more about cross-examination.

FORMULATING YOUR QUESTIONS

There are some basic rules to follow in formulating the questions for your witnesses during direct examination.

Ask One Question at a Time

Ask one question at a time, rather than multiple-part questions. For example, don't ask, 'Was a deposit paid or was the entire amount owing due on completion?" If the witness says "yes," it is not clear which question he or she is answering. Break it down into two separate questions.

Use Simple Language

Use simple language so that the witness and the decision-maker will understand what you are asking. For example, instead of asking, "What was the completed value of the projected construction renovation you were undertaking?" ask instead, "How much did the renovation cost?"

Do Not Ask Leading Questions

In direct examination, you are not allowed to ask leading questions. A **leading question** is one that suggests a desired answer or one that assumes a fact in dispute that has not yet been proved. Disallowing such questions prevents you from "feeding" answers to your witness. For example, consider the following question: "You were angry, weren't you?" This question clearly suggests the answer "yes." You should instead ask, "How did you feel?" A question such as "When did you deliver the appliances?" is leading if there has been no evidence before the court that the appliances had, in fact, been delivered, because it assumes this fact.

When preparing your direct examination questions, think about whether the question either assumes a fact or suggests a desired answer. If either of these is the case, rephrase the question so that it is non-leading. One way to help you avoid leading questions is by using the following introductory language: who, what, where, when, why, and how; tell me about …; what happened next?; explain …

The following table contains examples of leading versus non-leading questions.

TABLE 7.1 Leading Versus Non-Leading Questions

Leading Questions	Non-Leading Questions
You met with the landlord on March 1, didn't you?	Who did you meet with on March 1?
Were you going to talk to the landlord about terminating your lease?	Why were you at the landlord's office?
Was the landlord angry when she heard the news?	How did the landlord react when she heard the news?
Did the landlord yell at you after you told her the news?	What did the landlord do after you told her the news?
Did the landlord demand that you leave?	What did the landlord do next?

As you can see, leading questions can usually be answered only with "yes" or "no," while non-leading questions are open-ended.

The general rule is that you should not ask leading questions during direct examination, but there are some exceptions to this rule. For example, you can lead your witness when asking about a matter that

- is introductory—for example, "Do you work at Alice's Appliances?"
- is undisputed—for example, "Did you purchase a fridge?"

- is directing the witness to a specific subject, by way of introduction—for example, "At some point you had a meeting with the landlord; is that correct?" After the witness says "yes," you can go on to ask, "Can you tell me when that was?"

GUIDELINES FOR DIRECT EXAMINATION

When preparing and conducting the direct examination of your witness, you should follow these basic guidelines.

Keep the Focus on the Witness

As Thomas Mauet said, "[A] witness will be believed and remembered because of the manner and content of his or her testimony, not because the questions asked were so brilliant." The focus should be on the witness, not on you. Avoid behaviour that may distract the judge or other decision-maker from listening to what the witness is saying. For example, if you start pacing while your witness is speaking, you will draw attention to yourself and away from the witness. Also, many advocates have a habit of repeating the witness's answer. This is distracting and annoying, so do not do it. To have the testimony unfold as if the witness is telling a story, it should sound "natural" even though you have "rehearsed" it with your witness.

Listen to What Your Witness Says

Although you want to remain passive while the witness speaks, you should still show interest in what your witness is saying. Pay attention to and maintain interest in your witness's testimony. Make sure that your witness has answered your question fully. If he or she has not, ask additional questions. If the witness anticipates and answers several of your prepared questions at once, make sure you don't ask the questions he or she has already answered.

Direct the Witness's Testimony

You are the "director" of the examination, and your goal is to keep the testimony moving in a clear and logical manner. You accomplish this by directing the witness to the topics you will cover and then by asking questions that elicit a story that is understandable, logical, and convincing. The judge (and the witness) should know where you are headed with your questions. For example, assume your case involves a meeting that took place between a landlord and tenant on March 1. Do not simply ask the witness, "What did you do on March 1?" The witness probably did many things that day that have absolutely nothing to do with your case. Instead, you should say, "Ms. Lahari, you told us earlier about a problem you were having with your apartment. Did you ever meet with the landlord to discuss that problem?"

Admit Your Weak Facts

You can be sure that the other side has anticipated your theory and identified the weaknesses of your case. You can also be sure that if you do not mention your weak facts during direct examination, the opposing advocate will raise them in cross-examination! It is far better to admit your weak facts as part of your direct examination because you can control how and when the information comes out. More importantly, the witness can explain away the weakness in a logical and reasonable manner, something he or she will not be able to do during cross-examination. Admitting weaknesses up front also enhances the credibility of your case—it shows that you have nothing to hide.

Remember That Facts Outweigh Opinion

You call witnesses to testify at a trial or hearing because they have personal knowledge of events that are relevant to your case. In other words, they have directly seen, heard, or done something that is relevant to the issues in the case. When testifying, witnesses should relate facts, not their opinions. Factual evidence has more value than opinion evidence unless the witness is an expert (see below). For example, if a witness says, "I could see that the defendant was very upset," that is merely an opinion. You should then ask, "Why do you say that?" In this way, you can draw out the facts that caused the witness to form that opinion. The witness can then say, for example, "He became very quiet; he sat down; he had tears in his eyes."

Control the Speed of the Testimony

Many advocates rush through the witness's testimony. While both the advocate and his or her witness are familiar with the story, the judge or other decision-maker is not—this is the first time that he or she is hearing the story. You must pay attention to the judge or other decision-maker to make sure he or she has enough time to absorb what is being said and to write it down. Take your time. Pause after your witness answers a question—make sure the evidence is being heard and understood. If your witness is speaking too fast, slow him or her down. If your witness answers a question with a lot of information at once, be certain the judge has taken it all in. If you are in doubt, break down the witness's answer into small parts and review each part.

Finally, try to hold the attention of the decision-maker. If your questions are disorganized, irrelevant, and/or repetitive, he or she may become bored, inattentive, and annoyed. Thorough preparation will help you maximize the impact of your direct examination.

EXPERT WITNESSES

An expert witness is a witness who, because of his or her education, skill, or experience, has more knowledge than the average person about a particular subject matter in dispute. By virtue of his or her expertise, training, and specialized knowledge in a particular subject, the witness is considered to be an expert in that subject. Expert witnesses are allowed to give their expert opinions on matters that involve their area

BOX 7.1

Direct Examination of Alec Baldwin in the Kitchen Renovation Case

Q: What is your relationship to Baldwin Brothers Construction?
A: I'm an owner of the business together with my brother Stephen.

Q: Can you tell me a little bit about the business?
A: We're licensed contractors and have been in business for ten years. We do general contracting work, specializing in small renovation projects.

Q: What is your relationship with the defendants?
A: Six months ago Tina Fey hired us to renovate her kitchen.

Q: What renovations were you hired to do?
A: Tina told us she wanted the kitchen cabinets painted white, new hardware installed on the doors, a new countertop, and the existing lighting replaced with pot lights. She also wanted the kitchen walls and ceiling painted.

Q: How many pot lights were you supposed to install?
A: We talked about how many pot lights she would need to make her kitchen bright. I told her that pot lights normally cost $250 each installed, and that five would be the right number for her kitchen.

Q: Did you talk about the possibility of additional lights?
A: Yes. She asked what would happen if she wanted more light, and I said, "Then we can install more" even though I was sure five would be enough.

Q: Did you and Ms. Fey agree on a contract price?
A: Yes. Based on our discussions I gave her a price of $7,500 for all the work, and she agreed.

Q: Did you ask for a deposit before starting the work?
A: Yes, Ms. Fey gave me a deposit of $2,500.

Q: And did you in fact do the work?
A: Yes. We went to the house the following week to start the work. We installed the new countertop. After that I went to another job, and my brother completed the work at the Feys.

Q: How long did it take to complete the work?
A: Less than a week.

Q: Did you give the Feys an invoice for your work?
A: My brother dealt with the invoice and payment. ◇

of expertise, even though they do not have personal knowledge of events relating to the case. For example, a plumber can testify about the probable cause of toilet damage, even though he or she was not present when the toilet was damaged. If you call an expert witness, you must first demonstrate that the witness has the necessary background and expertise to give an opinion. The other side's advocate may challenge the witness's credentials and qualification as an expert, in which case it is up to the judge or other decision-maker to determine whether the witness qualifies as an expert.

Box 7.1 contains a sample direct examination of Alec Baldwin in the Kitchen Renovation Case.

REVIEW QUESTIONS

1. What is direct examination, and what is its purpose?
2. How should you design your direct examination questions?
3. How should you prepare yourself for direct examination?
4. In what areas must you prepare each witness?
5. What are the basic rules to follow when formulating the questions for your witnesses during direct examination?
6. What are the basic guidelines to follow when preparing and conducting the direct examination of your witnesses?
7. What is an expert witness, and how may his or her evidence differ from that of other witnesses?

DISCUSSION QUESTION

Prepare a direct examination of Tina Fey in the Kitchen Renovation Case.

CHAPTER 8

Cross-Examination of Witnesses

You present your version of the facts of your case through the direct examination of your witnesses, but your version of the facts does not go unchallenged. The advocate for the other side has the right to challenge your version of the facts by way of cross-examination of your witnesses. In addition, the other side will present another version of the facts through the direct examination of his or her witnesses. However, you too have the right to challenge those witnesses by cross-examination.

The importance of cross-examination to the success or failure of a case is generally overrated. In a criminal trial cross-examination takes on more importance if the defence chooses not to call any witnesses, but in a civil case, the theory of your case is presented through the direct examination of your own witnesses, and it is that evidence that will win your case. Cross-examination of the other party's witnesses generally serves only to confirm that evidence. Having said that, cross-examination is probably the most dreaded part of a trial—for both the questioner and the witness—and that is because it involves the unknown. Unlike direct examination, you do not have an opportunity to practise with the witness you are questioning; in fact, you do not know the witness at all, and you do not know for sure what the witness will say. However, it is possible to limit the risk inherent in cross-examination, and therefore the anxiety, through proper preparation.

This chapter discusses the purpose of and the preparation for the cross-examination of the other party's witnesses.

DEFINITION AND PURPOSE OF CROSS-EXAMINATION

Cross-examination is the questioning of a witness who was produced by the other side. It takes place immediately after the direct examination of that witness.

The two main goals of cross-examination are

- to get the witness to give evidence that is favourable to your case and
- to get the witness to give evidence that will discredit testimony given by that witness on direct examination that is unfavourable to your case.

In almost every case, the destruction of the witness is *not* your goal. Keep in mind that most witnesses are not lying when they testify in court. They may be mistaken or relying on bad information, but generally they are not lying. Even if your goal is to discredit the witness, your approach should be to attack the evidence, not the witness.

PREPARING FOR CROSS-EXAMINATION

Just because you cannot practise your cross-examination with the witness (as you were able to do with your direct examination) does not mean that you do not have to prepare. In fact, the opposite is true. Because there is the element of the unknown, planning and preparing are all the more important.

Prepare for cross-examination by doing the following:

- Before the trial or hearing,
  - ◇ know your case well and
  - ◇ select target areas for cross-examination.
- During the trial or hearing,
  - ◇ listen to what the witness says in direct examination,
  - ◇ listen to what the witness says during cross-examination, and
  - ◇ know when not to cross-examine.

Preparation Before the Trial or Hearing

The bulk of your preparation for cross-examination takes place before you go to court or appear before a tribunal.

KNOW YOUR CASE WELL

Learn everything you can about the evidence involved in your case. Review again the pleadings and documents. Think about who will be testifying for the other side. For each witness, ask:

- Why is this witness being called?
- What can this witness say to help the other side's case?
- What can this witness say to hurt your case?

Find out what the witness has already said about the case—for example, by way of a written statement or previous sworn testimony.

SELECT TARGET AREAS FOR CROSS-EXAMINATION

Your goals are to get the witness to give evidence that is favourable to your case and/or to get the witness to give evidence that will call into question unfavourable testimony given by the witness on direct examination. Consider how each witness fits within your theory of the case, and focus on the matters that are in dispute. Think about what you might say about this witness's evidence in closing, and then structure your cross-examination around these matters. For example, if you will try to prove that the witness's recollection of an event is unreliable, focus on facts that will support this: the witness was distracted by other events, the witness was talking to someone else at the time, and so on. You should have a purpose for every question you ask. If a question has no purpose, don't ask it.

Preparation During the Trial or Hearing

Given the nature of cross-examination, you cannot be fully prepared before the trial or hearing starts. You must continue to prepare even as the trial or hearing is going on.

LISTEN TO WHAT THE WITNESS SAYS IN DIRECT EXAMINATION

Take notes as the witness testifies. Pay particular attention to what the witness says in your "target areas." Leave room at the margin of your notes to insert, where appropriate, the questions you have already drafted. That way, when you ask the questions, you can refer to the witness's own testimony on the point. As you listen to the witness's testimony, you may have to change your questions, add questions, or abandon questions.

LISTEN TO WHAT THE WITNESS SAYS DURING CROSS-EXAMINATION

Your preparation for cross-examination continues until the minute you end your cross-examination. Every time the witness answers one of your questions, you have to decide what to do next: Continue on the line of questioning as previously planned? Pursue a new line of questioning? Abandon the line of questioning? You have to think on your feet!

KNOW WHEN NOT TO CROSS-EXAMINE

As you listen to the testimony of a witness, ask yourself whether the witness has said anything that hurts your case. If not, don't cross-examine unless you think you can get the witness to say something that will help your case.

FORMULATING YOUR QUESTIONS

The key to a successful cross-examination is control. You control the witness by asking leading questions. As discussed in Chapter 7, a leading question is one that suggests a desired answer or assumes a fact not yet proved. Unlike in direct examination, where generally you are not allowed to ask leading questions, in cross-examination you not only can, but should, lead the witness. By asking leading questions you tell the witness what to say; you suggest desired answers. The best way to maintain control of the witness is to ask short, single-fact questions that can be answered only by "yes" or "no."

While it is permissible and wise to use leading questions on cross-examination, do not make the mistake of trying to turn every question into a leading question. The use of open-ended questions can be quite effective if you are reasonably sure of the answer that you will get and if you can phrase your question in a way that limits the breadth of the response. Sometimes, you will have to ask an open-ended question to get the information you need. However, you should avoid questions that invite an explanation. You should never ask a question during cross-examination that starts with "why." Any question that gives the witness an opportunity to simply repeat his or her direct examination, or to explain or clarify, is a mistake.

The following pointers will help you plan and execute an effective cross-examination.

KEEP IT SHORT

Keep your cross-examination as short and succinct as possible. There are many opportunities for disaster in a cross-examination. The less time you spend cross-examining, the less likely you are to get into trouble. You should have only a few target areas for your cross-examination—once you hit them, stop. If you question on too many irrelevant areas, you risk boring the judge or other decision-maker, who may then not be paying attention when you ask a question about something important.

BE ORGANIZED

Deal with one target area at a time; do not jump around from one unrelated question to another. While moving around from subject to subject may keep the witness off-balance, it is also likely to confuse the judge or other decision-maker, who may then miss it when you make an important point.

BE SUBTLE

Within each target area, frame your questions so that you extract small pieces of information at a time. This approach has several advantages. First, the witness does not see where you are going until it is too late. Second, if the witness gives you answers that you do not like, you can readjust your questioning before too much damage is done.

DO NOT ASK THE WITNESS TO AGREE WITH YOUR CONCLUSION

Within each target area, ask only the questions that will get you the facts you need to support your conclusion about the evidence. Do not ask the witness to agree with your conclusion. First, you don't need the witness to agree with your conclusion; you need the judge or other decision-maker to agree with it. Think of the picture puzzle "connect the dots." Each dot is part of a picture that is not visible until all the dots are connected. In cross-examination, you know the picture you want to draw, and you are getting the witness to establish the dots for you. Do not ask the witness to connect the dots; you will do that when you present and discuss the evidence in your closing argument. Second, if you do ask the witness to agree with your conclusion, the odds are that the witness will not only disagree, but will explain away the facts you have already elicited that support your conclusion. For example, assume that you want to establish that a witness was not really paying attention when he claims he saw an event take place. That is your "picture"; your "dots" are the facts that support this conclusion—that he was distracted by a noise; that he turned away; that he bent down to tie his shoe; and so on. Ask questions only about these facts. In your closing, remind the judge of this evidence and submit that, as a result, the witness was not really paying attention. Do not ask the witness, "Since you were tying your shoes, you really weren't paying attention, were you?" First, it is unnecessary, and second, you will give the witness an opportunity to explain how he could do both at the same time. Save your conclusions for the judge.

DO NOT INVITE AN EXPLANATION

Focus your questions on getting only the facts you need to support your conclusions. Always avoid questions that invite an explanation. If the witness's answer does not make sense, or is false, avoid asking, "What do you mean?" or "How can you say that?" The answer will likely explain away the confusion and restore the witness's credibility. Avoid questions that are vague or contain a conclusion or judgment—these types of questions tend to provoke an explanation. Use questions that contain objective facts instead. For example, instead of asking, "You were distracted, weren't you?" you should ask, "You were talking to Ms. Bertelli at that moment, right?" or "You answered a phone call, isn't that right?"

KEEP YOUR QUESTIONS CLEAR AND SIMPLE

Use short, simple questions that focus on your target, and always use plain, basic words. As noted above, each question should be intended to elicit one fact only. For example, do not ask: "You were travelling in an easterly direction when you were operating your motor vehicle and it was dark out, isn't that right?" Instead ask, "You were driving your car east, is that right?" After the response, then ask, "And it was dark out, wasn't it?" Complex questions open the door to explanations. If your question invites an explanation, the witness must be given the opportunity to explain; you cannot cut the witness off. Shorter, more carefully phrased questions are more likely to result in single-word responses.

KEEP IT CIVIL

A witness will be more cooperative, and therefore more likely to give you the answers you are after, if you are polite and gentle than if you are rude and a bully.

PAY ATTENTION

Listen carefully to the answers given in cross-examination. If the witness does not answer your question, ask it again. If the witness offers more or different information than you expected, think about cross-examining on this new information. Pay attention to the answers and not to your next question!

KNOW THE ANSWER BEFORE YOU ASK THE QUESTION, OR AT LEAST KNOW THE RISK

A common wisdom of cross-examination is to ask only questions to which you already know the answer. However, it is difficult to achieve this level of certainty at tribunal and lower-level courts, because you do not have an opportunity to examine the other party under oath before the actual trial or hearing. If you are not sure what the answer to a question will be, weigh the potential benefit from the answer you want against the potential risk from the answer you do not want. If an unfavourable answer to a question can really hurt your case, it may be better not to ask that question. If an unfavourable answer will not really hurt, while a favourable answer will really help, you may want to risk asking the question.

DO NOT REPEAT THE OTHER SIDE'S DIRECT EXAMINATION

Do not give the witness an opportunity to repeat his or her testimony from the direct examination. That evidence helps the other side. You do not want the judge to hear it twice!

Box 8.1 contains a discussion of, and part of, a cross-examination of Alec Baldwin in the Kitchen Renovation Case.

BOX 8.1

Cross-Examination of Alec Baldwin in the Kitchen Renovation Case

In preparing to cross-examine Alec Baldwin, you must identify the target areas of your cross-examination. Those areas will come from those facts of the case that are in dispute. In this case Alec Baldwin's evidence is that there was an agreement to install five pot lights as part of the contract price and that installation of additional pot lights would cost $250 each. Tina Fey's evidence, on the other hand, is that there was an agreement to install all necessary pot lights, whatever number that would be. Alec suggested that five lights would be enough, but agreed to install more lights if necessary. He never said they would cost extra.

In cross-examining Alec Baldwin, the defendant will try to focus on the exact wording of the discussion between Alec and Tina, and try to establish that there was no clear agreement that she would have to pay extra if more than five lights were installed.

Q: You stated in your direct examination that you told Ms. Fey that five lights would be the right number for her kitchen. Is that correct?

A: Yes, that's correct.

Q: And you stated that you could install more lights if she wanted more?

A: Yes.

Q: Did you specifically tell her that any additional lights would cost extra?

A: I told her that pot lights cost $250 each.

Q: But did you specifically tell her that additional lights would cost extra?

A: No.

Q: Did either of the defendants ever specifically agree to pay extra for the additional lights?

A: No. ◇

REVIEW QUESTIONS

1. What is cross-examination and when does it take place?
2. What are the two main goals of cross-examination?
3. What questions should you ask yourself when preparing for cross-examination before the trial or hearing?
4. What should you consider when selecting target areas for cross-examination?
5. How should you prepare for cross-examination during the trial or hearing?
6. When should you not cross-examine a witness?
7. Why should you use leading questions during cross-examination?
8. When should you use open-ended questions during cross-examination?
9. What types of questions should you always avoid during cross-examination?

DISCUSSION QUESTION

Prepare a cross-examination of Tina Fey in the Kitchen Renovation Case.

CHAPTER 9

Re-examination

After the other side has finished cross-examining your witness, you have the chance to question your witness again by way of re-examination. Re-examination ends the questioning of the witness by the parties, and unless the judge has questions for the witness, the witness may return to his or her seat in the courtroom or hearing room.

SCOPE AND PURPOSE OF RE-EXAMINATION

The scope of re-examination is limited. You may question the witness only about matters arising out of the witness's answers in cross-examination. It is not an opportunity to have your witness repeat, correct, or add to evidence given in his or her direct examination. In other words, this is *not* a second chance at direct examination. This limitation arises as a matter of fairness: if you introduce new material after the cross-examination of your witness, that is evidence on which the other side has not had a chance to cross-examine.

The purpose of re-examination is to respond to, explain, or clarify matters raised during cross-examination, but only if explanation or clarification is needed. You can use re-examination to give your witness a chance to explain why a particular answer was given on cross-examination—especially helpful if the question limited your client to a "yes" or "no" answer. Of course, you should not ask for an explanation unless you are confident your client has one that is beneficial to your case.

In fact, it is often dangerous to re-examine. If your witness has given damaging evidence on cross-examination, and you cannot repair the damage, all you will do is reinforce or highlight the damaging information! If your client has given new information on cross-examination, but the information has not hurt your case, do not re-examine.

During re-examination, you may not use leading questions. Any explanation or clarification must come from the witness, not you. You cannot, for example, ask, "When you said Mr. Smith appeared confused, didn't you really mean he appeared drunk?" Instead, you would have to ask, "In your cross-examination, you stated that Mr. Smith appeared confused. Can you explain what you meant by that?"

PREPARING FOR AND CONDUCTING RE-EXAMINATION

Take notes while your witness is being cross-examined. Make a note of any new information given by your witness. Review this evidence to determine whether it is harmful. If so, consider whether your witness will improve the situation if you ask for an explanation.

If you decide to re-examine your witness, start each line of questioning with a reference to and a restatement of the particular evidence given on cross-examination, and then ask your questions. For example, "On your cross-examination you stated you didn't complain to the landlord about the other tenant; can you explain why you didn't complain?"

REVIEW QUESTIONS

1. What is the scope of re-examination?
2. What is the purpose of re-examination?
3. Why can it often be dangerous to re-examine your witness?
4. What types of questions can you ask during re-examination?
5. Briefly discuss how to prepare for and organize your re-examination.

CHAPTER 10

Exhibits

One of your key roles as an advocate is to prove your version of the facts to the judge or other decision-maker. This is done by way of your evidence, almost always in the form of oral testimony of witnesses who tell the judge or other decision-maker what happened in the case. Many cases also involve some sort of physical evidence—a signed contract, a letter, a photograph, the sunglasses that were allegedly stolen—something that you can show to the decision-maker to help prove your case. These objects cannot walk into the witness box and testify, but instead must be introduced as exhibits through the oral testimony of witnesses.

This chapter discusses the purpose of exhibits and sets out the steps for introducing exhibits as evidence.

DEFINITION AND PURPOSE OF EXHIBITS

An **exhibit** is an object that is introduced as evidence at a trial or hearing. An exhibit is any non-oral evidence that is made part of the record of the trial or hearing. Exhibits include documents, such as letters or contracts; physical evidence, such as property; and demonstrative evidence, such as photographs or diagrams.

An exhibit can provide objective, physical evidence to support and strengthen a witness's oral testimony. For example, assume a landlord is alleging that a tenant caused damage to the rental unit. The landlord can give oral testimony in which he or she describes the damage; however, a picture of the unit showing the damage is far more compelling and, as the saying goes, "A picture is worth a thousand words." As you prepare the direct examination of your witnesses, always consider whether there are exhibits available to support your witnesses' testimony. To be useful, an exhibit should either, in and of itself, prove a fact or help the judge or other decision-maker better understand the evidence.

USING EXHIBITS

Exhibits may be introduced during the direct examination of your witnesses or during the cross-examination of the other side's witnesses.

Using Exhibits in Direct Examination

Exhibits may be introduced during direct examination to confirm a fact being testified to. For example, assume your witness testifies that he had a written contract setting out the terms of a renovation project. You should introduce the contract itself as an exhibit. Doing so helps to prove both that the contract exists and that it was signed by both parties. The judge or other decision-maker can then actually read the terms of the contract. Or, assume your witness testifies about damage done to her sweater by a dry cleaner. Instead of merely describing the damage, you should introduce the sweater as an exhibit to allow the judge or other decision-maker to see the actual damage. Exhibits may also be used to help the judge or other decision-maker better understand the witness's testimony. For example, a diagram or photograph of an accident location may clarify the witness's testimony regarding the accident.

Using Exhibits During Cross-Examination

Exhibits may be introduced during cross-examination to help you discredit the witness's testimony. For example, the opposing witness, your client's landlord, has testified that he never received notice from your client that your client's apartment was in need of repairs. You should introduce as an exhibit a copy of the letter your client sent to the landlord complaining about the damage.

INTRODUCING EXHIBITS INTO EVIDENCE

You cannot simply give an object to the judge or other decision-maker to consider; you must introduce it as an exhibit through the testimony of a witness who has direct knowledge of the object and is able to verify its authenticity. You must also be able to establish that the exhibit is relevant to the facts of the case—the primary test of admissibility of all evidence—and that you have followed any other procedural steps required for admissibility. For example, under the Rules of the Small Claims Court, a written statement or document that has been served on all parties at least 14 days before the trial date must be received in evidence, unless the trial judge orders otherwise.

An exhibit may be introduced by asking a limited number of questions, and the process usually does not take long. However, those questions must cover a number of steps to properly introduce and use the exhibit.

1. Establish a context for the exhibit.
2. Set up the exhibit.
3. Show the exhibit to the witness and to the other side.
4. Have the witness authenticate the exhibit.
5. Enter the exhibit into evidence.
6. Use the exhibit.

1. Establish a Context for the Exhibit

Inexperienced advocates often introduce an exhibit first and then try to explain how it fits into the evidence. Instead, you should establish a context for the exhibit before you introduce it by steering the direct examination toward the matters or facts to which the exhibit relates.

2. Set Up the Exhibit

Once you have established a context for the exhibit, focus your questions on the exhibit itself, making sure to include enough information so that it is clear exactly what the exhibit is. For example, "I'm going to show you a lease agreement dated February 2, 2007." Your set-up should establish that the exhibit has probative value or will assist the witness with his or her oral testimony. Often, this is obvious by the very nature of the exhibit.

The following examples illustrate the right way and the wrong way to establish a context for and set up an exhibit (that is, steps 1 and 2).

Your client is a landlord and has testified that the original rent for an apartment was $1,000 per month. You are now trying to establish that the rent has been increased to $1,014 by way of a notice of rent increase (as required by legislation).

The wrong way:

Paralegal: I'm showing you a notice of rent increase dated December 1, 2007. Can you explain what this is?

The right way:

Paralegal: Is the monthly rent still $1,000 per month?
Landlord: No. I increased the rent effective March 1, 2008.

Paralegal: What did you do to increase the rent?
Landlord: I served the tenant with a notice of rent increase.

Paralegal: I'm showing you a notice of rent increase dated December 1, 2007. Is this the notice of rent increase you served?
Landlord: Yes.

3. Show the Exhibit to the Witness and to the Other Side

Show the exhibit to the witness and then hand it to him or her. You must also show the exhibit to the other side, unless you have already provided a copy, in which case, tell the judge or other decision-maker that you have done so.

4. Have the Witness Authenticate the Exhibit

Once the witness has the exhibit, you must connect the exhibit to the witness to establish that the witness is qualified to testify about it. In other words, the witness must have some direct involvement with or knowledge of the exhibit. For example, a party would be qualified to give evidence in court about an exhibit if he or she

- prepared the exhibit,
- received the exhibit from another party, or
- discovered the exhibit.

Make sure that the witness confirms the identity of the document. For example:

Paralegal: I'm showing you a notice of rent increase dated December 1, 2007. Is this the notice of rent increase you served?
Landlord: Yes it is.

You must also prove that the exhibit is authentic—in other words, it is what you say it is. If the exhibit is property, such as a sweater damaged by a dry cleaner, you must establish that it has not been tampered with in any way before trial. If the exhibit is a photograph or diagram, you must establish that it is accurate and does not in any way distort the evidence it illustrates. If the exhibit is a document, you must show that it has not been amended or modified in any way.

5. Enter the Exhibit into Evidence

After the witness identifies the exhibit, take it back from the witness and hand it to the judge or other decision-maker (or to the clerk, if there is one, who will hand it to the decision-maker). Ask the decision-maker to enter it into evidence as an exhibit by stating, "I would ask that this (document) be introduced as Exhibit (X)." The decision-maker will briefly state the nature of the exhibit and then assign the exhibit a number. For example, if you introduce a lease as the second exhibit of a trial, the judge might state: "Lease agreement dated February 2, 2007, marked as Exhibit #2."

Keep a list of all the exhibits entered during the trial or hearing. Record the number of each exhibit and a brief description. The list will help you both keep track of the number to be assigned to the next exhibit and retrieve an exhibit if you need to use it again. If you are about to enter an exhibit and cannot remember what number it will be, simply ask that it be marked as the next exhibit.

6. Use the Exhibit

Having gone to all this trouble to enter the exhibit, make sure that you actually use it! Ask your witness questions about the exhibit. You may use the exhibit to help your witness with details of his or her evidence. For example, your witness may have testified that he or she signed a written contract for the renovation of a bathroom, and you entered the contract as an exhibit. Have your witness look at the exhibit while asking questions about the terms of the contract instead of having the witness recall the details of the contract from memory. At the very least, draw the attention of the decision-maker to the key aspects of the exhibit.

The decision-maker may ask you whether you want the exhibit back after he or she marks it and enters it into evidence. If you are not asked, then ask the decision-maker or clerk for the exhibit and give it to the witness. Then, ask questions about it. When you are finished with the exhibit, be sure to return it to the decision-maker or clerk.

WORKING WITH EXHIBITS THAT HAVE ALREADY BEEN ENTERED

You may want to refer a witness to an exhibit that has been entered into evidence earlier in the trial through another witness. In that case, ask for the exhibit using the number and description assigned to it by the judge or other decision-maker. For example, "Your Honour, may I please have Exhibit #5, the lease agreement." Present it to the witness by saying, "I am showing you Exhibit #5." Remember to return the exhibit to the decision-maker or clerk when you are finished using it.

REVIEW QUESTIONS

1. What is an exhibit? Provide an example.
2. Why are exhibits useful at trial?
3. Provide an example of how exhibits may be used during direct examination.
4. Provide an example of how exhibits may be used during cross-examination.
5. What are the six steps you should follow to properly introduce and use an exhibit? Briefly summarize each step.
6. How do you use an exhibit that has already been entered into evidence earlier in the trial through another witness?

DISCUSSION QUESTION

Your witness is a residential landlord who entered into a written tenancy agreement with Tom Tenant on January 15, 2008 for a one-year term starting February 1, 2008 at a monthly rent of $1,000. Prepare the part of the landlord's direct examination in which you introduce the tenancy agreement as an exhibit, and question the landlord about the exhibit.

CHAPTER 11

Closing Argument

After the last witness is excused, the advocate for each side is given an opportunity to summarize his or her case for the judge or other decision-maker.

In Chapter 6, the following rule for public speaking was discussed: start by telling your audience what you are going to tell them; tell them; then tell them what you have told them. Think of the trial or hearing as a speech: you tell the judge or other decision-maker what you are going to tell him or her in your opening statement; you do the telling with your evidence; and then you tell the judge or other decision-maker what you have told him or her in your closing argument. The closing argument is your last chance to persuade the judge or other decision-maker to decide the case in favour of your client.

This chapter discusses the closing argument—its purpose, how to prepare one, and how to present it.

PURPOSE OF CLOSING ARGUMENT

The purpose of the closing argument is to persuade the judge or other decision-maker to choose your theory of the case over that of the other side. At the conclusion of the trial or hearing, the judge, justice of the peace, or adjudicator will make a decision either for or against your client by first determining the facts of the case and then applying the relevant law to those facts. In order to win, you have to be successful on both the facts and the law, and a closing argument addresses both.

With respect to the facts, the purpose of the closing argument is to summarize your version of the facts and persuade the judge or other decision-maker to prefer your version of the facts to that of the other side. This is the time to "connect the dots" of your evidence—to advise the judge or other decision-maker of the reasonable inferences and logical conclusions to be drawn from the evidence presented during the trial, both through the direct examination of your witnesses and the cross-examination of the witnesses for the other side.

With respect to the law, the purpose of the closing argument is to advise the judge or other decision-maker of the relevant law and to demonstrate how the law should be applied to your facts so that you win.

PREPARING YOUR CLOSING ARGUMENT

Most of your closing argument can be—and in fact should be—prepared before the trial or hearing starts. If you have properly prepared for your trial or hearing, you will have developed your theory of the case and will therefore know what the evidence will be and what the relevant law is. You should also be able to anticipate the evidence that will be presented by the other side and what your witnesses will be asked on cross-examination—although you cannot know for sure. As a result, you will have to finalize your closing argument during the trial or hearing, after all the evidence has been presented, to make sure that your conclusions and inferences are supported by the evidence as actually given. However, if you are well prepared going into the trial or hearing, there should not be too many, if any, surprises during the trial or hearing.

You should keep in mind the following guidelines as you prepare your closing argument.

Use Common Sense

Your closing argument should be logical, credible, and easy for the judge or other decision-maker to follow. It should be based on the facts and supported by the law, and not be based on wishful thinking.

Do Not Argue Facts Not in Evidence

You can refer only to evidence that has in fact been presented during the trial or hearing. Any conclusion that you draw must be supported by the facts established during direct examination of your witnesses or cross-examination of the witnesses of the other side. You cannot assume facts in your closing argument. You are, however, allowed to argue matters of general knowledge or common sense.

Do Not Misstate the Law or the Evidence

You must present the law and the evidence accurately. When summarizing or paraphrasing legal principles, be careful not to change their meaning. When referring to evidence, present it in an impartial and fair manner. Remain neutral—do not let your bias or prejudice in the case influence you to misrepresent the evidence.

Do Not State Your Personal Belief

Do not state your personal views about your client, your witnesses, or the case, and avoid using any language that may suggest a personal opinion or belief of the worthiness of your case or the credibility of your witnesses. For example, do not introduce arguments with the words "I believe" or "I think." It doesn't matter what you think or believe; what matters is what the judge is persuaded to think or believe. The facts and the law should speak for themselves.

Remember that your closing argument is your last opportunity to speak to the judge or other decision-maker—use it wisely! Weave all the evidence together into a compelling, logical, and persuasive argument that supports your theory of the case, and that is consistent with the facts and supported by the law.

FORMAT OF CLOSING ARGUMENT

Your closing argument should be a clear, concise, and persuasive synopsis of the issues, the evidence, and the law. Your closing argument should walk the judge or other decision-maker through your theory of the case and lead him or her to the conclusion that your case should prevail. Proper organization is crucial.

There is no prescribed format for a closing argument, but the following structure is suggested:

1. Outline the issues you will deal with in your closing argument.
2. Deal with each issue in turn, addressing the facts and the law relating to the issue.
3. State the relief you are seeking.

1. Outline the Issues

Start by telling the judge or other decision-maker how many issues you will be dealing with. For example, "Your Honour, there are three issues in this case." Then, set out each issue: "The first issue is whether … ." These issues should be the same ones you set out in your opening statement. However, instead of simply stating the issues, you also state your position on each issue. For example, "Your Honour, there are three issues in this case. The first issue is whether there was a contract between the parties, and we submit that there was."

2. Deal with Each Issue

For each issue you identify, start by summarizing the evidence adduced at the trial or hearing in keeping with your theory of the case. Your goal is to convince the judge or other decision-maker to accept your version of the facts. Start with the evidence about which the parties agree. Then, discuss the evidence that is in dispute, and give the judge or other decision-maker some reason to prefer your version of the evidence. This is the time to draw logical inferences and conclusions that clearly favour your theory and support your view of the disputed evidence. Think of ways you can strengthen the evidence—for example, by convincing the judge or other decision-maker that your witnesses are more believable, and by identifying corroboration, consistency, and impartiality within the testimony. Raise inconsistencies, contradictions, or bias apparent in the evidence presented by the other side. Tie the evidence together to present a convincing case that supports your theory. Make sure you have explained away any unfavourable evidence—do not leave any loose ends.

After summarizing the facts, move on to a discussion of the relevant law—statute law or case law or both—that applies to each issue. When referring to a statutory provision, state the name of the statute and the applicable section. If the section is not too long, read it; otherwise, summarize it, being careful not to change the meaning. When referring to case law, give the case name and then summarize the principle of law underlying the case. You may also quote directly from the case. As you refer to each statutory provision or case, state how the legal principle applies to the facts of the case. You should be sure to provide the judge or decision-maker with a book of authorities, containing copies of the statutory provisions and/or cases to which you make reference. Also, refer the judge or decision-maker to the appropriate pages in the book of authorities as you discuss each one. See Chapter 14 for a more complete discussion of the book of authorities.

After you have finished your discussion of the relevant statutes and/or cases, state your conclusion for the particular issue.

Repeat this process for each issue you identified in the introduction to your closing argument.

3. State the Relief You Are Seeking

When you are finished discussing each issue, state the relief or judgment you are seeking. For example, if you are representing a defendant, you will likely be asking that the plaintiff's case be dismissed.

ADJUST YOUR LANGUAGE FOR ORAL PRESENTATION

Keep in mind that you will be delivering your closing argument orally; the judge or other decision-maker will not be reading what you have written. Accordingly, after you prepare your closing argument using the above format, read through it and adjust your language so that it is appropriate for an oral presentation. The following pointers may be helpful:

- *Keep your sentence structure simple and your sentences short.* Complex sentences that may be simple to read are difficult for a listener to understand.
- *Use introductory sentences to take the place of headings.* State what you will be talking about at the start of each part of the closing argument. For example, when dealing with each issue, start by saying, "I would now like to deal with the second issue, which is … (restate the issue)."
- *Use words you know how to pronounce.* Make sure you will be able to deliver your closing argument without tripping over any of your words.
- *Use language that is persuasive and respectful, not argumentative.* Although it is called a closing *argument*, you should never argue with the judge or other decision-maker! The term *argument* refers to the fact that you are trying to persuade the judge or decision-maker. Use language and sentence structure that show respect for the authority of the judge, justice of the peace, or adjudicator to make the final decision. Never tell the decision-maker what to do—for example, "You should prefer the evidence of the plaintiff." Instead, submit or suggest—for example, "I submit that the plaintiff's evidence should be preferred to that of the defendant."

PRACTISE YOUR CLOSING ARGUMENT

Practise delivering your closing argument so that your delivery will enhance, and not diminish, your argument's effectiveness.

You should be familiar enough with your closing argument so that you do not have to read it. Instead, try to talk to the judge or decision-maker and tell him or her about your case. However, you do not have to memorize your closing argument. You may look to your notes, read a passage, pause, and look at the judge or other decision-maker. Sometimes, working from memory may cause your delivery to be stilted. Instead, use your notes to help you with your pacing. Block your argument out; use large print so that you will be forced to read only small bits at a time, and will not lose your place. Leave lots of white space between ideas to remind yourself to pause.

Practise speaking slowly so that the judge or decision-maker will be able to follow and absorb what you have to say. Speak a lot more slowly than you think you need to.

Use pacing to reinforce the organization and meaning of your closing argument. Pause between sentences; pause longer between paragraphs. Your pacing takes the place of commas, periods, and paragraphs.

Practise using the appropriate honorific: Your Honour, Your Worship, Ms. Adjudicator, as the case may be.

Practise speaking loudly. The judge or decision-maker must be able to hear you if he or she is to understand you.

Finally, practise speaking with expression. If you speak in a monotone, you will bore the decision-maker and lose his or her attention. Make a special effort to avoid "up-talk," the tendency, especially among young people, to express statements as if they were questions. "Up-talk" makes a speaker sound nervous and tentative, rather than confident and persuasive.

Box 11.1 contains a sample closing argument for the plaintiff in the Kitchen Renovation Case.

BOX 11.1

Plaintiff's Closing Argument in the Kitchen Renovation Case

Your Honour, the issue in this case is whether the defendants breached their contract with the plaintiff by failing to pay the cost of installation of three pot lights, and we submit that they have.

The facts of the case are as follows:

Both parties agree that they entered into a contract for minor renovations to the defendants' kitchen in the amount of $7,500. Both parties also agree that the contract required the plaintiff to install pot lights in the kitchen. The evidence of the parties differs, however, with respect to the exact number of pot lights that were included in the contract price. The defendants' evidence is that the contract price included the installation of all necessary pot lights to make the kitchen bright. The plaintiff's evidence is that the contract price included the installation of only five pot lights, and that any additional pot lights requested would cost extra.

We submit that the evidence of the plaintiff should be preferred on this point because it is not reasonable to assume that a contractor would agree to provide an undefined number of lights.

This case involves common-law principles of contract law, in particular contract interpretation. We submit that there is clearly a contract between the parties, and the only issue is one of interpretation. We submit that, in interpreting contracts, the court should try to give effect to the intention of the parties based on the clear meaning of the words they used, and that each party must persuade the court that his or her interpretation of the contract is the correct one.

In this case, the evidence of the parties about the exact words used differs. However, if Your Honour prefers the evidence of the plaintiffs, as we submit Your Honour should, then Your Honour should conclude that the contract provided for five pot lights only, and additional pot lights were to cost extra.

We therefore submit that the defendants are responsible for the cost of supplying and installing the three additional pot lights at a cost of $250 each.

The plaintiffs therefore ask for damages in the amount of $750 for the cost of supplying and installing the additional three pot lights. ◇

REVIEW QUESTIONS

1. What is the purpose of the closing argument?
2. When should you prepare your closing argument?
3. What is the recommended format for a closing argument? Briefly describe what should be included in each step.
4. How and why should you adjust the language of your closing argument so that it is appropriate for an oral presentation?
5. Why is it important to practise delivering your closing argument?

DISCUSSION QUESTION

Prepare a closing argument for the defendant in the Kitchen Renovation Case.

CHAPTER 12

Additional Submissions

After closing arguments the judge, justice of the peace, or adjudicator will give his or her decision in the case. After delivery of the decision, you may be called upon to make additional submissions on costs, interest, or sentence, depending on the nature of the matter.

COSTS

If you are successful at your hearing or trial, your client may be able to recover fees and expenses incurred in the conduct of your case by way of an award of **costs**. Sometimes, the judge or other decision-maker may simply fix costs, without requiring either advocate to make any submissions. For example, in Small Claims Court, the judge will typically award as costs the court fees (filing fee, set-down fee) and a preparation fee. At the Landlord and Tenant Board, the adjudicator will award a successful applicant the fees he or she paid to file his or her application.

The judge or other decision-maker may, however, ask both parties to make submissions on the issue of costs. These submissions are usually made right after the judge or other decision-maker delivers his or her decision. You should therefore be prepared to speak to costs.

Small Claims Court

Section 19 of the Rules of the Small Claims Court sets out the costs recoverable by a successful party. Generally speaking, the winning party is entitled to have his or her reasonable disbursements paid by the losing party. If the amount claimed in the action is over $500, exclusive of interest and costs, and the successful party is represented by a lawyer, student-at-law, or agent, the court may also award the party a reasonable representation fee at trial. Under s. 29 of the *Courts of Justice Act*, an award of costs in the Small Claims Court, other than disbursements, cannot exceed 15 percent of the amount claimed.

Before preparing your submission as to costs, you should review the relevant provisions of the Act and the Rules, so that you may refer to the rules on which you rely in support of your claim for costs. You should also prepare a detailed list of all the procedural steps taken and legal fees and disbursements incurred. Make sure you keep a copy of all your receipts, invoices, or cancelled cheques to prove that you paid the amounts claimed.

After the judge makes his or her decision (and if you are the successful party), wait for the judge to ask you whether you would like to speak to costs. Then, stand up, and state the amounts you are seeking and the authority for those amounts.

Tribunals

The *Statutory Powers Procedure Act* allows a tribunal to make its own rules about costs. At the Landlord and Tenant Board, costs are dealt with in the *Residential Tenancies Act, 2006* and the Rules of Practice of the Landlord and Tenant Board. Costs are also dealt with in an Interpretation Guideline. Review the Interpretation Guideline and Rules when you prepare your submissions.

Provincial Offences Court

Under the *Provincial Offences Act*, a person who is convicted of an offence may be ordered to pay costs in addition to any fine. The regulations to the Act set out the amount of costs payable. For example, if convicted, the defendant must pay costs in the amount of $5 for service of the offence notice or summons. Although the amount of costs payable is fixed by the regulations, the parties are given an opportunity to make submissions about costs. If your client has financial difficulties, you should ask to make submissions about costs to try to minimize the costs (and fine payable) as much as possible. You may also want to ask that the time given to pay the costs (and fine) be extended beyond the deadline imposed by the legislation

INTEREST

Generally speaking, a party who is awarded money at a trial or hearing is entitled to interest on the amount awarded. There are two kinds of interest: **pre-judgment interest** is calculated from the date the cause of action arose to the date of judgment and **post-judgment interest** is calculated from the date of judgment to the date payment is made. Both types of interest may be awarded at the Small Claims Court; only post-judgment interest may be awarded at the Landlord and Tenant Board.

The interest rate for both types of interest is set by law. However, there is discretion to change the interest rate or the period of time for which interest is allowed. For example, interest may be awarded at a lower rate than that prescribed by law if a party can establish that the circumstances of the case warrant it. As an advocate, you should be prepared to speak to the amount of interest awarded.

No interest is payable on fines imposed by the Provincial Offences Court. If payment is not made by the due date, the defendant's driver's licence can be suspended.

SENTENCE

If a person is convicted of an offence at Provincial Offences Court, he or she will be sentenced by the justice of the peace. The **sentence** is the penalty imposed for the offence committed. The sentence could be, for example, a set fine with or without costs, probation, licence suspension, or imprisonment. Before the sentence is imposed, the justice of the peace must ask both the prosecutor and the advocate for the defendant whether they have anything to say about the sentence.

You should be prepared to make submissions about the penalty that may be imposed. For example, if your client cannot afford to pay a fine, you can ask the court to reduce or waive the fine. If a minimum penalty is prescribed for an offence that includes imprisonment, you can ask the court to impose a fine of not more than $5,000 in lieu of imprisonment. When a fine is imposed, the defendant is given 15 days to pay it. If you think that your client will not be able to pay the fine on time, you should ask the court for more time to pay.

REVIEW QUESTIONS

1. How can a successful party recover the fees and expenses incurred in the conduct of his or her case?
2. What costs are recoverable by a successful party at the Small Claims Court?
3. What should you do when preparing your submissions as to costs in Small Claims Court?
4. When do you speak to costs in Small Claims Court?
5. How do you speak to costs in Small Claims Court?
6. How are costs dealt with at the Landlord and Tenant Board?
7. How are costs dealt with at Provincial Offences Court?
8. In what situation should you make submissions about costs at Provincial Offences Court?
9. How is pre-judgment interest calculated?
10. How is post-judgment interest calculated?
11. Why should you be prepared to speak to the amount of interest awarded?
12. What types of sentences may be imposed by the justice of the peace upon conviction in the Provincial Offences Court?
13. Briefly describe what submissions can be made about sentencing in Provincial Offences Court.

CHAPTER 13

Objections

A trial or hearing is a highly structured proceeding in which each party's advocate addresses the court or tribunal at a specified time. Under the rules of courtroom etiquette an advocate is required to listen quietly and respectfully when the opposing advocate is speaking. However, an advocate is permitted to speak out of turn, as it were, when making an objection.

This chapter discusses the purpose of objections, how they are made, and when they are made.

PURPOSE OF OBJECTIONS

Objections are used primarily to prevent improper evidence from being presented and considered by the court or tribunal. For example, objections may be made with respect to

- questions asked by an advocate,
- a witness's testimony, and
- the introduction or use of exhibits.

Less commonly, objections may also be used to object to the behaviour of the other advocate.

When made with respect to evidence, the purpose of the objection is to draw the decision-maker's attention to the impropriety of the evidence and to ask him or her to rule on its admissibility. If the decision-maker agrees with the objection, the objection is sustained and the evidence is excluded. If the decision-maker disagrees with the objection, the objection is overruled and the evidence is admitted.

How to Object

Make an objection by providing both notice of your objection and the grounds for your objection. Always direct your objection toward the judge or other decision-maker, not to the other advocate. It is important to be polite and respectful at all times, and not to shout or become argumentative.

Stand up and say, "I object, Your Honour." Then, state the reason for your objection, keeping it simple, yet specific. For example, "I object, Your Honour. The question is leading." The other side is given an opportunity to respond to your objection, and finally you have the opportunity to reply to that response. Remain standing until the judge or other decision-maker has made his or her ruling on the objection, and then sit down. Thank the decision-maker whether or not he or she rules in your favour.

TYPES OF OBJECTIONS

As stated earlier, objections are used primarily to prevent improper evidence from being presented and considered by the court or tribunal. As a result, most objections are made during the examination of witnesses. Some objections are based on the form in which the question is asked. Other objections are based on the substance of the evidence that the witness is being asked to give.

Objections to the Form of the Question

It is possible to object to the form in which a question is asked by the opposing advocate, even though the information being sought may be perfectly admissible. For example, you might object because a question is

- *leading* (on direct examination)—the question suggests the desired answer or assumes facts not in evidence;
- *compound*—the question asks two or more questions;
- *vague, ambiguous, or confusing*—the question is too general, has more than one meaning, or is confusing;
- *argumentative*—the question is an attempt to get the witness to agree with the questioner's conclusions or inferences rather than to agree with a statement of fact—the question is asked not to elicit information but rather to persuade the judge; or
- *repetitive*—the question has already been asked and answered (by the same witness).

These types of objections may be corrected by rephrasing the question.

Objections to the Substance of the Evidence

Objections to the substance of the evidence are based on the admissibility of evidence being asked for, and not on the question itself. The most common admissibility grounds are

- *hearsay*—the witness is stating what another person has said as proof of the truth of a relevant fact,
- *opinion*—the witness is not a qualified expert and is stating his or her opinion,
- *relevancy*—the evidence is not relevant to the issues of the case,
- *speculation*—the witness does not know the answer and is speculating about what the answer might be, and
- *privilege*—the evidence is protected by solicitor–client privilege.

Sometimes it is apparent from the question itself that the answer will contain evidence that should be excluded as inadmissible. For example, the question "What did your partner tell you about the quality of the goods your partnership sold?" is clearly asking for hearsay evidence if the quality of the goods is at issue in the proceeding. You may object to the question without waiting for the answer. Other times, the question is appropriate, but the answer given includes inadmissible evidence. For example, the question "What do you know about the quality of the goods your partnership sold?" is an acceptable question. However, if the witness responds, "My partner told me that the quality was high," that is hearsay, and you may object to the answer. In other words, you may object to a question if it clearly calls for inadmissible evidence; you may object to an answer if it contains such evidence.

If you are going to object, you should do so as soon as you realize that an objection is called for. For example, if you are objecting to a leading question, object as soon as the question is asked—don't wait to hear the answer! You should generally not interrupt the questioner unless the question is objectionable because of what it asserts. For example, if the questions starts, "When you signed the contract," you may object before the question is finished if there has been no evidence that a contract was signed. In this case, the question asserts the existence of a contract. If the question is objectionable only because of what it asks, then you should wait until the question is complete before making your objection. For example, the question "What do you think he meant by that?" is objectionable because it calls for an answer that is speculative.

WHEN OBJECTIONS ARE RAISED

As stated earlier, objections are used primarily to prevent improper evidence from being presented and considered by the court or tribunal. As a result, most objections are made during the examination of witnesses, although they can be made at other times as well.

Direct Examination

During direct examination by the opposing advocate of his or her witnesses, objections are made to limit the admission of evidence that is helpful to the other side. Objections may be made to either the question asked or to the evidence given. The most common objections are

- the question is leading;
- the question calls for hearsay evidence or the witness is giving hearsay evidence; and
- the question calls for an opinion or the witness is giving opinion evidence, and the witness is not a qualified expert.

Cross-Examination

During cross-examination of your witness by the opposing advocate, objections are designed to prevent your witness from giving evidence that is harmful to your case or to protect your witness from mistreatment. Objections may be made to the question asked, not to the answer given. The most common objections are that the question is

- argumentative;
- repetitive;

- compound;
- vague, ambiguous, or confusing;
- seeking privileged information; or
- seeking evidence that is not relevant.

Re-examination

During re-examination by the opposing advocate of his or her witnesses, again, objections are designed to limit the admission of evidence that is helpful to the other side. Objections are generally made to the question asked. The most common objections are

- the question is leading,
- the question is asking for information already given on direct examination, and
- the question is asking for information that should have been dealt with in direct examination.

Introduction of Exhibits

You should object to the introduction of an exhibit by the opposing advocate if the witness cannot authenticate the exhibit.

Opening Statement and Closing Argument

Objections are rarely made during the opening statement and closing argument. However, during the opening statement it is possible to object if the opposing advocate is presenting argument, referring to inadmissible evidence, or stating his or her personal opinion; and during the closing argument, it is possible to object if he or she is misstating the law or the evidence, arguing facts that have not been entered into evidence, or expressing his or her personal opinion.

THE WISDOM OF OBJECTING

Certainly you should never object unless your objection deserves to be sustained. You will lose credibility with the judge or other decision-maker if you repeatedly make objections that are unfounded and therefore overruled. Even if you have good grounds to object, you should consider whether it is wise to object. Some objections will hurt more than help your case. An objection interrupts the trial or hearing and shifts the attention to the objectionable evidence. The other side is given an opportunity to explain this evidence when responding to your objection. The process may increase the decision-maker's focus on the evidence.

When deciding whether to object, think about your theory of the case, and consider how the objectionable evidence affects your theory. If exclusion of the evidence is required to support your theory of the case, then you should object. If the objectionable evidence does not hurt your case, you may be wiser not to object to it. This is not an easy decision to make, and you do not have a lot of time in which to make it.

RESPONDING TO OBJECTIONS

Unless the judge or other decision-maker immediately overrules an objection made by the other side, you will be given the opportunity to respond. Your response should explain why the evidence is being presented to the court or tribunal and why it is admissible.

Part of trial or hearing preparation involves considering the admissibility of the evidence you intend to present to the court. You should also consider the form and substance of the questions you intend to ask during direct examination and cross-examination. For every question you ask, you should have a purpose; every question should support and advance your theory of the case. Reviewing these matters will prepare you to respond to objections at the trial or hearing.

REVIEW QUESTIONS

1. What is the purpose of objections?
2. Provide an example of what you might object to during a trial or hearing.
3. What happens if the decision-maker agrees with your objection?
4. What happens if the decision-maker disagrees with your objection?
5. What is the proper way to object?
6. List and briefly describe the types of objections that may be made to the form of the question being asked by the opposing advocate.
7. List and briefly describe the types of objections that may be made to the substance of the evidence that the witness is being asked to give.
8. When should you object?
9. What are the most common objections made during direct examination of the other side's witness?
10. What are the most common objections made during cross-examination of your witness by the opposing advocate?
11. What are the most common objections made during re-examination by the opposing advocate of his or her witness?
12. When should you object to the introduction of an exhibit by the opposing advocate?
13. When should you object during the opening statement and closing argument of the opposing advocate?
14. How do you decide whether or not to object?
15. How do you respond to an objection made by the other side?

DISCUSSION QUESTION

You are acting on a residential landlord and tenant matter for the landlord. The paralegal for the tenant is conducting a direct examination of her client, the tenant and asks the following question: "You and the landlord orally agreed to the termination of your tenancy, isn't that correct?" Prepare an objection to that question.

PART V

Final Preparation

CHAPTER 14

Final Preparation for the Trial or Hearing

Previous chapters have discussed the preparation for a trial or hearing from the development of your theory of the case through every stage of the actual trial or hearing itself—opening statement, submission of evidence, and closing argument. That part of your preparation should take place well in advance of the actual trial or hearing date. As the actual trial or hearing date draws closer, there are several additional matters to attend to:

- ensuring that your witnesses will attend,
- ensuring that your documentary evidence will be admitted,
- preparing a trial or hearing notebook,
- preparing a book of authorities, and
- practising your presentation skills.

This chapter discusses these matters.

ENSURING THAT YOUR WITNESSES WILL ATTEND

It is essential to the success of your case that all of your witnesses show up at the trial or hearing. Advise your witnesses of the trial or hearing date as soon as you are advised of it, and confirm that they are willing and able to appear on that date. Make sure they know where the trial or hearing will take place. If the witness refuses or is unwilling to testify, ask the court or tribunal to issue a **summons** to compel the witness's attendance.

Often witnesses will agree to come to the trial or hearing when you ask them. However, unless you are 100 percent confident that a witness will attend, you should arrange to have a summons issued to protect your client in the event that the witness fails to appear.

A summons is a legal document requiring a person to attend a trial or hearing as a witness. It may also require that person to bring specified documents to the court or tribunal. A witness who receives a summons must appear in the court or tribunal on the date and time specified in the summons. A witness who fails to do so is subject to arrest.* A witness who is not served with a summons is under no

* The power to issue a warrant for the arrest of a witness who does not appear at a Small Claims Court trial is given to the trial judge under the Rules of the Small

legal obligation to attend at the trial or hearing, and you may be forced to proceed with your trial or hearing without the witness.

A summons to a witness is issued by the court or tribunal at the request of a party to the proceeding. You will need to obtain the appropriate form and attend at the court or tribunal office to have it properly issued. Once the summons is issued, you must serve it on the witness. If the witness does not attend the trial or hearing, you will be required to prove that you served the witness with the summons.

ENSURING THAT YOUR DOCUMENTARY EVIDENCE WILL BE ADMITTED

If you are relying on any documentary evidence, you must comply with any procedural requirements of the court or tribunal as to disclosure or notice of those documents. For example, the Rules of the Small Claims Court provide that a document that has been served at least 30 days before the trial date shall be received in evidence, unless the trial judge orders otherwise.

PREPARING A TRIAL OR HEARING NOTEBOOK

A **trial or hearing notebook** contains all the important information you will need at the trial or hearing in a secure and organized format. It allows you to find documents and information quickly and easily; as a result, you are more likely to remain calm and in control throughout the proceeding, and appear confident and ready for the trial or hearing to both the judge or other decision-maker and the other side.

Create your notebook using a three-ring binder with tabs or dividers to separate the sections. Do not simply place everything in a folder, because if you drop it, all of your papers can fall out. Your notebook should be organized so that you will be able to easily and quickly find any information or documents you need.

Your notebook should contain the following sections:

1. *Title page*—Set out the names of the parties to the case, your client's contact information, and the name and contact information of the advocate for the other side.

2. *Summary of the facts of the case*—If you have a busy practice, you may have several cases on the go at the same time for which you may have prepared some time before the actual trial or hearing date. The summary will help to refresh your memory of the case.

3. *Pleadings*—Insert all the court or tribunal documents in chronological order—for example, in a Small Claims Court trial, include the plaintiff's claim and the defence.

Claims Court; the power to issue a warrant for the arrest of a witness at a provincial offences trial is given to provincial judges under the *Provincial Offences Act*; the power to issue a warrant for the arrest of a witness at a tribunal hearing is given to a judge of the Superior Court by the *Statutory Powers Procedure Act*.

4. *Trial checklist*—List the facts you must prove at the trial or hearing to establish the necessary legal elements of your case (go back to your theory of the case). Next to each fact, set out the name of the witness you will call and any documentary evidence you will be relying on to establish that fact.
5. *Witness list*—List the witnesses in the order in which you plan to call them, including contact information for each witness.
6. *Documents/exhibits*—Insert copies of all documents you intend to use during the trial or hearing. If there are a lot of documents, you may want to include an index at the beginning of this section. Do not punch holes in the original documents or insert them into the notebook. Instead, keep them in a folder or sleeve, and insert the folder or sleeve into the binder. This section should also include several blank pages for you to make an exhibit list, setting out the number and a brief description of each exhibit as it is entered into evidence. This lets you keep track of exhibits so that when you need to use them, you can quickly and easily identify them by exhibit number.
7. *Opening statement*—Insert the notes you have prepared for the delivery of your opening statement.
8. *Direct examination*—For each witness, insert notes setting out the questions you will ask together with the answers you expect. Include some blank pages so that you can take notes, if necessary.
9. *Cross-examination*—For each witness, insert notes setting out the target areas you have identified and the questions you have prepared on a preliminary basis. Also insert blank pages so that you can take notes on the direct examination of each witness you will be cross-examining. Draw a vertical line two-thirds of the way across the page. To the left of the line, write down what the witness says. To the right of the line, make notes on how to tie those statements to questions you have already prepared and/or to any additional questions you should ask.
10. *Closing argument*—Insert the notes of the draft closing argument you have prepared. Insert blank pages so that you can make notes of any additions or revisions required if the evidence does not unfold exactly as you anticipated.

PREPARING A BOOK OF AUTHORITIES

During your closing argument you must provide the judge or decision-maker with a copy of any case or statutory provision on which you are relying. If you are relying on only one or two cases or statutory provisions, you may simply provide the judge or other decision-maker with copies of each as you go. However, if you are relying on multiple cases or statutory provisions, you should prepare a **book of authorities** into which you insert a copy of each case or statutory provision, separated by numbered tabs. Insert a list of the authorities at the front of the book, setting out the full name and citation of each case and statute.

PRACTISE YOUR PRESENTATION SKILLS

As an advocate, you must not only plan and prepare for *what* you will say, you must also pay attention to *how* you will say it. While some people are naturally gifted public speakers, most are not, and will need to develop presentation skills to improve their performance at the trial or hearing. It is likely that, as a new advocate, you will be nervous about appearing in court or before a tribunal. This is perfectly normal. The best way to combat your nerves is to be as well prepared as possible; this preparation includes practising your presentation skills.

Appearance

Dress appropriately for your trial or hearing. Pay attention to your hair, clothing, and accessories. First impressions can be very important and may influence the attitude of the judge, justice of the peace, or adjudicator toward you.

Body Language and Mannerisms

Stand straight and hold your head up during your presentation, and avoid slouching, pacing, shuffling about, or fidgeting. Try to be aware of any mannerisms you might have while speaking that might be irritating and/or distracting and that will detract from your presentation.

Use of Language

Consider whether the language you are using is appropriate for an oral presentation. Often, words look fine on the page but sound awkward or unduly complicated when spoken. Sentences should be shorter and sentence structure simpler in an oral presentation. Use introductory sentences to take the place of headings so that the judge or other decision-maker can follow what you are saying. Finally, use words you know how to pronounce. Make sure you check the pronunciation of unusual or foreign words that you will be using.

Volume and Clarity

Make sure your voice is loud enough, but not too loud. Adjust your volume to the size of the courtroom or tribunal room. Some courtrooms or tribunal rooms are large and the judge or other decision-maker may be seated quite a distance away from you, in which case you need to be able to project your voice and speak clearly so that the judge or other decision-maker can hear you.

Speed

Speak more slowly than you think you need to. Most people naturally speak too quickly. If you sound to yourself like you are speaking too slowly, it is probably the right speed. Keep in mind that the judge or other decision-maker will be taking notes and needs time to process what you are saying.

Pacing

Think of pacing like punctuation in a written presentation; in an oral presentation, pacing takes the place of commas, periods, and paragraphs. Pause briefly between sentences, and pause longer between ideas.

Expression

Speak with interest. Do not use a monotone. Avoid "up-talk"—ending your sentences with the intonation you use when asking a question. "Up-talk" is extremely irritating and makes the speaker sound tentative and uncertain. Pay attention to your intonation so that you appear confident and certain about what you are saying.

Attention to the Decision-Maker

Watch the judge, justice of the peace, or adjudicator to help you monitor the speed of your presentation. If the judge or decision-maker is writing notes, pause until you see that he or she has stopped writing or has otherwise indicated to you that he or she is ready for you to proceed.

Do Not Read

Do not read from your prepared notes. Look at the judge or decision-maker and talk to him or her—it sounds very different from reading. You should be so well prepared and familiar with your case that you will not have to read. You can, of course, use notes to help you with your delivery. But do not rely on them too heavily. Look at them to refresh your memory, pause, and then resume eye contact with the judge or decision-maker. Prepare your notes so that they will help you in your delivery. Use large print and large blocks of white space to remind you to look at the judge or decision-maker. This encourages you to read only small bits of text at a time and helps you to easily find your place when you need to check your notes.

Practise

Finally, practise your presentation before your court or tribunal appearance! Stand in front of a mirror or, better yet, ask someone to observe your presentation and critique your delivery and demeanour.

REVIEW QUESTIONS

1. What should you do to ensure that all of your witnesses will show up at the trial or hearing?
2. What is a summons?
3. What should you do to ensure that your documentary evidence will be admitted?

4. What is a trial or hearing notebook?
5. How should you prepare a trial or hearing notebook?
6. Briefly describe what sections your notebook should contain.
7. When should you prepare a book of authorities, and what should you put in it?

PART VI

Ethical Issues in Advocacy

CHAPTER 15

Paralegal Advocacy Rules and Guidelines

Paralegals who appear as advocates before a court or tribunal are now regulated by the Law Society of Upper Canada. Paralegals must abide by the Paralegal Rules of Conduct, which set out the paralegal's professional and ethical obligations. The Rules include general paralegal duties and duties to the courts, tribunals, other paralegals, and the Law Society of Upper Canada. The Law Society has also created Paralegal Professional Conduct Guidelines to assist paralegals in interpreting and applying the Rules.

Rule 4 and Guideline 12 provide specifically for advocacy-related matters, including the paralegal's duty toward clients, tribunals, and others while acting as an advocate. "Tribunal" is defined in the Rules to include "courts, boards, arbitrators, mediators, administrative agencies, and bodies that resolve disputes, regardless of their function or the informality of their procedures."

Rule 4 and Guideline 12 are reproduced below. Appendixes C and D contain additional Rules and Guidelines that are also relevant to advocacy-related matters. The complete set of rules is available online at http://www.lsuc.on.ca/media/paralegal_rules_conduct.pdf.

RULE 4: ADVOCACY

4.01 The Paralegal as Advocate

Duty to Clients, Tribunals and Others

4.01(1) When acting as an advocate, the paralegal shall represent the client resolutely and honourably within the limits of the law while, at the same time, treating the tribunal and other licensees with candour, fairness, courtesy and respect.

(2) This rule applies to appearances and proceedings before all tribunals in which the paralegal may appear.

(3) This rule does not require a paralegal, except as otherwise provided in these Rules, to assist an adversary or advance matters derogatory to the client's case.

(4) Without restricting the generality of subrule (1), the paralegal shall,

(a) raise fearlessly every issue, advance every argument, and ask every question, however distasteful, that the paralegal thinks will help the client's case;

(b) endeavour, on the client's behalf, to obtain the benefit of every remedy and defence authorized by law;

(c) never waive or abandon a client's legal rights, for example, an available defence under a statute of limitations, without the client's informed consent; and

(d) avoid and discourage the client from resorting to frivolous and vexatious objections, or from attempts to gain advantage from mistakes or oversights not going to the merits, or from tactics designed to merely delay or harass the other side.

The Paralegal and the Tribunal Process

(5) When acting as an advocate, the paralegal shall not,

(a) abuse the process of the tribunal by instituting or prosecuting proceedings which, although legal in themselves, are clearly motivated by malice on the part of the client and are brought solely for the purpose of injuring the other party;

(b) knowingly assist or permit the client to do anything that the paralegal considers to be dishonest or dishonourable;

(c) knowingly attempt to deceive a tribunal or influence the course of justice by offering false evidence, misstating facts or law, presenting or relying upon a false or deceptive affidavit, suppressing what ought to be disclosed, or otherwise assisting in any deception, crime or illegal conduct;

(d) deliberately refrain from informing the tribunal of any binding authority that the paralegal considers to be directly on point and that has not been mentioned by an opponent;

(e) appear before a judicial officer when the paralegal, a partner of the paralegal, a paralegal employed by the paralegal firm or the client has a business or personal relationship with the officer that gives rise to, or might reasonably appear to give rise to, pressure, influence or inducement affecting the impartiality of the officer;

(f) knowingly assert as true, a fact when its truth cannot reasonably be supported by the evidence or as a matter of which notice may be taken by the tribunal;

(g) endeavour or allow anyone else to endeavour, directly or indirectly, to influence the decision or action of the tribunal or any of its officials in any case or matter by any means other than open persuasion as an advocate;

(h) knowingly misstate the contents of a document, the testimony of a witness, the substance of an argument or the provisions of a statute or like authority;

(i) knowingly permit a witness or party to be presented in a false or misleading way or to impersonate another;

(j) needlessly abuse, hector, harass or inconvenience a witness;

(k) dissuade a witness from giving evidence or suggest that a witness be absent;

(l) when representing a complainant or potential complainant, attempt to gain a benefit for the complainant by threatening the laying of a criminal charge or by offering to seek or to procure the withdrawal of a criminal charge; or

(m) needlessly inconvenience a witness.

Disclosure of Documents

(6) If the rules of a tribunal require the parties to produce documents, a paralegal, when acting as an advocate,

(a) shall explain to his or her client the necessity of making full disclosure of all documents relating to any matter in issue and the duty to answer to the best of his or her knowledge, information and belief, any proper question relating to any issue in the action;

(b) shall assist the client in fulfilling his or her obligation to make full disclosure; and

(c) shall not make frivolous requests for the production of documents or make frivolous demands for information.

Errors and Omissions

(7) A paralegal who does, or fails to do, something which may involve a breach of this rule, shall, subject to rule 3.03 relating to confidentiality, disclose the error or omission and do all that can reasonably be done in the circumstances to rectify it.

Agreement on Guilty Pleas

(8) Before a charge is laid or at any time after a charge is laid, a paralegal acting for an accused or potential accused may discuss with the prosecutor the possible disposition of the case, unless the client instructs otherwise.

(9) A paralegal, on behalf of his or her client, may enter into an agreement with a prosecutor about a guilty plea, if, following investigation,

(a) the paralegal advises the client about the prospects for an acquittal or finding of guilt;

(b) the paralegal advises the client of the implications and possible consequences of a guilty plea and particularly of the sentencing authority and discretion of the court, including the fact that the court is not bound by any agreement about a guilty plea;

(c) the client is prepared voluntarily to admit the necessary factual and mental elements of the offence charged; and

(d) the client voluntarily instructs the paralegal to enter into an agreement as to a guilty plea.

4.02 Interviewing Witnesses

Interviewing Witnesses

4.02(1) Subject to subrules (2) and (3), a paralegal may seek information from any potential witness, whether under subpoena or not, but shall disclose the paralegal's interest and take care not to subvert or suppress any evidence or procure the witness to stay out of the way.

(2) A paralegal shall not approach or deal with a person who is represented by another licensee, except through or with the consent of that licensee.

(3) A paralegal retained to act for a party in a matter involving a corporation or organization represented by another licensee shall not, without the other licensee's consent or unless otherwise authorized or required by law,

(a) approach directors, officers or persons likely involved in the decision-making process for the corporation or organization; or

(b) approach employees and agents of the corporation or organization whose acts or omissions in connection with the matter may expose the corporation or organization to quasi-criminal, criminal or civil liability.

(4) This rule applies to communications with any person, whether or not a party to a formal adjudicative proceeding, contract, or negotiation, who is represented by a licensee concerning the matter to which the communication relates.

(5) The prohibition on communications with a represented person applies if the paralegal has direct knowledge of the representation or if he or she should be able to infer the representation from the circumstances.

Definition

(6) In this rule,

"organization" includes a partnership, limited partnership, sole proprietorship, association, union, unincorporated group, government department, government agency, tribunal, and regulatory body.

4.03 Communication with Witnesses Giving Testimony

Communication with Witnesses Giving Testimony

4.03(1) Subject to the direction of the tribunal, a paralegal shall observe the following rules respecting communication with witnesses giving evidence:

1. During examination-in-chief, the examining paralegal may discuss with the witness any matter that has not been covered in the examination up to that point.
2. During examination-in-chief by another licensee of a witness who is unsympathetic to the paralegal's cause, the paralegal not conducting the examination-in-chief may discuss the evidence with the witness.
3. Between completion of examination-in-chief and commencement of cross-examination of the paralegal's own witness, the paralegal ought not to discuss the evidence given in chief or relating to any matter introduced or touched on during the examination-in-chief.
4. During cross-examination by an opposing licensee, the witness's own representative ought not to have any conversation with the witness about the witness's evidence or any issue in the proceeding.
5. Between completion of cross-examination and commencement of a re-examination, a paralegal who is going to re-examine the witness ought not to have any discussion about evidence that will be dealt with on re-examination.
6. During cross-examination by the representative of a witness unsympathetic to the cross-examiner's cause, the paralegal may discuss the witness's evidence with the witness.
7. During cross-examination by the representative of a witness who is sympathetic to that licensee's cause, any conversations ought to be restricted in the same way as communications during examination-in-chief of one's own witness.
8. During re-examination of a witness called by an opposing licensee, if the witness is sympathetic to the paralegal's cause, the paralegal ought not to discuss the evidence to be given by that witness during re-examination. The paralegal may, however, properly discuss the evidence with a witness who is adverse in interest.

(2) With the consent of the opposing licensee or with leave of the tribunal, a paralegal may enter into discussions with a witness that might otherwise raise a question under this rule as to the propriety of the discussions.

(3) This rule applies, with necessary modifications, to examinations out of court.

4.04 The Paralegal as Witness

The Paralegal as Witness

4.04(1) Subject to any contrary provisions of the law or the discretion of the tribunal before which a paralegal is appearing, the paralegal who appears as an advocate shall not submit his or her own affidavit to the tribunal.

(2) Subject to any contrary provisions of the law or the discretion of the tribunal before which a paralegal is appearing, a paralegal who appears as an advocate shall not testify before the tribunal unless permitted to do so by the rules of the court or the rules of procedure of the tribunal, or unless the matter is purely formal or uncontroverted.

(3) A paralegal who is to testify before a tribunal shall entrust the conduct of the case to another licensee.

(4) A paralegal shall not express personal opinions or beliefs or assert as a fact anything that is properly subject to legal proof, cross-examination or challenge.

4.05 Dealing with Unrepresented Persons

4.05 When a paralegal is dealing on a client's behalf with an unrepresented person, the paralegal shall,

(a) urge the unrepresented person to obtain independent representation;

(b) take care to see that the unrepresented person is not proceeding under the impression that his or her interests will be protected by the paralegal; and

(c) make clear to the unrepresented person that the paralegal is acting exclusively in the interests of the client and accordingly his or her comments may be partisan.

GUIDELINE 12: ADVOCACY

Definitions

Rule Reference: Rule 4

Rule 1.02 definition of "tribunal"

1. An *advocate* is someone who speaks and acts on behalf of others. Rule 4 outlines a paralegal's duties when appearing as an advocate before a tribunal. Rule 4 applies to all appearances and all proceedings before all tribunals. A *tribunal* can be either an administrative board or a court of law. An *adjudicator* is any person who hears or considers any type of proceeding before a tribunal and renders a decision with respect to that proceeding.

General

Rule Reference: Rule 4

2. The paralegal has a duty to represent his or her client diligently and fearlessly. Generally, the paralegal has no obligation to assist an opposing party, or to advance matters harmful to the client's case. However, these general principles do not mean that, when acting as advocate for a client before a tribunal, the paralegal can behave as he or she likes or, in some cases, as his or her client may instruct. Rule 4 describes the professional obligations that a paralegal owes to opposing parties, other paralegals and lawyers, the tribunal and the administration of justice. These obligations are paramount, and must be met by the paralegal in each and every tribunal proceeding in which the paralegal acts as advocate for a client.

Candour, Fairness, Courtesy and Respect

Rule Reference: Rule 4.01(1), 4.01(4)(d)
Rule 7.01(3)

3. A paralegal should not engage in rude and disruptive behaviour before a tribunal, or uncivil correspondence, language or behaviour towards opposing parties or their advocates.

Malicious Proceedings

Rule Reference: Rule 4.01(5)(a)

4. A paralegal should not help a client to bring proceedings that have no merit. Claims that have no merit waste the time of the tribunal and its officers, and do not further the cause of justice.

Misleading the Tribunal Rule

Reference: Rule 4.01(5)(c), (d) & (h)

5. A paralegal must ensure that neither the paralegal nor his or her client(s) misleads the tribunal. For a tribunal to decide a matter effectively and appropriately, the tribunal must have access to everything that is relevant to the issues to be decided.

Improperly Influencing the Tribunal

Rule Reference: Rule 4.01(5)(e) & (g)

6. For the public to have respect for the administration of justice, tribunals must be fair, objective, independent and neutral. There should be no personal connection between an adjudicator and any of the parties to a proceeding or their advocates.

7. The only appropriate way to influence the tribunal's decision is through open persuasion as an advocate. This is done by making submissions based on legal principles and offering appropriate evidence before the tribunal in the presence of, or on notice to, all parties to the proceeding, or as otherwise permitted or required by the tribunal's rules of procedure. A paralegal should not communicate directly with the adjudicator in the absence of the other parties, unless permitted to do so by the tribunal's rules of procedure.

Dishonest Conduct

Rule Reference: Rule 4.01(5)(b), (c) & (f)

8. Acting with integrity before a tribunal means being honest and acting with high ethical principles.

Admissions by the Client

Rule Reference: Rule 4.01(5)(b), (c) & (f)

9. When defending an accused person, a paralegal's duty is to protect the client from being convicted, except by a tribunal of competent jurisdiction and upon legal evidence sufficient to support a conviction for the offence with which the client is charged. Accordingly, a paralegal may properly rely on any evidence or defences, including "technicalities," as long as they are not known to be false or fraudulent.

10. However, admissions made by a client to a paralegal may impose strict limitations on the paralegal's conduct of the client's defence. The client should be made aware of this by the paralegal. Where the client has admitted to the paralegal any or all of the elements of the offence with which the client is charged, a paralegal must not do or say anything before the tribunal, including calling any evidence, that would contradict the facts admitted by the client to the paralegal. This would be misleading the court.

11. Where the client has admitted to the paralegal all the elements of the offence, and the paralegal is convinced that the admissions are true and voluntary, the paralegal may properly take objection to the jurisdiction of the tribunal, or to the form, admissibility or sufficiency of the evidence. The paralegal could not suggest that someone else committed the offence, try to establish an alibi or call any evidence which, by reason of the admissions, the paralegal believes to be false. Admission by the client to the paralegal of all of the elements of the offence with which the paralegal is charged also limits the extent to which the paralegal may attack the evidence for the prosecution. The paralegal may test the evidence given by each witness for the prosecution and may argue that the evidence, as a whole, is not enough to prove the client guilty. The paralegal should go no further than that.

Witnesses

Rule Reference: Rule 4.01(5)(i), (j), (k) & (m)
Rule 4.02
Rule 4.03
Rule 7.01(6)

12. As an advocate, a paralegal may contact all possible witnesses for both sides of a matter, but the paralegal must be fair and honest when dealing with them. This includes the paralegal speaking to the opposing party or co-accused. The paralegal must make it clear to the witness who is the paralegal's client(s) and that that the paralegal is acting only in the interests of his or her client(s). As part of this disclosure, the paralegal should give the witness his or her name, tell the witness that he or she is a paralegal, the name of the client(s) he or she represents in the matter, and his or her status in the proceeding. A paralegal should make an extra effort to be clear when the witness does not have legal representation. Note that, although a paralegal may ask to speak to a potential witness, the witness does not have to speak to the paralegal.

13. During a hearing, a paralegal's ability to speak with a witness giving testimony is limited. This ensures that the paralegal does not influence the evidence the witness will give. A comment made by the paralegal to the paralegal's own witness during court recess, for example, may result in a breach of the *Rules*. The witness may return to the witness box and, as a result of the communication with the paralegal, offer evidence that is slanted to benefit the paralegal's client. Such evidence is no longer neutral and could mislead the tribunal.

Disclosure of Documents

Rule Reference: Rule 4.01(6)

14. The rules of procedure of the tribunal may require parties to produce documents and information to the tribunal or to the other parties in the matter. Timely, complete and accurate disclosure helps settlement efforts and makes the hearing process more effective and fair.

Agreement on Guilty Pleas

Rule Reference: Rule 4.01(8) & (9)

15. As an advocate for a person accused in a criminal or quasi-criminal matter, the paralegal should take steps reasonable in the circumstances to satisfy himself or herself that the client's instructions to enter into the agreement on a guilty plea is informed and voluntary. The paralegal should ensure the client's instructions to enter into an agreement on a guilty plea are in writing.

The Paralegal as Witness

Rule Reference: Rule 4.04

16. As an advocate, the paralegal's role is to further the client's case within the limits of the law. The role of a witness is to give evidence of facts that may or may not assist in furthering the case of any of the parties to a proceeding. Because these roles are different, a person may not be able to carry out the functions of both advocate and witness at the same time.

17. When acting as an advocate for his or her client before a tribunal, the paralegal should not appear to be giving unsworn testimony. This is improper and may put the paralegal's own credibility in issue. A paralegal who has appeared as a witness on a matter should not act as an advocate or legal representative in any appeal of that matter.

Dealing with Unrepresented Persons

Rule Reference: Rule 4.05

18. The paralegal has a special duty when representing a client and an opposing party is not represented by a paralegal or a lawyer.

19. To avoid misunderstandings, it will helpful for the paralegal to confirm in writing the steps he or she takes to fulfill the requirements of Rule 4.05.

Withdrawal and Disclosure Obligations

Rule Reference: Rule 4.01(7)
Rule 3.08

20. If, after explanation and advice from the paralegal, the client persists in instructing the paralegal to engage in or continue a type of conduct prohibited by Rule 4, the paralegal must withdraw from representing the client in the matter. (See Guideline 11: Withdrawal of Representation.)

REVIEW QUESTION

What Rules must paralegals abide by when appearing as advocates before a court or tribunal?

DISCUSSION QUESTIONS

1. Licensed paralegal Harry Hothead is appearing before the Landlord and Tenant Board on behalf of a tenant. The adjudicator renders her decision against Harry's client. Harry slams his hand down on the table, shouts "What a load of garbage!" and storms out of the hearing room. Referring to Rule 4 and Guideline 12, what has Harry done wrong?

2. Licensed paralegal Eric Eager is representing a plaintiff in the Small Claims Court. Eric has just completed direct examination of his client when the judge orders a short recess. During the recess, Eric meets with the client to discuss the evidence he just gave and to give him some pointers about the cross-examination that will start after the recess. Referring to Rule 4 and Guideline 12, what has Eric done wrong?

Appendixes

APPENDIX A

Small Claims Court: Guide to Getting Ready for Court

INTRODUCTION

If your Small Claims Court case is going to court—whether it is for a settlement conference, assessment hearing or trial, you will probably have a lot of questions. This three-part guide will try to answer most of them.

Part One describes the settlement conference, its purpose and what you can do to prepare for it.

Part Two describes what happens during a trial and sets out additional steps to take to get your case ready.

Part Three describes the assessment hearing process and when you would need one.

The steps set out in Part One of this guide refer to preparation for a settlement conference. However, very similar steps also apply to preparation for an assessment hearing or a trial. So, if you are preparing for an assessment hearing or trial, read Part One, but keep in mind that you are not preparing for a settlement conference.

PART ONE: SETTLEMENT CONFERENCE

What is the purpose of the settlement conference?

If the defendant files a defence, the parties will receive a notice of settlement conference in the mail from the court office indicating the date, time and location of the settlement conference. A settlement conference should be held within 90 days after the first defence is filed.

The purpose of a settlement conference is to:

- resolve or narrow down the issues in the action;
- expedite the disposition of the action (that is, to help to resolve the dispute faster);

- encourage settlement of the action;
- assist the parties with effective trial preparation; and
- provide full disclosure between the parties of the relevant facts and evidence.

Try to be reasonable. Think about what you want from your case, but also determine what you can "live with." Think about what is acceptable to you. For example:

- If you are suing a contractor over a job that was not done to your satisfaction, you probably want the work done and done right.
- If you are the contractor, you will want to at least break even on the job, but you may be willing to apply some of your profits towards repair work.
- If you are being sued for money you owe someone, maybe you agree that you owe the money and only need more time to pay.

Try not to think in terms of winning and losing. Think instead, "What is my 'bottom line' in this case? What is the minimum acceptable to the other side? Is there any possible solution that we both can live with?"

Even if the whole case cannot be resolved, the settlement conference is a good opportunity to work out an agreement on at least some of the issues, so that the trial can be less expensive, easier and quicker.

If there is going to be a trial, the settlement conference is also an opportunity to help you get prepared for the trial. The judge may make recommendations about your case. Also, there are a number of orders the judge might make.

At the end of the settlement conference, if the parties do not settle the case, the Rules provide that the judge will give the clerk a memorandum listing the issues remaining in dispute, matters agreed on, and information related to scheduling. The memorandum will be provided to the trial judge. The judge who conducts your settlement conference will not preside at the trial.

After the settlement conference, the clerk will provide the parties with a copy of the endorsement record, either in person or by mail. The endorsement record contains any orders that the judge made at the settlement conference.

Remember, the settlement conference and any settlement discussions between the parties are private and cannot be disclosed to others, unless you have the consent of all of the parties to do so.

Who attends the settlement conference?

A judge usually presides at the settlement conference. The parties must attend, but the witnesses **do not** attend. If any of the parties has a lawyer or agent, the lawyer or agent may attend as well but the parties must always be there.

The people who attend must have the authority to settle the case. For example, if one of the parties is a company, or if a party requires another person's approval before agreeing to a settlement, then that party must arrange to have ready telephone access to the other person throughout the conference.

If you would like to have someone other than your lawyer or agent attend to support you, you must ask the judge for permission at the start of the settlement conference.

What if I cannot attend on the date set for the settlement conference?

If you are unable to attend on the date set for the settlement conference, you can ask the court to adjourn the settlement conference and reschedule it on another date. Contact the court office for assistance.

If the judge allows the request and makes an order, the clerk will notify the parties of the new settlement conference date.

If the settlement conference is not adjourned before the scheduled date you, or someone on your behalf, must attend the settlement conference to request the adjournment. If a judge allows the request and makes an order adjourning the settlement conference, the clerk will notify the parties of the new settlement conference date.

Can I attend the settlement conference by telephone or video conference?

A settlement conference can be heard or conducted by telephone or video conference if the facilities are available at the court. A party can file a **Request for Telephone or Video Conference** [**Form 1B**]. Make the request as soon as you are aware you need this arrangement and indicate the reasons for your request. If the judge grants the request, the court will make the necessary arrangements and notify the parties.

What if I do not go to the settlement conference?

If you do not attend the settlement conference, an order can be made against you, including an order requiring you to pay the other party's costs. The judge can also order you to attend an additional settlement conference.

In the event that a defendant fails to attend a settlement conference, a second settlement conference may be scheduled. If the defendant fails to attend again, the judge can order final judgment in the case. No trial will be held.

How should I prepare for the settlement conference?

Get organized. The better prepared you are for your settlement conference, the more you may gain from it. Being well prepared may make it possible for you to avoid the expense and risks of having to go to trial. It is a good idea to do most of your preparation before the settlement conference. If you do have a trial, you will simply have to refresh your memory and make sure that you take into account any recommendations or orders made by the judge at the settlement conference.

More importantly, if you are not prepared and the settlement conference cannot be properly conducted, it could cost you money. For example, if you do not have the necessary documents with you, the judge could order you to pay the other party's expenses for having to come to the settlement conference, and then everyone might still have to come back a second time.

IF YOU ARE THE PLAINTIFF

There are two basic parts to your case if you are a plaintiff (proving either a plaintiff's claim or a defendant's claim):

1. **You have to prove liability.** That means you must prove that the defendant did something wrong to you for which you should be compensated.
2. **You have to prove the amount owing.** For example, it is not enough to prove that the dry cleaner ruined your suit. You have to prove what the suit was worth, or what it cost to repair the damage.

"Evidence" is whatever you will use at trial to prove your case. You have to think about it now because how you intend to prove your case will likely be discussed at the settlement conference. There are several different kinds of evidence. Those most often used are:

1. Oral testimony: a witness comes to court and answers questions at the trial. Witnesses **do not** attend settlement conferences.
2. Documentary evidence: documents, such as business records and written estimates, are presented in court either by a witness or a party.
3. Expert reports: reports prepared by an expert in the field (e.g., a building inspector).
4. Photographs: photographs are sometimes used as evidence if the person who took them can properly identify them.

Try to break down your case into individual facts and decide what evidence you will use to prove each point. The best way to do this is to review the claim form and defence form closely. Use these documents as a reference and then make a worksheet from them.

Well in advance of the court date, each party must decide if there is any document not attached to his or her claim or defence form that the party wants to use at trial to prove his or her case. If so, at least 14 days before the date scheduled for the settlement conference, the document must be served on every other party and filed with the court. Make detailed notes of when and how you served the document in case the court requires you to file an affidavit of service sometime later.

In our example, the documents would include the contract, invoices, bill of sale and written estimates. Some of these documents would already have been attached to the plaintiff's claim and served on the defendant. Any new documents (for example, the report prepared by the building inspector or copies of photographs) would have to be served on the defendant and filed with the court at least 14 days before the settlement conference.

The clerk will send each party a blank **List of Proposed Witnesses [Form 13A]** together with the notice of settlement conference. At least 14 days before the date of the settlement conference, the plaintiff and the defendant must fill out the form and serve it on each other as well as any other party involved **and** file the documents with the court. You should not bring any witnesses to the settlement conference, but you should be prepared to briefly explain what your witnesses will say if they come to the trial.

For example, you would not bring the building inspector but you could say, "The building inspector told me that the reason the roof leaks is because the flashing

Example 1

We will use the same roofer example that we talked about in the "Guide to Making a Claim." You will recall that you hired a roofer to put a new roof on your house. The roof leaks, so you sue ZC Roofing Ltd.

Worksheet

Suppose your claim says this in the "Reasons for Claim and Details" section:

1. ZC Roofing Ltd. put a new roof on my house at 123 King Street, Barrie, ON.
2. The roof leaks and ZC Roofing Ltd. has refused to fix it.
3. My furniture and carpeting were damaged and I had to hire another roofer to fix the leak.
   How much?

a) Cost of replacing chair	$ 479
b) Cost of cleaning carpet	$ 135
c) Cost of repairing roof	$1,250
TOTAL	$1,864

You could prepare a worksheet like this:

	FACT		EVIDENCE
A	ZC Roofing put the roof on my house	A	Signed contract with ZC Roofing and invoice marked "PAID"
B	The roof leaks	B	Photos taken by me
C	The leak was caused by ZC's poor workmanship	C	Report of building inspector Evidence of foreman from YZ Roofing who repaired the roof
D	It will cost $1,250 to repair the roof	D	Estimates from three roofing companies
E	The leak caused damage to my carpets and furniture	E	My own testimony and photos taken by me
F	It cost $135 to clean the carpet	F	Invoice from Columbia Carpet Cleaners
G	It cost $479 to replace my chair	G	Bill of sale from Peg's Furniture Mart for new chair

was not properly installed and the shingles around the chimney and eaves have to be removed and replaced."

Tip: A good way to organize your papers to ensure nothing is overlooked is to cross-index them with your worksheet. To do this:

- Paperclip each document to a page in a three-ring binder.
- Mark each of the pages in the upper right hand corner with the letters from your worksheet.
- Make the worksheet the first page in the binder, to serve as a Table of Contents.

IF YOU ARE THE DEFENDANT REPLYING TO EITHER A PLAINTIFF'S CLAIM OR A DEFENDANT'S CLAIM

Begin by closely reviewing the claim and your defence. For example:

- Do you disagree with the plaintiff's version of "Reasons for Claim and Details"? Make a note of exactly what you agree or disagree with and be prepared to briefly explain why to the judge.
- Do you disagree with the amount that the plaintiff says you owe? Be prepared to show what the correct amount is and how you arrived at that figure.
- Do you agree you owe what the plaintiff claims, but simply cannot pay it all at once? If that is the case, bring proof of your financial situation (e.g., recent pay stubs and last year's income tax return). Be prepared to tell the judge what sort of payment terms you are capable of making. If you can pay something right away, all the better.
- Do you agree that you may owe the plaintiff some money, but not the amount claimed? If that is the case be prepared to explain the reasons for your position and what you think would be reasonable.

> **Example 2**
>
> Suppose you agree to pay the plaintiff $1,000. You might say, "I will pay $200 today, and then $200 at the end of each month until it is paid."

Here are a few other things to keep in mind

First, has the correct defendant been named in the claim?

> **Example 3**
>
> In Example 1, the plaintiff had a contract with ZC Roofing Ltd. If he named Zoro Carey as the defendant (the one who owns the company and did the work) and not the company, Mr. Carey could reply to the claim by saying that he did not enter into an agreement with the plaintiff in his personal capacity and therefore the plaintiff has no case against him.

Second, if the plaintiff has suffered the damage described, has it been proven that it was your fault?

Third, carefully examine the amount of the claim. Is the plaintiff asking for a much more expensive chair to replace the original one that was old and worn? Can this be justified?

Organize your case following the process described earlier in this guide for the plaintiff. Use a worksheet listing the points you wish to make and the evidence you will use to prove those points. Refer to the worksheet in Example 1.

You must serve on the plaintiff any document that was not already attached to your defence and file it with the court at least 14 days before the settlement conference. You must also complete a **List of Proposed Witnesses [Form 13A]**, serve it on the plaintiff and file it with the court at least 14 days before the settlement conference.

Finally, like the plaintiff, you must come to the settlement conference prepared, or risk having to pay the other side's expenses.

What will happen at the settlement conference?

The settlement conference will usually be held in an office or meeting room. This is a less formal procedure than a trial and all parties will sit at a table with the judge. The settlement conference is a private meeting. Members of the public are not allowed.

Judges may conduct settlement conferences in different ways, but usually the judge will say a few words and then ask each party to give a brief summary of his or her case. You do not need to write this out in full but you should have a list of the points you wish to make. If you made a worksheet, use that.

If all parties agree on a final settlement, the judge may make an order which disposes of the case and you will not need to go to trial. If a settlement is not reached, the settlement conference is an opportunity to try to resolve some issues before the trial and to assist in preparing for the trial.

Example 4

Going back to the claim in Example 1, the parties might agree that the carpet damage was not the roofer's fault, because the homeowner had agreed to remove it before the roof was repaired. They might also agree that the chair was old and only worth $150. They will have a trial but it will be shorter and simpler because they only have to deal with issues about the $1,250 repair job.

Once the settlement conference is completed, the clerk will provide the parties with a copy of the endorsement record.

At the bottom of the endorsement record there is a notice that states that, if the action is not disposed of within 30 days after the settlement conference, one of the parties must request a trial date and pay the fee for setting the action down for trial. Failure to set the action down for trial will result in the clerk eventually sending you a notice of approaching dismissal.

Is there a special rule for claims less than $500?

If the claim is for less than $500 ($500 is the minimum claim that can be appealed under the *Courts of Justice Act*), there is a special procedure available to parties who consent to it. The parties can file a signed **Consent [Form 13B]** (before the settlement conference) indicating that they wish to have final judgment at the settlement conference. If the parties do not reach a settlement the judge can then make a final judgment at the settlement conference. If you consent to this procedure, this will be the final judgment in your case and you will not have to attend again for a trial, or pay the trial fee.

What if we settle the case after the settlement conference?

Even though you have been through a settlement conference and your case has been set for trial, it does not mean that you have to go to trial. If you keep talking to one another after the settlement conference, and you agree to settle, you can fill out and sign a **Terms of Settlement [Form 14D]**. File the terms of settlement, signed by all parties, as soon as possible in order to notify the court that the action has been settled. If a trial date has been scheduled, notify the court of the settlement before the scheduled trial date, if possible.

If one party fails to abide by the terms of the settlement, the other party can make a motion to the court to either:

- ask for judgment in the terms of the settlement, or
- go to trial as if there had been no settlement.

What is an "Offer to Settle"?

An "Offer to Settle" is the name given to a formal written offer made by one party to the other party. Either party can make a written offer to settle to the other party at any time until a judge disposes of the case. The party may use the **Offer to Settle [Form 14A]**, or may write a letter setting out the terms of the offer.

If you have made or received an offer to settle and it has not been accepted, **you cannot file the offer to settle at the court office**.

If you have made or received an offer to settle and it has not been accepted **you must not mention the offer to settle or any negotiations relating to it to the judge during the trial** until a final disposition has been made of all issues of liability and relief, except for costs.

I want to discuss settlement with the other party. Do I have to make an offer to settle?

No. The offer to settle process is a special process which may be used, but it is not required. The use of the offer to settle has several important consequences which are discussed below. If you and the other party want to settle your case, it is not necessary to use the offer to settle process.

The simplest way to settle an action is to talk with the other side until you come to an agreement. Write down the details and sign your agreement in the presence of a witness who also signs the document. You may use the **Terms of Settlement [Form 14D]** noted above and file it with the court.

However, if you are not sure that the other side is willing to settle, you can make a written offer to settle using the **Offer to Settle [Form 14A]**. Keep in mind that you do not have to use this form, but it is provided for your convenience.

I received a written offer to settle. What can I do now?

Carefully consider any written offer that is made to you.

If you do not accept an offer to settle, and if the offer to settle was made at least 7 days before trial, there is a chance that you could end up being penalized with an order for costs made against you. For example:

- the judge may order extra costs **against a defendant** who rejects an offer to settle when the judgment at trial is as favourable as, or more favourable than, the plaintiff's offer to settle, or
- the judge may order costs **against a plaintiff** when the judgment is as favourable as, or less favourable than, the defendant's offer to settle.

Remember: An offer to settle which is not accepted may be disclosed to the trial judge only when all issues of liability and relief have been determined, and only costs remain to be determined.

Example 5

Referring back to the claim in Example 1, the parties are scheduled to go to trial over whether the $1,250 repair job is necessary.

The plaintiff sends the defendant a letter with an offer to settle for $1,000 so that he can avoid the time and expense of trial. The offer to settle is made in writing and is served on the defendant more than 7 days before the trial date. The defendant does not accept the offer to settle.

At trial the judge finds for the plaintiff and awards the plaintiff judgment for $1,250 plus costs of $75. After the judge gives the judgment, the plaintiff shows the judge his offer to settle. The judge then awards the plaintiff an additional $75 in costs because the defendant failed to accept the offer to settle.

In an alternative example, the defendant makes an offer to settle for $850 plus costs. The offer to settle is made in writing and is served on the plaintiff more than 7 days before trial. The plaintiff does not accept the offer to settle.

At trial the judge awards the plaintiff $750. After the judge gives the judgment, the defendant shows the judge his offer to settle. The judge awards the defendant costs of $100.

Remember, an offer to settle may be accepted until the time specified in the offer, or until the judge makes a final decision in the case, if no time for expiry is specified in the offer.

I want to make a formal offer to settle. What can I do?

You can make a written offer to settle using the **Offer to Settle [Form 14A]**. Keep in mind that you do not have to use this form, but it is provided for your convenience.

You can specify a date after which the offer is no longer available for acceptance. If the offer has not been accepted by that date, the offer is deemed to have been withdrawn. If you change your mind and want to withdraw your offer to settle before that, you can serve a **Notice of Withdrawal of Offer to Settle [Form 14C]** on the party to whom the offer was made. However, you cannot withdraw your offer if the party has already accepted it.

If the other party wishes to accept your offer, he or she must do so in writing and serve the acceptance on you. The party can complete an **Acceptance of Offer to Settle [Form 14B]** or write a letter. Once the offer to settle is accepted, the settlement is then binding on both you and the other party.

What can I do if the offer to settle is not accepted?

If you have made or received an offer to settle, and it has not been accepted, **you cannot file the offer to settle at the court office, and you must not mention the offer to settle during the trial**. You may only mention the offer to settle when the judge has decided all issues of liability and relief, except costs.

If you made a written offer to settle that was not accepted, you may bring it with you to the trial to show the judge **after** a final judgment on all issues of liability and relief, except costs, has been made in the case.

PART TWO: TRIAL

What is the difference between a settlement conference and a trial?

There are a number of differences between a settlement conference and a trial. A settlement conference is a private discussion between the parties, with the assistance of the judge. The purpose is to see whether the parties can agree on a settlement. A trial is a public process where each party tells his or her own side of the case to a judge who makes a decision about the issues in the case. You will have a different judge at the trial than you have at the settlement conference.

Sworn evidence may be heard from witnesses at a trial. At a settlement conference the parties simply tell the judge what the witnesses would say if they were present.

How do I prepare for trial?

If you followed the information in this guide about preparing for the settlement conference, much of your work is already done. Start by going back and reviewing these documents:

- the claim;
- the defence;
- the defendant's claim (if any);
- your worksheet;
- the settlement conference endorsement record (containing court orders made at the settlement conference);
- any direction given or recommendations made by the judge at the settlement conference; and
- any documents or other evidence you may have.

You will likely be the main witness for your case, and you may be asked to tell your story, so prepare what you will say. Usually the best way to organize a story is in the order that the events actually happened. Think about how you would explain the case to another person who does not know you or the other people involved. Make a list of all the points you want to cover.

The plaintiff should be prepared to start by telling the judge briefly with the case is about, remembering to mention any facts the parties have agreed to.

Remember, under no circumstances should either party mention to others anything about discussions at the settlement conference. Also remember that under no circumstances should either party mention to the judge anything about an offer to settle that has not been accepted. The offer to settle can only be discussed when the trial is over and all issues of liability and relief, except costs, have been determined.

Tip: If possible, try to go to court and watch some cases being tried. Small Claims Courts are open to the public. Unless the judge orders otherwise you are allowed to sit and watch any day the court is in session.

Are there special rules about how to behave in court?

Yes, there are special rules about how to behave in court:

- The judge in Small Claims Court is called "Your Honour."
- Everyone stands when the judge enters or leaves the courtroom.
- You must stand whenever you are speaking to the judge or the judge is speaking to you. You will also stand while questioning your witnesses.
- Remember, it is improper for you to attempt to have any out-of-court communication with a judge unless the judge specifically orders it.

There are signs posted in the courthouse about other behaviours which are not permitted. You must abide by these rules to show respect for the court.

What evidence can I present at trial?

Evidence that may help prove your case at trial might include: documents, records (including audio or visual records), or written statements.

Examples of documents which might be used as evidence include: hospital records, medical reports, financial records, receipts, bills, estimates, photographs identified by the person who took them, and other documents that show the party's loss or property damage.

The Rules provide for copies of written statements, documents and records to be served on all parties at least 30 days before the trial date. You may have already served most of this material before the settlement conference.

If you serve on another party a written statement or document described in subrule 18.02(2) of the Rules, you must include:

- the name, telephone number and address for service of the witness or author; and
- if the witness or author is to give expert evidence, you must also include a summary of his or her qualifications.

> **Example 6**
>
> Referring back to Example 1, the plaintiff in this case would serve the written statement of the building inspector indicating that the leak was caused by ZC's poor workmanship. The plaintiff would also include the inspector's name, telephone number, address for service and a summary of the inspector's qualifications.

If you want to ask questions of the author of another party's written report or document, you can summons the author as described below in the discussion about witnesses. You must also serve a copy of your summons to witness form on all parties in the case. If you do not, a party who has not been served may request an adjournment of the trial and, if granted, you may be ordered to pay costs.

You should bring the original documents and at least three copies of each document to the trial. The original may be entered by the court as an exhibit. The copies are for the judge, the other party (or parties) and yourself.

Check with the court office prior to the scheduled trial date to ensure that any equipment you may require is available in the courtroom (e.g., a television and VCR if you have footage that you would like to show the judge). You may be required to bring the necessary equipment with you.

What witnesses can I have?

When you are thinking about possible witnesses, remember that the best witnesses are usually those who have personal, first-hand knowledge of the facts. You may also want to have expert witnesses that you think will assist your case, for example, a report of the building inspector. The judge will determine what evidence given by the witness will be allowed.

Think carefully about the questions you will ask your witness in order to get the evidence you think you will need, and write those questions down.

It is alright for you to review the questions with your witnesses beforehand, but you must not tell them what to say. Be sure to tell them this so they won't be concerned if they are asked in court whether they've discussed the case with you.

At the trial, witnesses will be required to swear or affirm that they will tell the truth.

How do I make sure my witnesses will come to court?

You can fill out a **Summons to Witness [Form 18A]** form and file it at the Small Claims Court office. The court will issue the summons. There is a fee to issue the summons.

The summons to witness must be served personally on the witness at least 10 days before the trial date together with attendance money. Attendance money includes a witness fee and travel expenses. Refer to the "Guide to Serving Documents" and the "Guide to Fee Schedules" for more information.

You may be required to file an **Affidavit of Service [Form 8A]** to prove service of the summons and attendance money so make sure you keep a record of the details such as the date, time, and address where the summons was served.

Example 7

Referring back to Example 1, the plaintiff in this case wishes to have the foreman from YZ Roofing, who was in charge of the repair of the roof, testify about the problems with the original roofing job and the work required to repair the roof.

The defendant would ask the court clerk to issue a blank summons to witness form and pay the fee.

Once he filled in the witness details for the witness, he would make a photocopy for himself and then personally serve the original summons to witness form on the witness together with attendance money.

Then, from his copy, he would make enough photocopies to serve on every other party.

Remember that it is your responsibility, and in your own best interests, to make sure your witnesses attend. You do not have to serve a summons on the witness, but if you do not and your witness does not appear, you may have to proceed without the witness.

If a witness fails to attend trial after being properly served with a summons to witness and attendance money, the trial judge may issue a warrant for his or her arrest.

If the court finds a party has abused the power to summons a witness, the judge may order the party to pay money to the witness to compensate him or her for inconvenience and expense.

What if my witness requires an interpreter?

If a witness who is summonsed requires an interpreter, the court will provide an interpreter from English to French or French to English or visual language interpretation.

It is the responsibility of the party summonsing the witness to arrange for interpretation for other languages. Failure to do so may result in an adjournment of the trial and an award of costs against you.

The court will provide an interpreter for other languages to parties who have qualified for a fee waiver.

For more information see the "What is Small Claims Court?" guide.

What can I do when a witness for the other side says something I do not agree with?

When you are in court, when it is the other party's turn to say what happened or ask his or her witness questions, you should not interrupt.

When a witness for the other side has finished giving evidence, the judge may allow you to ask the witness questions.

What if I cannot be ready in time, or cannot attend, on the date set for the trial?

If you do not attend at trial, judgment may be granted against you or your claim may be dismissed. If you have a very good reason for being unable to attend on the date set for trial, you can ask the court to adjourn the trial and reschedule it to another date. Contact the court office for assistance. If the judge allows the request and makes an order, the clerk will notify the parties of the new trial date.

If the trial is not adjourned before the scheduled date, you or someone on your behalf must attend court on the trial date to request the adjournment. If a judge allows your request and makes an order adjourning the trial, the clerk will notify the parties of the new trial date.

If an adjournment is granted and a new trial date is set, make sure you notify all of your witnesses about the new date. It may be necessary for you to prepare and serve a summons with the new date and attendance money on each witness.

If a trial has been adjourned two or more times, any further adjournment may be made only on motion, with notice to all parties who were served with a trial notice, unless the court orders otherwise. Refer to the "Guide to Motions and Clerk's Orders" for more information.

What is a judgment?

The judgment is the decision of the judge who heard your case. Usually, a judge in Small Claims Court will give judgment in court right after both sides have finished presenting their cases. Sometimes, however, the judge may not give the judgment right away but will give the decision later (this is called reserving judgment). In this case, a copy of any reasons for judgment or an endorsement record will be mailed to each party when the judgment is made.

A judgment is an order of the court; it is not a guarantee of payment. Refer to "After Judgment—Guide to Getting Results" for information about what you can do to attempt to collect your money or property after you get your judgment.

Can I appeal a judgment?

You can appeal a judgment to a higher court if the amount of the judgment, not including court costs, is more than $500, or there is an order directing recovery of personal property valued at more than $500. This is set out in the *Courts of Justice Act*.

An appeal is based upon your belief that a judge made a significant mistake. It is not an opportunity to retell your story. The judge who hears the appeal will not hear any new evidence; he or she will rely entirely on the transcript of the trial and the court record.

For more information about appeals, the Ontario Courts website at www.ontariocourts.on.ca contains useful self-help information. From the home page:

- click on "Superior Court of Justice"
- click on "Divisional Court"
- scroll down to "Divisional Court Information" and click on "Appeal Information Package."

What if judgment is made against a party who did not appear at trial?

In some circumstances, a party who did not appear at trial may make a motion to set aside or vary at judgment obtained against them. The motion must be made within 30 days after becoming aware of the judgment, unless the court extends the time. See the "Guide to Motions and Clerk's Orders" for more information on making a motion.

Can either party ask for a new trial?

In very limited circumstances, which are set out in the Rules, a party can ask for a new trial. A motion for a new trial must be made within 30 days after the final order at the trial, unless the court orders otherwise. To do so, serve and file:

1. A **Notice of Motion [Form 15A]** and **Affidavit [Form 15B]** setting out your reasons for asking for a new trial; and
2. A document proving that you have made a request to a court reporter to make a transcript, or partial transcript, of your trial. You can obtain a transcript by contacting the court office to order it. There will be a fee for this process. Refer to the "Guide to Fee Schedules" for more information.
3. If available, you must also serve a copy of the transcript on all parties who were served with the notice of trial, and file it, with proof of service, at least three days before the hearing date. For information on service, see the "Guide to Serving Documents."

Under the Rules, you may request a new trial only where:

- there was a purely arithmetical (mathematical) error in the determination of the amount of damages awarded at trial; or
- there is relevant evidence that was not available to the party at the time of the original trial and could not reasonably have been expected to be available at that time.

If your request for a new trial is based on a mathematical error, your affidavit must show the error in calculating in the judgment and the correct calculations. For more information about requesting a new trial, refer to Rule 17.04 of the *Rules of the Small Claims Court.*

Checklist: Getting ready for trial

Follow this checklist when getting ready for your trial:

1. Review the claim, defence (if any) and any other documents that have been filed.
2. Review the results of your settlement conference. Make a note of all points that were agreed to which are no longer in dispute and any direction given by the judge.
3. List the points you need to prove.
4. Consider how you will prove each point.
5. Gather the original documents you need and organize them in logical order.
6. If you have not already done so, serve on all other parties the documents and witness statements that you will use at least 30 days before trial, and include contact information and the address for service for each document's author.
7. Contact any witnesses you decide are necessary.
8. If you decide to summons any witness(es), serve a copy of the summons and attendance money on your witness(es) at least 10 days before the trial.
9. Obtain statements from expert witnesses, if any, and serve copies on the other parties together with the expert's contact information, address for service, and qualifications.
10. Prepare a list of questions for your witnesses.
11. Prepare a list of questions that you would like to ask the witnesses for the other party or parties.
12. On your trial date, dress appropriately and give yourself plenty of time to travel to the courthouse and find your courtroom.

If you have prepared your case well, you will be much more relaxed in court and you will be able to present your case to its best advantage.

PART THREE: ASSESSMENT HEARING

Where a defendant does not file a defence to a claim for an unliquidated amount, the plaintiff can ask the clerk to note the defendant in default and request an assessment hearing before a judge to prove the amount the defendant owes. An unliquidated claim is a claim where the amount in dispute is not fixed under an express agreement (for example, damage to property or a personal injury). For more information, refer to the "Guide to Making a Claim."

Note: You may also make a motion in writing for an assessment of damages, rather than scheduling an assessment hearing. For information about motions in writing for an assessment of damages, refer to the "Guide to Motions and Clerk's Orders."

How do I prepare for an assessment hearing?

An assessment hearing proceeds as a trial except the defendant is not present. Because the defendant did not file a defence, the defendant is considered to have admitted the claims you made against him or her. As a result, you do not have to prove the defendant's liability (i.e., that the defendant does, in fact, owe you something). You must only prove the amount that the defendant should pay to compensate you.

The information about preparing your case in Parts One and Two of this guide will help you prepare for an assessment hearing. It is a good idea to prepare your case as suggested in Parts One and Two. The sections you may find particularly helpful are:

- how to prepare your case in Part One;
- information on witnesses and documents in Part Two (but keep in mind that you are not required to serve the defendant with these materials); and
- information on how to behave in court in Part Two.

Source: Ministry of the Attorney General, *Small Claims Court Guides to Procedures: Guide to Getting Ready for Court*, www.attorneygeneral.jus.gov.on.ca/english/courts/guides.

Tips on Completing Forms in Small Claims Court

1. **BE NEAT.** These are court documents. All court forms must be typed, handwritten or printed legibly. It may cause delays if your forms cannot be read.
2. How to **COUNT DAYS FOR TIMELINES** in the Rules of the Small Claims Court:

   When calculating timelines in the Rules, count the days by excluding the first day and including the last day of the period; if the last day of the period of time falls on a holiday, the period ends on the next day that is not a holiday.

   Holidays include:

   - any Saturday or Sunday
   - New Year's Day
   - Family Day
   - Good Friday
   - Easter Monday
   - Victoria Day
   - Canada Day
   - Civic Holiday
   - Labour Day
   - Thanksgiving Day
   - Remembrance Day
   - Christmas Day
   - Boxing Day
   - any special holiday proclaimed by the Governor General or the Lieutenant Governor

   NOTE: If New Year's Day, Canada Day or Remembrance Day falls on a Saturday or Sunday, the following Monday is a holiday. If Christmas Day falls on a Saturday or Sunday the following Monday and Tuesday are holidays, and if Christmas Day falls on a Friday, the following Monday is a holiday.

   The court can order, or the parties can consent to, the shortening or lengthening of the time prescribed by the Rules.
3. At the top of the forms, fill in the **NAME AND ADDRESS OF THE COURT** where you are filing the documents.
4. Once court staff provides a **COURT FILE NUMBER**, make sure it is written on the upper right-hand corner of **ALL** your documents.
5. Make enough **COPIES** of your completed forms. The court will stamp and return your copy of the forms so you can make copies for service. Usually you will require one copy for each party who must be served and one copy for your own records. In most cases, the court will keep the original form. There is a fee to have copies made at the court office. Refer to the "Guide to Fee Schedules" for more information.
6. **COURT FEES** must be paid to issue and file specific documents. A listing of Small Claims Court fees can be viewed at the Ministry of the Attorney General website at www.attorneygeneral.jus.gov.on.ca or you can refer to the "Guide to Fee Schedules." Fees are payable in Canadian funds, and can be paid by cash, cheque or money order payable to the Minister of Finance.
7. An **AFFIDAVIT** can be sworn before:

   - a Small Claims Court staff member who has been appointed a commissioner for taking affidavits (there is no fee for this service);
   - a lawyer who is entitled to practice law in Ontario;
   - a notary public; or
   - any other person who has been appointed a commissioner for taking affidavits in connection with court documents.

   The affidavit must be signed in the presence of the person before whom it is sworn.

   NOTE: It is a criminal offence to knowingly swear a false affidavit.
8. If your **ADDRESS FOR SERVICE** changes, you must serve written notice of the change on the court and all other parties within seven (7) days after the change takes place.

APPENDIX B

Rules of the Small Claims Court

Ontario Regulation 258/98

RULE 17 TRIAL

Failure to Attend

17.01(1) If an action is called for trial and all the parties fail to attend, the trial judge may strike the action off the trial list.

(2) If an action is called for trial and a party fails to attend, the trial judge may,

(a) proceed with the trial in the party's absence;

(b) if the plaintiff attends and the defendant fails to do so, strike out the defence and dismiss the defendant's claim, if any, and allow the plaintiff to prove the plaintiff's claim, subject to subrule (3);

(c) if the defendant attends and the plaintiff fails to do so, dismiss the action and allow the defendant to prove the defendant's claim, if any; or

(d) make such other order as is just.

(2.1) In the case described in clause (2)(b) or (c), the person with the claim is not required to prove liability against the party who has failed to attend but is required to prove the amount of the claim.

(3) In the case described in clause (2)(b), if an issue as to the proper place of trial under subrule 6.01(1) is raised in the defence, the trial judge shall consider it and make a finding.

Setting Aside or Variation of Judgment

(4) The court may set aside or vary, on such terms as are just, a judgment obtained against a party who failed to attend at the trial.

Conditions to Making of Order under Subrule (4)

(5) The court may make an order under subrule (4) only if,

(a) the party who failed to attend makes a motion for the order within 30 days after becoming aware of the judgment; or

(b) the party who failed to attend makes a motion for an extension of the 30-day period mentioned in clause (a) and the court is satisfied that there are special circumstances that justify the extension.

Adjournment

17.02(1) The court may postpone or adjourn a trial on such terms as are just, including the payment by one party to another of an amount as compensation for inconvenience and expense.

(2) If the trial of an action has been adjourned two or more times, any further adjournment may be made only on motion with notice to all the parties who were served with the notice of trial, unless the court orders otherwise.

Inspection

17.03 The trial judge may, in the presence of the parties or their representatives, inspect any real or personal property concerning which a question arises in the action.

Motion for New Trial

17.04(1) A party may make a motion for a new trial within 30 days after a final order is made.

Transcript

(2) The moving party shall serve and file proof that a transcript of evidence, or that portion of the transcript that is relevant, has been requested, in addition to the notice of motion (Form 15A) and affidavit (Form 15B) required under rule 15.01.

Service and Filing of Transcript

(3) If available, a copy of the transcript or partial transcript of evidence shall, at least three days before the hearing date,

(a) be served on all parties who were served with the original notice of trial; and

(b) be filed, with proof of service.

Powers of Court on Motion

(4) On the hearing of the motion, the court may,

(a) if the party demonstrates that a condition referred to in subrule (5) is satisfied,

(i) grant a new trial, or

(ii) pronounce the judgment that ought to have been given at trial and order judgment accordingly; or

(b) dismiss the motion.

Conditions

(5) The conditions referred to in clause (4)(a) are:

1. There was a purely arithmetical error in the determination of the amount of damages awarded.

2. There is relevant evidence that was not available to the party at the time of the original trial and could not reasonably have been expected to be available at that time.

RULE 18 EVIDENCE AT TRIAL

Affidavit

18.01 At the trial of an undefended action, the plaintiff's case may be proved by affidavit, unless the trial judge orders otherwise.

Written Statements, Documents and Records

18.02(1) A document or written statement or an audio or visual record that has been served, at least 30 days before the trial date, on all parties who were served with the notice of trial, shall be received in evidence, unless the trial judge orders otherwise.

(2) Subrule (1) applies to the following written statements and documents:

1. The signed written statement of any witness, including the written report of an expert, to the extent that the statement relates to facts and opinions to which the witness would be permitted to testify in person.

2. Any other document, including but not limited to a hospital record or medical report made in the course of care and treatment, a financial record, a receipt, a bill, documentary evidence of loss of income or property damage, and a repair estimate.

Details about Witness or Author

(3) A party who serves on another party a written statement or document described in subrule (2) shall append to or include in the statement or document,

(a) the name, telephone number and address for service of the witness or author; and

(b) if the witness or author is to give expert evidence, a summary of his or her qualifications.

(4) A party who has been served with a written statement or document described in subrule (2) and wishes to cross-examine the witness or author may summon him or her as a witness under subrule 18.03(1).

Where Witness or Author is Summoned

(5) A party who serves a summons to witness on a witness or author referred to in subrule (3) shall, at the time the summons is served, serve a copy of the summons on every other party.

(6) Service of a summons and the payment or tender of attendance money under this rule may be proved by affidavit (Form 8A).

Adjournment

(7) A party who is not served with a copy of the summons in accordance with subrule (5) may request an adjournment of the trial, with costs.

Summons to Witness

18.03(1) A party who requires the attendance of a person in Ontario as a witness at a trial may serve the person with a summons to witness (Form 18A) requiring him or her to attend the trial at the time and place stated in the summons.

(2) The summons may also require the witness to produce at the trial the documents or other things in his or her possession, control or power relating to the matters in question in the action that are specified in the summons.

(3) A summons to witness (Form 18A) shall be served in accordance with subrule 8.01(7).

(4) Service of a summons and the payment or tender of attendance money may be proved by affidavit (Form 8A).

(5) A summons to witness continues to have effect until the attendance of the witness is no longer required.

Interpreter

(5.1) If a party serves a summons on a witness who requires an interpreter, the party shall arrange for a qualified interpreter to attend at the trial unless the interpretation is from English to French or French to English and an interpreter is provided by the Ministry of the Attorney General.

(5.2) If a party does not comply with subrule (5.1), every other party is entitled to request an adjournment of the trial, with costs.

Failure to Attend or Remain in Attendance

(6) If a witness whose evidence is material to the conduct of an action fails to attend at the trial or to remain in attendance in accordance with the requirements of a summons to witness served on him or her, the trial judge may, by warrant (Form 18B) directed to all police officers in Ontario, cause the witness to be apprehended anywhere within Ontario and promptly brought before the court.

Identification Form

(6.1) The party who served the summons on the witness may file with the clerk an identification form (Form 20K) to assist the police in apprehending the witness.

(7) On being apprehended, the witness may be detained in custody until his or her presence is no longer required or released on such terms as are just, and may be ordered to pay the costs arising out of the failure to attend or remain in attendance.

Abuse of Power to Summon Witness

(8) If satisfied that a party has abused the power to summon a witness under this rule, the court may order that the party pay directly to the witness an amount as compensation for inconvenience and expense.

RULE 19 COSTS

Disbursements

19.01(1) A successful party is entitled to have the party's reasonable disbursements, including any costs of effecting service and expenses for travel, accommodation, photocopying and experts' reports, paid by the unsuccessful party, unless the court orders otherwise.

(2) The clerk shall assess the disbursements in accordance with the regulations made under the *Administration of Justice Act* and in accordance with subrule (3); the assessment is subject to review by the court.

(3) The amount of disbursements assessed for effecting service shall not exceed $20 for each person served unless the court is of the opinion that there are special circumstances that justify assessing a greater amount.

Limit

19.02 Any power under this rule to award costs is subject to section 29 of the *Courts of Justice Act*, which limits the amount of costs that may be awarded.

Preparation and Filing

19.03 The court may award a successful party an amount not exceeding $50 for preparation and filing of pleadings.

Representation Fee

19.04(1) If the amount claimed in an action exceeds $500, exclusive of interest and costs, and the successful party is represented by a lawyer, student-at-law or agent, the court may award the party a reasonable representation fee at trial or at an assessment hearing.

(2) In the case of a student-at-law or an agent, the representation fee shall not exceed half of the maximum costs that may be awarded under section 29 of the *Courts of Justice Act.*

Compensation for Inconvenience and Expense

19.05 The court may order an unsuccessful party to pay to a successful party an amount not exceeding $500 as compensation for inconvenience and expense, if,

(a) the successful party is self-represented; and

(b) the amount claimed in the action exceeds $500, exclusive of interest and costs.

Penalty

19.06 If the court is satisfied that a party has unduly complicated or prolonged an action or has otherwise acted unreasonably, the court may order the party to pay an amount as compensation to another party.

Source: *Rules of the Small Claims Court,* O. Reg. 258/98, as amended. www.canlii.org/on/laws/regu/1998r.258/20080821/whole.html.

APPENDIX C

Selected Paralegal Rules of Conduct*

RULE 2: PROFESSIONALISM

2.01 Integrity and Civility

INTEGRITY

2.01(1) A paralegal shall conduct himself* or herself in such a way as to maintain the integrity of the paralegal profession.

CIVILITY

(2) A paralegal shall be courteous and civil, and shall act in good faith with all persons with whom he or she has dealings in the course of his or her practice.

OUTSIDE INTERESTS AND PUBLIC OFFICE

(3) A paralegal who engages in another profession, business, occupation or other outside interest or who holds public office concurrently with the provision of legal services, shall not allow the outside interest or public office to jeopardize the paralegal's integrity, independence, or competence.

(4) A paralegal shall not allow involvement in an outside interest or public office to impair the exercise of his or her independent judgment on behalf of a client.

ACTING AS MEDIATOR

(5) A paralegal who acts as a mediator shall, at the outset of the mediation, ensure that the parties to it understand fully that the paralegal is not acting as a representative for either party but, as mediator, is acting to assist the parties to resolve the issues in dispute.

2.02 Undertakings

2.02(1) A paralegal shall fulfil every undertaking given and shall not give an undertaking that cannot be fulfilled.

* The Law Society of Upper Canada may add to or revise these Rules without notice.

(2) Except in exceptional circumstances, a paralegal shall give his or her undertaking in writing or confirm it in writing as soon as practicable after giving it.

(3) Unless clearly stated in the undertaking, a paralegal's undertaking is a personal promise and it is his or her personal responsibility.

2.03 Harassment and Discrimination

APPLICATION OF *HUMAN RIGHTS CODE*

2.03(1) The principles of the Ontario *Human Rights Code* and related case law apply to the interpretation of this rule.

(2) A term used in this rule that is defined in the *Human Rights Code* has the same meaning as in the *Human Rights Code*.

HARASSMENT

(3) A paralegal shall not engage in sexual or other forms of harassment of a colleague, a staff member, a client or any other person on the ground of race, ancestry, place of origin, colour, ethnic origin, citizenship, creed, sex, sexual orientation, age, record of offences, marital status, family status or disability.

DISCRIMINATION

(4) A paralegal shall respect the requirements of human rights laws in force in Ontario and without restricting the generality of the foregoing, a paralegal shall not discriminate on the grounds of race, ancestry, place of origin, colour, ethnic origin, citizenship, creed, sex, sexual orientation, age, record of offences, marital status, or disability with respect to the employment of others or in dealings with other licensees or any other person.

(5) The right to equal treatment without discrimination because of sex includes the right to equal treatment without discrimination because a woman is or may become pregnant.

SERVICES

(6) A paralegal shall ensure that no one is denied services or receives inferior service on the basis of the grounds set out in this rule.

EMPLOYMENT PRACTICES

(7) A paralegal shall ensure that his or her employment practices do not offend this rule.

RULE 3: DUTY TO CLIENTS

3.01 Competence

3.01(1) A paralegal shall perform any services undertaken on a client's behalf to the standard of a competent paralegal.

(2) A paralegal shall be alert to recognize any lack of competence for a particular task and the disservice that would be done to the client by undertaking that task and shall not undertake a matter without being competent to handle it or being able to become competent without undue delay or expense to the client.

(3) If a paralegal discovers that he or she lacks the competence to complete the task for which he or she has been retained, the paralegal shall either decline to act or obtain the client's consent to retain, consult or collaborate with another licensee who is competent and licensed to perform that task.

WHO IS COMPETENT

(4) For the purposes of this rule, a competent paralegal is one who has and applies the relevant skills, attributes, and values appropriate to each matter undertaken on behalf of a client including,

(a) knowing general legal principles and procedures and the substantive law and procedures for the legal services that the paralegal provides;

(b) investigating facts, identifying issues, ascertaining client objectives, considering possible options, and developing and advising clients on appropriate courses of action;

(c) implementing, as each matter requires, the chosen course of action through the application of appropriate skills, including,

(i) legal research,

(ii) analysis,

(iii) application of the law to the relevant facts,

(iv) writing and drafting,

(v) negotiation,

(vi) alternative dispute resolution,

(vii) advocacy, and

(viii) problem-solving ability;

(d) representing the client in a conscientious, diligent, and cost-effective manner;

(e) communicating with the client at all stages of a matter in a timely and effective manner that is appropriate to the age and abilities of the client and engaging the services of an interpreter when necessary;

(f) answering reasonable client requests in a timely and effective manner;

(g) ensuring that all applicable deadlines are met;

(h) managing one's practice effectively;

(i) applying intellectual capacity, judgment, and deliberation to all functions;

(j) pursuing appropriate training and development to maintain and enhance knowledge and skills;

(k) adapting to changing requirements, standards, techniques and practices; and

(l) complying in letter and in spirit with these Rules.

3.02 Advising Clients

GENERAL

3.02(1) A paralegal shall be honest and candid when advising clients.

(2) A paralegal shall not undertake or provide advice with respect to a matter that is outside his or her permissible scope of practice.

DISHONESTY, FRAUD, ETC. BY CLIENT

(3) A paralegal shall not knowingly assist in or encourage any dishonesty, fraud, crime, or illegal conduct when advising a client and he or she shall not instruct the client on how to violate the law and avoid punishment.

(4) A paralegal shall take all reasonable measures to avoid becoming the tool or dupe of an unscrupulous client or persons associated with such a client.

(4.1) When a paralegal is employed or retained by an organization to act in a matter and the paralegal knows that the organization intends to act dishonestly, fraudulently, criminally, or illegally with respect to that matter, then in addition to his or her obligations under subrules (3) and (4), the paralegal shall

(a) advise the person from whom the paralegal takes instructions that the proposed conduct would be dishonest, fraudulent, criminal or illegal,

(b) if necessary, because that person refuses to cause the proposed wrongful conduct to be abandoned, advise the organization's chief legal officer, or both the chief legal officer and the chief executive officer, that the proposed conduct would be dishonest, fraudulent, criminal or illegal,

(c) if necessary because the chief legal officer or the chief executive officer of the organization refuses to cause the proposed conduct to be abandoned, advise progressively the next highest persons or groups, including ultimately, the board of directors, the board of trustees, or the appropriate committee of the board, that the proposed conduct would be dishonest, fraudulent, criminal, or illegal, and

(d) if the organization, despite the paralegal's advice, intends to pursue the proposed course of conduct, withdraw from acting in the matter in accordance with rule 3.08.

(4.2) When a paralegal is employed or retained by an organization to act in a matter and the paralegal knows that the organization has acted or is acting dishonestly, fraudulently, criminally, or illegally with respect to that matter, then in addition to his or her obligations under subrules (3) and (4), the paralegal shall

(a) advise the person from whom the paralegal takes instructions and the chief legal officer, or both the chief legal officer and the chief executive officer, that the conduct was or is dishonest, fraudulent, criminal, or illegal and should be stopped,

(b) if necessary because that person, the chief legal officer, or the chief executive officer refuses to cause the wrongful conduct to be stopped, advise progressively the next highest persons or groups, including ultimately, the board of directors, the board of trustees, or the appropriate committee of the board, that the conduct was or is dishonest, fraudulent, criminal, or illegal and should be stopped, and

(c) if the organization, despite the paralegal's advice, continues with the wrongful conduct, withdraw from acting in the matter in accordance with rule 3.08.

[New October 2008]

SETTLEMENT

(5) A paralegal shall advise and encourage a client to compromise or settle a dispute whenever it is possible to do so on a reasonable basis, and shall discourage the client from commencing ill-advised legal proceedings.

(6) The paralegal shall consider the use of alternative dispute resolution for every dispute, and,

(a) if appropriate, the paralegal shall inform the client of the client's alternative dispute resolution options; and

(b) if so instructed, take steps to pursue those options.

CLIENT UNDER A DISABILITY

(7) If a client's ability to make decisions is impaired because of minority, mental disability or for some other reason, the paralegal shall, as far as reasonably possible, maintain a normal professional relationship with that client.

(8) If the disability of the client is such that the client no longer has the legal capacity to manage his or her legal affairs, the paralegal shall take such steps as are appropriate to have a lawfully authorized representative appointed.

MEDICAL-LEGAL REPORTS

(9) A paralegal who receives a medical-legal report from a physician or health professional that is accompanied by a proviso that it not be shown to the client, shall return the report immediately to the physician or health professional, without making a copy, unless the paralegal has received specific instructions to accept the report on that basis.

(10) A paralegal who receives a medical-legal report from a physician or health professional containing opinions or findings that, if disclosed, might cause harm or injury to the client, shall attempt to dissuade the client from seeing the report but, if the client insists, the paralegal shall produce the report.

(11) If a client insists on seeing a medical-legal report about which the paralegal has reservations for the reasons noted in subrule (10), the paralegal shall recommend that the client attend at the office of the physician or health professional to see the report, in order that the client will have the benefit of the expertise of the physician or health professional in understanding the significance of the conclusions contained in the medical-legal report.

ERRORS

(12) If, in connection with a matter for which a paralegal is responsible, the paralegal discovers an error or omission that is or may be damaging to the client and that cannot be rectified readily, the paralegal shall,

(a) promptly inform the client of the error or omission, being careful not to prejudice any rights of indemnity that either of them may have under an insurance, client's protection or indemnity plan, or otherwise;

(b) recommend that the client obtain legal advice elsewhere concerning any rights the client may have arising from the error or omission; and

(c) advise the client that in the circumstances, the paralegal may no longer be able to act for the client.

(13) A paralegal shall give prompt notice of any circumstances that he or she may reasonably expect to give rise to a claim, to an insurer or other indemnitor so that the client's protection from that source will not be prejudiced.

OFFICIAL LANGUAGE RIGHTS

(14) A paralegal shall, where appropriate, advise a client who speaks French of the client's language rights, including the right of the client to be served by a paralegal who is competent to provide legal services in the French language.

CLAIMS UNDER STATUTORY ACCIDENT BENEFITS SCHEDULE

(15) In addition to complying with these Rules, a paralegal when acting as an adviser, consultant or representative to a person making a claim under the Statutory Accident Benefits Schedule to the *Insurance Act* shall comply with that Act, the regulations under that Act and the Code of Conduct for Statutory Accident Benefit Representatives.

3.03 Confidentiality

CONFIDENTIAL INFORMATION

3.03(1) A paralegal shall, at all times, hold in strict confidence all information concerning the business and affairs of a client acquired in the course of their professional relationship and shall not disclose any such information unless expressly or impliedly authorized by the client or required by law to do so.

(2) The duty of confidentiality under subrule (1) continues indefinitely after the paralegal has ceased to act for the client, whether or not differences have arisen between them.

(3) The paralegal shall keep the client's papers and other property out of sight, as well as out of reach, of those not entitled to see them.

JUSTIFIED OR PERMITTED DISCLOSURE

(4) A paralegal shall disclose confidential information when required by law or by order of a tribunal of competent jurisdiction.

(5) If a paralegal believes upon reasonable grounds that there is an imminent risk to an identifiable person or group of death or serious bodily harm, including serious psychological harm that substantially interferes with health or well-being, the paralegal may disclose, pursuant to judicial order where practicable, confidential information if it is necessary to do so in order to prevent the death or harm.

(6) In order to defend against the allegations, a paralegal may disclose confidential information if it is alleged that the paralegal or his or her employees are,

(a) guilty of a criminal offence involving a client's affairs;

(b) civilly liable with respect to a matter involving a client's affairs; or

(c) guilty of malpractice or misconduct.

(7) A paralegal may disclose confidential information in order to establish or collect his or her fees.

(8) A paralegal shall not disclose more information than is necessary when he or she discloses confidential information as required or permitted by subrules (4), (5), (6) and (7).

3.04 Conflicts of Interest—General

DEFINITION

3.04(1) In this rule and rule 3.05,

"conflict of interest" or "conflicting interest" means an interest, financial or otherwise,

(a) that would be likely to affect adversely a paralegal's judgment on behalf of, or loyalty to, a client or prospective client; or

(b) that a paralegal might be prompted to prefer over the interests of a client or prospective client.

AVOIDANCE OF CONFLICTS OF INTEREST

(2) A paralegal shall not advise or represent more than one side of a dispute.

(3) A paralegal shall not act or continue to act in a matter when there is, or is likely to be, a conflicting interest unless, after disclosure adequate to make an informed decision, the client or prospective client consents.

ACTING AGAINST CLIENTS

(4) Unless the client and those involved or associated with the client consent, a paralegal who has acted for a client in a matter shall not thereafter act against the client or against persons who were involved or associated with the client in that matter,

(a) in the same matter;

(b) in any related matter; or

(c) except as provided by subrule (6), in any new matter, if the paralegal has obtained from the other retainer, relevant confidential information.

(5) If a paralegal has acted for a client and obtained confidential information relevant to a matter, the paralegal's partner or employee may act in a subsequent matter against that client, if,

(a) the former client consents to the paralegal's partner or employee acting; or

(b) the paralegal's firm establishes that it is appropriate to act in the new matter having regard to all the circumstances, including,

(i) the availability of suitable alternative representation,

(ii) the measures in place to ensure that no disclosure of the former client's confidential information to the partner or employee having carriage of the new matter will occur,

(iii) the extent of prejudice to any party,
(iv) the good faith of the parties, and
(v) issues affecting the public interest.

(6) If a partner or paralegal employed in a paralegal firm has obtained confidential information from a former client that is relevant to a new matter, no partner or paralegal employed in the firm may act against the former client in the new matter unless the requirements of subrule (5) have been satisfied.

(7) A paralegal may act against a client in a fresh, independent and unrelated matter if previously obtained confidential information is irrelevant to that matter.

JOINT RETAINERS

(8) Before agreeing to act for more than one client in a matter or transaction, a paralegal shall advise the clients that,

(a) the paralegal has been asked to act for both or all of them;

(b) no information received in connection with the matter from one client can be treated as confidential so far as any of the others are concerned; and

(c) if a conflict develops that cannot be resolved, the paralegal cannot continue to act for both or all of them and may have to withdraw completely.

(9) If a paralegal has a continuing relationship with a client for whom he or she acts regularly, before agreeing to act for that client and another client in a matter or transaction, the paralegal shall advise the other client of the continuing relationship and recommend that the client obtain independent legal advice about the joint retainer.

(10) If a paralegal has advised the clients, as provided under subrules (8) and (9), and the parties are content that the paralegal act for both or all of them, the paralegal shall obtain their consent.

(11) Although all parties concerned may consent, a paralegal shall avoid acting for more than one client if it is likely that an issue contentious between them will arise or their interests, rights, or obligations will diverge as the matter progresses.

(12) Except as provided by subrule (14), if a paralegal's clients have consented to a joint retainer and an issue contentious between them or some of them arises, the paralegal shall not advise them on the contentious issue, but shall refer the clients to other licensees, unless,

(a) the contentious issue does not involve the provision of legal services; and

(b) the clients are sophisticated.

(13) If the conditions set out in clauses (a) and (b) of subrule (12) are met, the clients may settle the contentious issue by direct negotiation in which the paralegal does not participate.

(14) If a paralegal's clients consent to a joint retainer and also agree that if a contentious issue arises the paralegal may continue to advise one of them and a contentious issue does arise, the paralegal may advise the one client about the contentious matter and shall refer the other or others to another licensee.

(15) A paralegal in a multi-discipline practice shall ensure that non-licensee partners and associates observe this rule for the provision of legal services and for any other business or professional undertaking carried on by them outside the professional business.

(16) Where there is an affiliation, before accepting a retainer to provide legal services to a client jointly with non-legal services of an affiliated entity, a paralegal shall disclose to the client

(a) any possible loss of confidentiality because of the involvement of the affiliated entity, including circumstances where a non-licensee or staff of the affiliated entity provide services, including support services, in the paralegal's office,

(b) the paralegal's role in providing legal services and in providing non-legal services or in providing both legal and non-legal services, as the case may be,

(c) any financial, economic or other arrangements between the paralegal and the affiliated entity that may affect the independence of the paralegal's representation of the client, including whether the paralegal shares in the revenues, profits or cash flows of the affiliated entity; and

(d) agreements between the paralegal and the affiliated entity, such as agreements with respect to referral of clients between the paralegal and the affiliated entity, that may affect the independence of the paralegal's representation of the client.

(17) Where there is an affiliation, after making the disclosure as required by subrule (16), a paralegal shall obtain the client's consent before accepting a retainer under subrule (16).

(18) Where there is an affiliation, a paralegal shall establish a system to search for conflicts of interest of the affiliation.

[New October 2008]

3.05 Conflicts of Interest—Transfers

APPLICATION OF RULE

3.05(1) This rule applies where a paralegal transfers from one paralegal firm ("former paralegal firm") to another ("new paralegal firm"), and either the transferring paralegal or the new paralegal firm is aware at the time of the transfer or later discovers that,

(a) the new paralegal firm represents a client in a matter that is the same as or related to a matter in which the former paralegal firm represents its client ("former client");

(b) the interests of those clients in that matter conflict; and

(c) the transferring paralegal actually possesses relevant information respecting that matter.

PARALEGAL FIRM DISQUALIFICATION

(2) If a transferring paralegal actually possesses information respecting a former client that is confidential and that, if disclosed to a paralegal in the new paralegal firm, may prejudice the former client, the new paralegal firm shall cease representation of its client unless the former client consents to the new paralegal firm's continued representation or the new paralegal firm establishes that it is in the interests of justice that it continue to represent the client.

(3) In deciding whether or not it is appropriate to continue to act for a client, the new paralegal firm shall consider all the circumstances including,

(a) the adequacy and timing of the measures taken to ensure that no disclosure to any paralegal of the new paralegal firm of the former client's confidential information will occur;

(b) the availability of suitable alternative representation;

(c) the measures taken to ensure that no disclosure of the former client's confidential information, to any paralegal in the new paralegal firm, will occur;

(d) the extent of any prejudice to any party;

(e) the good faith of the parties; and

(f) issues affecting the public interest.

(4) If a transferring paralegal actually possesses relevant information respecting a former client but that information is not confidential information as described in subrule (2), the paralegal shall execute an affidavit or solemn declaration to that effect, and the new paralegal firm shall,

(a) notify its client and the former client, or if the former client is represented in that matter by a licensee, notify that licensee, of the relevant circumstances and its intended action under this rule; and

(b) deliver to the persons referred to in clause (a) a copy of the paralegal's affidavit or solemn declaration executed under this subrule.

TRANSFERRING PARALEGAL DISQUALIFICATION

(5) A transferring paralegal described in subrule (2) or (4) shall not, unless the former client consents,

(a) participate in any manner in the new paralegal firm's representation of its client in that matter; or

(b) disclose any confidential information respecting the former client.

(6) No paralegal in the new paralegal firm shall, unless the former client consents, discuss with a transferring paralegal described in subrule (2) or (4) the new paralegal firm's representation of its client or the former paralegal firm's representation of the former client in that matter.

(7) Anyone who has an interest in, or who represents a party in, a matter referred to in this rule may apply to a tribunal of competent jurisdiction for a determination of any aspect of this rule.

3.06 Doing Business with a Client

INVESTMENT BY CLIENT WHERE PARALEGAL HAS AN INTEREST

3.06(1) Subject to subrule (2), if a client intends to enter into a transaction with a paralegal who is representing the client, or with a corporation or other entity in which the paralegal has an interest other than a corporation or other entity whose securities are publicly traded, the paralegal, before accepting any retainer,

(a) shall disclose and explain the nature of the conflicting interest to the client, or, in the case of a potential conflict, how and why it might develop later;

(b) shall recommend independent legal representation and shall require that the client receive independent legal advice; and

(c) if the client requests the paralegal to act, shall obtain the client's written consent.

(2) If a client intends to pay for legal services by transferring to a paralegal a share, participation or other interest in property or in an enterprise, the paralegal shall recommend, but need not require, that the client receive independent legal advice before agreeing to act for the client.

(3) This rule does not apply to a transfer of a non-material interest in a publicly traded enterprise.

(4) If the paralegal does not choose to make disclosure of the conflicting interest or cannot do so without breaching a confidence, the paralegal shall decline the retainer.

BORROWING FROM CLIENTS

(5) A paralegal shall not borrow money from a client unless,

(a) the client is a lending institution, financial institution, insurance company, trust corporation or any similar institution whose business includes lending money to members of the public; or

(b) the client is a related person as defined by the Income Tax Act (Canada) and the paralegal is able to discharge the onus of proving that the client's interests were fully protected by the nature of the case and by independent legal advice or independent legal representation.

GUARANTEES BY PARALEGAL

(6) Subject to subrule (7), a paralegal shall not guarantee personally, or otherwise provide security for, any indebtedness in respect of which a client is a borrower or lender.

(7) A paralegal may give a personal guarantee if,

(a) the lender is a lending institution, financial institution, insurance company, trust company or any similar corporation whose business includes lending money to members of the public, and the lender is directly or indirectly providing funds solely for the paralegal, the paralegal's spouse, parent or child;

(b) the transaction is for the benefit of a non-profit or charitable institution where the paralegal as a member or supporter of such institution is asked, either individually or together with other members or supporters of the institution to provide a guarantee; or

(c) the paralegal has entered into a business venture with a client and the lender requires personal guarantees from all participants in the venture as a matter of course and,

(i) the paralegal has complied with the requirements of these Rules regarding the avoidance of conflicts of interest, and

(ii) the lender and the participants in the venture who are or were clients of the paralegal have received independent legal representation.

3.07 Client Property

PRESERVATION OF CLIENT'S PROPERTY

3.07(1) A paralegal shall care for a client's property as a careful and prudent owner would when dealing with like property and shall observe all relevant rules and law about the preservation of property entrusted to a fiduciary.

NOTIFICATION OF RECEIPT OF PROPERTY

(2) A paralegal shall promptly notify the client of the receipt of any money or other property of the client, unless satisfied that the client is aware they have come into the paralegal's custody.

IDENTIFICATION OF PROPERTY

(3) A paralegal shall clearly label and identify the client's property and place it in safekeeping, distinguishable from the paralegal's own property.

(4) A paralegal shall maintain such records as necessary to identify a client's property that is in the paralegal's custody.

ACCOUNTING AND DELIVERY

(5) A paralegal shall account promptly for a client's property that is in the paralegal's custody and upon request, shall deliver it to the order of the client.

(6) If a paralegal is unsure of the proper person to receive a client's property, the paralegal shall apply to a tribunal of competent jurisdiction for direction.

3.08 Withdrawal from Representation

WITHDRAWAL FROM REPRESENTATION

3.08(1) A paralegal shall not withdraw from representation of a client except for good cause and upon notice to the client appropriate in the circumstances.

OPTIONAL WITHDRAWAL

(2) Subject to subrules (7), (8) and (9) and the direction of the tribunal, a paralegal may withdraw if there has been a serious loss of confidence between the paralegal and the client.

(3) Without limiting subrule (2), a paralegal may withdraw if the client deceives the paralegal or refuses to accept and act upon the paralegal's advice on a significant point.

(4) A paralegal shall not use the threat of withdrawal as a device to force a hasty decision by the client on a difficult question.

MANDATORY WITHDRAWAL

(5) Subject to subrules (7), (8) and (9) and the direction of the tribunal, a paralegal shall withdraw if,

(a) discharged by the client;

(b) the paralegal is instructed by the client to do something inconsistent with the paralegal's duty to the tribunal and, following explanation, the client persists in such instructions;

(c) the client is guilty of dishonourable conduct in the proceedings or is taking a position solely to harass or maliciously injure another;

(d) it becomes clear that the paralegal's continued representation will lead to a breach of these Rules; or

(e) the paralegal is not competent to handle the matter.

NON-PAYMENT OF FEES

(6) Subject to subrules (7), (8) and (9) and the direction of the tribunal, unless serious prejudice to the client would result, a paralegal may withdraw from a case if, after reasonable notice, the client fails to provide funds on account of disbursements or fees.

WITHDRAWAL FROM QUASI-CRIMINAL AND CRIMINAL CASES

(7) A paralegal who has agreed to act in a quasi-criminal or criminal case may withdraw if the interval between the withdrawal and the trial of the case is sufficient to enable the client to obtain alternate representation and to allow such other licensee adequate time for preparation and if the paralegal,

(a) advises the client, preferably in writing, that the paralegal is withdrawing and the reason for the withdrawal;

(b) accounts to the client for any monies received on account of fees and disbursements;

(c) notifies the prosecution in writing that the paralegal is no longer acting; and

(d) in a case where the paralegal's name appears in the records of the court as acting for the accused, notifies the clerk or registrar of the appropriate court in writing that the paralegal is no longer acting.

(8) A paralegal who has agreed to act in a quasi-criminal or criminal case may not withdraw because of non-payment of fees if the date set for trial is not far enough removed to enable the client to obtain the services of another licensee or to enable another licensee to prepare adequately for trial and if an adjournment of the trial date cannot be obtained without adversely affecting the client's interests.

(9) If,

(a) a paralegal is justified in withdrawing from a quasi-criminal or criminal case for reasons other than non-payment of fees; and

(b) there is not a sufficient interval between a notice to the client of the paralegal's intention to withdraw and the date when the case is to be tried to enable the client to obtain the services of another licensee and to enable the new licensee to prepare adequately for trial,

the paralegal, unless instructed otherwise by the client, shall attempt to have the trial date adjourned and may withdraw from the case only with permission of the court before which the case is to be tried.

MANNER OF WITHDRAWAL

(10) When a paralegal withdraws, he or she shall try to minimize expense and avoid prejudice to the client and shall do all that can reasonably be done to facilitate the orderly transfer of the matter to the successor licensee.

(11) Upon discharge or withdrawal, a paralegal shall,

(a) deliver to or to the order of the client, all papers and property to which the client is entitled;

(b) give the client all information that may be required in connection with the case or matter;

(c) account for all funds of the client then held or previously dealt with, including the refunding of any monies not earned during the representation;

(d) promptly render an account for outstanding fees and disbursements; and

(e) cooperate with the successor licensee so as to minimize expense and avoid prejudice to the client.

DUTIES OF SUCCESSOR PARALEGAL

(12) Before agreeing to represent a client of a predecessor licensee, a successor paralegal shall be satisfied that the predecessor has withdrawn or has been discharged by the client.

RULE 6: DUTY TO THE ADMINISTRATION OF JUSTICE

6.01 Encouraging Respect for the Administration of Justice

GENERAL DUTY

6.01(1) A paralegal shall encourage public respect for, and try to improve, the administration of justice.

(2) A paralegal shall take care not to weaken or destroy public confidence in legal institutions or authorities by making irresponsible allegations or comments particularly when commenting on judges or members of a tribunal.

SECURITY OF COURT FACILITIES

(3) Subject to Rule 3.03 relating to confidentiality, a paralegal who has reasonable grounds for believing that a dangerous situation is likely to develop at a court facility shall inform the local police force and give particulars.

PUBLIC APPEARANCES AND STATEMENTS

(4) So long as there is no infringement of the paralegal's obligation to the client, the paralegal profession, the courts, or the administration of justice, a paralegal may communicate information to the media and may make public appearances and statements.

(4.1) A paralegal shall not communicate information to the media or make public statements about a matter before a tribunal if the paralegal knows or ought to know that the information or statement will have a substantial likelihood of materially prejudicing a party's right to a fair trial or hearing.

[New October 2008]

WORKING WITH OR EMPLOYING UNAUTHORIZED PERSONS

(5) A paralegal shall assist in preventing the unauthorized practice of law and the unauthorized provision of legal services.

(6) Without the express approval of a committee of Convocation appointed for the purpose, a paralegal shall not retain, occupy office space with, use the services of, partner or associate with, or employ in any capacity having to do with the provision of legal services any person who, in Ontario or elsewhere,

(a) is disbarred and struck off the Rolls,

(b) is a person whose license to practice law or to provide legal services is revoked,

(c) as a result of disciplinary action, has been permitted to resign his or her membership in the Law Society or to surrender his or her licence to practise law or to provide legal services, and has not had his or her license restored,

(d) is suspended,

(e) is a person whose license to practise law or to provide legal services is suspended, or

(f) is subject to an undertaking not to practise law or to provide legal services.

[Amended January 2008]

PRACTICE BY SUSPENDED PARALEGAL PROHIBITED

(7) A paralegal whose license to provide legal services is suspended shall comply with the requirements of the By-laws and shall not

(a) provide legal services; or

(b) represent or hold himself or herself out as a person entitled to provide legal services.

[New January 2008]

UNDERTAKINGS NOT TO PROVIDE LEGAL SERVICES

(8) A paralegal who gives an undertaking to the Law Society not to provide legal services shall not,

(a) provide legal services; or

(b) represent or hold himself or herself out as a person entitled to provide legal services.

[New January 2008]

UNDERTAKINGS TO PROVIDE LEGAL SERVICES SUBJECT TO RESTRICTIONS

(9) A paralegal who gives an undertaking to the Law Society to restrict his or her provision of legal services shall comply with the undertaking.

[New January 2008]

RULE 7: DUTY TO LICENSEES AND OTHERS

7.01 Courtesy and Good Faith

(1) A paralegal shall avoid sharp practice and shall not take advantage of or act without fair warning on slips, irregularities or mistakes on the part of other licensees not going to the merits or involving the sacrifice of a client's rights.

(2) A paralegal shall agree to reasonable requests concerning trial dates, adjournments, waiver of procedural formalities and similar matters that do not prejudice the rights of the client.

(3) A paralegal shall not, in the course of a providing legal services, communicate, in writing or otherwise, with a client, another licensee, or any other person in a manner that is abusive, offensive, or otherwise inconsistent with the proper tone of a professional communication from a paralegal.

(4) A paralegal shall not engage in ill-considered or uninformed criticism of the competence, conduct, advice or charges of other licensees, but should be prepared, when requested, to represent a client in a complaint involving another licensee.

(5) A paralegal shall answer with reasonable promptness, all professional letters and communications from other licensees that require an answer, and a paralegal shall be punctual in fulfilling all commitments.

(6) A paralegal shall not communicate with or attempt to negotiate or compromise a matter directly with any person who is represented by another licensee, except with the consent of that licensee.

(7) A paralegal shall not use a tape recorder or other device to record a conversation between the paralegal and a client or another licensee, even if lawful, without first informing the other person of the intention to do so.

Source: Paralegal Rules of Conduct, Law Society of Upper Canada, October 2008, www.lsuc.on.ca/paralegals/a/paralegal-rules-of-conduct.

APPENDIX D

Selected Paralegal Professional Conduct Guidelines*

GUIDELINE 1: PROFESSIONALISM—INTEGRITY & CIVILITY

General

RULE REFERENCE: RULE 1.03
RULE 2.01(1) & (2)

1. A paralegal should inspire the respect and confidence of Ontarians. Even the appearance of inappropriate conduct should be avoided.

Integrity and Civility

RULE REFERENCE: RULE 2.01(1), (2) & (3)

2. Acting with *integrity* means that a paralegal will be honest and will act with high ethical and moral principles. If integrity is lacking, the paralegal's usefulness to the client and reputation within the profession will be destroyed regardless of how competent the paralegal may be.

3. Acting with *civility* means that a paralegal will communicate politely and respectfully and act in a manner that does not cause unnecessary difficulty or harm to another.

4. The obligation to show courtesy and good faith extends to clients, opposing parties, other paralegals and lawyers, support staff, adjudicators, court and tribunal officers and staff and representatives of the Law Society. This obligation applies regardless of where the paralegal may be appearing or at what stage of the process the matter may be. Public confidence in the administration of justice and in the paralegal profession may be eroded by a paralegal's unprofessional conduct.

* The Law Society of Upper Canada may add to or revise these Guidelines without notice.

GUIDELINE 2: OUTSIDE INTERESTS

General

RULE REFERENCE: RULE 2.01(4) & (5)

1. The term "outside interest" covers the widest range of activities. It includes activities that may overlap or be connected with provision of legal services, for example, acting as a director of a corporation or writing on legal subjects, as well as activities less connected such as, for example, a career in business, politics, broadcasting or the performing arts.

2. It is the paralegal's responsibility to consider whether the outside interest may impair his or her ability to act in the best interest of his or her client(s). If so, the paralegal must withdraw, either from representation of the client or from the outside interest.

3. When acting in another role, the paralegal must continue to fulfill his or her obligations under the *Rules*, for example, to

- act with integrity,
- be civil and courteous,
- be competent in providing legal services,
- avoid conflicts of interest, and
- maintain confidentiality.

Acting as a Mediator

RULE REFERENCE: RULE 2.01(6)

4. A mediator works with disputing parties to help them resolve their dispute. A paralegal acting as a mediator is not providing legal services to either party—the relationship is not a paralegal-client relationship.

5. When acting as a mediator, the paralegal should guard against potential conflicts of interest. For example, neither the paralegal nor the paralegal's partners or associates should provide legal services to the parties. Further, a paralegal-mediator should suggest and encourage the parties to seek the advice of a qualified paralegal or a lawyer before and during the mediation process if they have not already done so. Refer to Guideline 9: Conflicts of Interest for more information on how a paralegal's outside interests may conflict with the paralegal's duty to his or her clients.

GUIDELINE 3: UNDERTAKINGS

General

RULE REFERENCE: RULE 2.02

1. An *undertaking* is a *personal promise*. Rule 2.02 sets out a paralegal's obligations in relation to undertakings.

2. A paralegal could, for example, give an undertaking to complete a task or provide a document. Fulfilling that promise is the responsibility of the paralegal giving the undertaking.

3. The person who accepts the paralegal's undertaking is entitled to expect the paralegal to carry it out personally. Using the phrase "on behalf of my client," even in the undertaking itself, may not release the paralegal from the obligation to honour the undertaking. If a paralegal does not intend to take personal responsibility, this should be clearly outlined in the written undertaking. In those circumstances, it may only be possible for the paralegal to personally undertake to make "best efforts."

4. A court or a tribunal may enforce an undertaking. The paralegal may be brought before a court or tribunal to explain why the undertaking was not fulfilled. The court or tribunal may order the paralegal to take steps to fulfill the undertaking and/or pay damages caused by the failure to fulfill the undertaking.

5. To avoid misunderstandings and miscommunication, a paralegal should remember the following points about undertakings. A paralegal

- should ensure that the wording of the undertaking is clear. If a paralegal is the recipient of an undertaking given by another paralegal or a lawyer, the paralegal should ensure that the wording is clear and consistent with his or her understanding of the undertaking. The paralegal should contact the other paralegal or lawyer to clarify the issue as soon as possible if this is not the case.
- should consider specifying a deadline for fulfilling the undertaking.
- should ensure that the undertaking provides for contingencies (e.g. if the obligations in the undertaking rely on certain events occurring, the paralegal should indicate what will happen if these events do not occur).
- should confirm whether or not the individual providing the undertaking is a paralegal or a lawyer.

GUIDELINE 6: COMPETENCE

General

1. A licensed paralegal is held out to be knowledgeable, skilled and capable in his or her permissible area of practice. A client hires a legal service provider because the client does not have the knowledge and skill to deal with the legal system on his or her own. When a client hires a paralegal, the client expects that the paralegal is competent and has the ability to properly deal with the client's case.

The Required Standard of Competence

RULE REFERENCE: RULE 3.01(1)
RULE 3.01(4)

Knowledge

RULE REFERENCE: RULE 3.01(4)(A) & (B)

2. The competent paralegal will ensure that only after all necessary information has been gathered, reviewed and considered does he or she advise the client as to the course(s) of action that will most likely meet the client's goals, taking care to ensure that the client is made aware of all foreseeable risks and/or costs associated with the course(s) of action.

Client Service and Communication

RULE REFERENCE: RULE 3.01(4)(D), (E), (F) & (G)

3. Client service is an important part of competence. Most of the complaints received by the Law Society relate to client service, such as not communicating with a client, delay, not following client instructions and not doing what the paralegal or lawyer was retained to do.

4. Rule 3.01(4) contains important requirements for paralegal-client communication and service. In addition to those requirements, a paralegal can provide more effective client service by

- keeping the client informed regarding his or her matter, through all stages of the matter and concerning all aspects of the matter,
- managing client expectations by clearly establishing with the client what the paralegal will do or accomplish and at what cost, and
- being clear about what the client expects, both at the beginning of the retainer and throughout the retainer.

Practice Management

RULE REFERENCE: RULE 3.01(4)(H)
BY-LAW 9

5. In a busy office, practice management includes ensuring that there is sufficient staff to assist the paralegal in fulfilling his or her professional responsibilities, for example, ensuring that communications from clients, other paralegals or lawyers are responded to and that financial records are kept in accordance with the requirements of By-Law 9.

6. Competent practice management requires that the paralegal effectively manage his or her staff, time, finances and client information. A paralegal should consider the following practice management tools:

- workplace policies and business procedures for staff,
- planning and reminder systems, and time docketing systems for time management, and
- filing, organizational and storage systems for management of client information and a system for effectively identifying and avoiding conflicts.

Applying Skills & Judgment

RULE REFERENCE: RULE 3.01(4)(C), (I) & (L)

7. When serving clients, or otherwise acting in a professional capacity, a competent paralegal should understand the legal concepts, issues and facts, give careful consideration to the matters he or she handles and make decisions that are reasoned and make sense in the client's circumstances.

8. A competent paralegal knows the *Rules* and understands why each *Rule* is important. The paralegal uses this knowledge and understanding to guide his or her own conduct.

Continuing Education/Professional Development

RULE REFERENCE: RULE 3.01(4)(J) & (K)

9. A paralegal is responsible to remain competent throughout his or her career. A competent paralegal understands that maintaining competence is an ongoing professional commitment that requires the paralegal to constantly assess his or her knowledge and skills.

Failing to Be Competent

RULE REFERENCE: RULE 3.01

10. The *Rules* do not require a standard of perfection. An error or omission, even though it might be actionable for damages in negligence or contract, will not necessarily constitute a breach of Rule 3.01. Conversely, incompetent professional practice may constitute professional misconduct whether or not the error or omission is actionable through the courts for professional negligence.

GUIDELINE 7: ADVISING CLIENTS

General

RULE REFERENCE: 3.02(1) & (2)

1. A paralegal must honestly and candidly advise the client regarding the law and the client's options, possible outcomes and risks of his or her matter, so that the client is able to make informed decisions and give the paralegal appropriate instructions regarding the case. Fulfillment of this professional responsibility may require a difficult but necessary conversation with a client and/or delivery of bad news. It can be helpful for advice that is not well-received by the client to be given or confirmed by the paralegal in writing.

When advising a client, a paralegal

- should explain to and obtain agreement from the client about what legal services the paralegal will provide and at what cost. Subject to any specific instructions or agreement, the client does not direct every step taken in a matter. Many decisions made in carrying out the delivery of legal services are the responsibility of the paralegal, not the client, as they require the exercise of professional judgment. However, the paralegal and the client should agree on the specific client goals to be met as a result of the retainer.

- should explain to the client under what circumstances he or she may not be able to follow the client's instructions (for example, where the instructions would cause the paralegal to violate the *Rules*).
- should ensure that clients understand that the paralegal is not a lawyer and should take steps to correct any misapprehension on the part of a client, or prospective client.

Dishonesty, Fraud or Crime by Client

RULE REFERENCE: RULE 3.02(3), (4), (4.1) & (4.2)
RULE 3.08
BY-LAW 9

2. A paralegal must be alert to the warning signs that may indicate dishonesty or illegal conduct by a client. The paralegal may need to, or be forced to, withdraw from representing the client where the client takes part in this type of dishonourable conduct.

3. Before accepting a retainer or during a retainer, if a paralegal has suspicions or doubts about whether he or she might be assisting a client in dishonesty, fraud, crime or illegal conduct, the paralegal should make reasonable inquiries to obtain information about the client and about the purpose of the retainer. For example, if a paralegal is consulted by a prospective client who requests the paralegal to deposit an amount of cash into the paralegal's trust account but is vague about the purpose of the retainer, the paralegal has an obligation to make further inquiries about the retainer. (The paralegal should also have regard to the provisions of By-Law 9 regarding cash transactions.) The paralegal should make a record of the results of these inquiries.

4. Rules 3.02(4.1) and (4.2) speak of conduct that is dishonest, fraudulent, criminal or illegal, and this conduct would include acts of omission as well as acts of commission. Conduct likely to result in substantial harm to the organization, as opposed to genuinely trivial misconduct by an organization, would invoke these rules.

Dispute Resolution

RULE REFERENCE: RULE 3.02(5), (6)

5. A paralegal has an important role to play in both commencing and settling legal proceedings.

6. The paralegal should assist the client in his or her decision about commencing legal proceedings by reviewing the reasons for and against starting the proceeding, and explaining the potential consequences of a decision to commence litigation.

7. In the course of the proceedings, the paralegal should seek the client's instructions to make an offer of settlement to the other party as soon as reasonably possible. As soon as possible after receipt of an offer of settlement from the other party, the paralegal must explain to the client the terms of the offer, the implications of accepting the offer and the possibility of making a counter-offer. When making an offer of settlement, a paralegal should allow the other party reasonable time for review and acceptance of the offer. The paralegal should not make, accept or reject an offer of settlement without the client's clear and informed instructions. To avoid any misunderstandings, the paralegal should confirm the client's instructions in writing.

Client Under a Disability

RULE REFERENCE: RULE 3.02(7), (8)
RULE 2.03

8. A paralegal must be particularly sensitive to the individual needs of a client under a disability. The paralegal should maintain a good professional relationship with the client, even if the client's ability to make decisions is impaired because of minority, mental disability or some other reason. The paralegal should also be aware of his or her duty to accommodate a client with a disability.

Medical-Legal Reports

RULE REFERENCE: RULE 3.02 (9), (10), (11)

9. On occasion, in the course of representing and advising a client, a paralegal may need to obtain a report from an expert to help the client's case. Since a medical-legal report may contain information sensitive to the client, a paralegal has special responsibilities where such reports are concerned.

10. After an expert has been hired, but before the report has been prepared, the paralegal should speak to the expert to see if the findings in the report will advance the client's cause. If the findings do not, and subject to any legal requirements, the paralegal may decide not to obtain a *written* report.

Official Language Rights

RULE REFERENCE: RULE 3.02(14)

11. When advising French-speaking clients, a paralegal should advise a client of his or her French language rights under each of the following (where appropriate):

- Subsection 19(1) of the *Constitution Act, 1982* on the use of French or English in any court established by Parliament,
- Section 530 of the *Criminal Code* (Canada) on an accused's right to a trial before a court that speaks the official language of Canada that is the language of the accused,

- Section 126 of the *Courts of Justice Act* that requires that a proceeding in which the client is a party be conducted as a bilingual (English and French) proceeding, and
- Subsection 5(1) of the *French Language Services Act* for services in French from Ontario government agencies and legislative institutions.

Errors

RULE REFERENCE: RULE 3.02(12), (13)

12. When providing legal services, the paralegal may make a mistake or fail to do something he or she should have done. When the paralegal realizes this has happened, he or she must fulfill specific duties to the client.

Multi-Discipline Practices

RULE REFERENCE: RULE 3.04(15)
RULE 8.01(5)
RULE 1.02 DEFINITION OF "ASSOCIATE"
RULE 9.01(13) DEFINITION OF "PROFESSIONAL MISCONDUCT"
BY-LAW 7

13. In a multi-discipline practice, a paralegal should be particularly alert to ensure that the client understands that he or she is receiving legal services only from the paralegal. If advice or service is sought from non-licensed members of the firm, it should be sought and provided independently of and outside the scope of the retainer for the provision of legal services. A paralegal should also be aware that advice or services provided by a non-licensed member of the firm will be subject to the constraints outlined in the relevant by-laws and rules governing multi-discipline practices. One way to distinguish the advice or services of non-licensed members of the firm is to ensure that such advice or services is provided from a location separate from the premises of the multi-discipline practice.

Affiliations

RULE REFERENCE: RULE 3.04(16) & (17)
RULE 1.02 DEFINITIONS OF "AFFILIATED ENTITY" AND "AFFILIATION"
BY-LAW 7

14. Before accepting a retainer, the *Rules* impose certain disclosure and consent requirements on a paralegal providing legal services jointly with non-legal services of an affiliated entity.

GUIDELINE 8: CONFIDENTIALITY

General

RULE REFERENCE: RULE 3.03(1)

1. A paralegal cannot render effective professional service to a client, unless there is full and unreserved communication between them. The client must feel completely secure that all matters discussed with the paralegal will be held in strict confidence. The client is entitled to proceed on this basis, without any express request or stipulation.

2. A paralegal's duty of loyalty to a client prohibits the paralegal from using any client information for a purpose other than serving the client in accordance with the terms of the retainer. A paralegal cannot disclose client information to serve another client or for his or her own benefit.

What Information Must Be Protected?

RULE REFERENCE: RULE 3.03(1)

3. The obligation to protect client information extends to information that is either relevant or irrelevant to the matter for which the paralegal is retained. The source of the information does not matter. The information could be received from the client or from others. The information may come in any form—the spoken word, paper, computer documents, e-mails, audio or video recordings. The obligation also extends to the client's papers and property, the client's identity and the facts the client has consulted or retained the paralegal.

How Long Does the Duty Last?

RULE REFERENCE: RULE 3.03(2)

4. The Rules provide that the duty of confidentiality lasts indefinitely. The duty continues, even after the client or former client dies.

5. Problems can arise when information is provided to a paralegal or a paralegal firm by a prospective client. For lawyers, the duty to protect confidential information begins when a prospective client first contacts the lawyer or law firm. The courts may determine that a paralegal also owes a duty of confidentiality to prospective clients, even if the paralegal is never actually retained by the prospective client.

Who Owes the Duty?

RULE REFERENCE: RULE 3.03(1) & (3)
RULE 8.01(1)

6. The paralegal, and all other employees of the paralegal firm, owe the duty of confidentiality to every client. A paralegal must ensure that his or her employees, and anyone involved with the client's matter, understand the duty of confidentiality as set out in the *Rules*. The paralegal is ultimately responsible, if someone employed by the paralegal discloses confidential information without client authorization or as permitted by the *Rules*.

When, If Ever, is Disclosure of Confidential Information Permitted?

Disclosure With Client Authority

RULE REFERENCE: RULE 3.03(1)

7. Disclosure of confidential information may be authorized by the client. This authorization may be express or implied. For example, where a paralegal is retained to represent a client in a Small Claims Court matter, the paralegal has the client's implied authority to disclose enough information to complete the necessary forms.

8. When disclosing confidential information on the express authority of the client, the paralegal should consider

- whether the client understands his or her right to confidentiality,
- whether the client understands the potential implications of disclosure,
- whether the client has shown a clear, informed and voluntary intention to forego the right to confidentiality, and
- whether, in the particular circumstances, it would be prudent to obtain the client's written authorization to disclose.

Disclosure Without Client Authority

RULE REFERENCE: RULE 3.03(4), (5), (6), (7) & (8)

9. Rule 3.03 identifies a number of situations in which a paralegal *must* or *may* disclose confidential client information, whether or not the client consents to the disclosure.

10. This rule does not permit the paralegal to reveal confidential information about past criminal conduct, or to prevent future illegal or criminal conduct that does not involve death or serious bodily or psychological harm.

11. If a paralegal wishes to use a collection agency for an outstanding account, the information provided to the collection agency should be limited to that necessary to collect the fees. Information contained in documents that is not necessary to enforce payment should either be deleted or blocked out.

Other Obligations Relating to Confidential Information—Security of Court Facilities and Misconduct

RULE REFERENCE: RULE 3.03
RULE 6.01(3)
RULE 9.01(2)

12. The *Rules* require a paralegal to disclose confidential client information in other circumstances—for the security of court facilities, and to report certain acts of misconduct to the Law Society.

13. Where a paralegal discloses confidential information to prevent a dangerous situation from developing at a court facility, the paralegal should consider providing this information to the court facility anonymously or through another paralegal or a lawyer.

Avoiding Inadvertent Disclosure

RULE REFERENCE: RULE 3.03(1)

14. The following steps may assist a paralegal in meeting his or her obligation to protect confidential client information:

- not disclosing having been consulted or retained by a particular person unless the nature of the matter requires disclosure,
- taking care not to disclose to one client confidential information about another client and declining any retainer that might require such disclosure,
- avoiding indiscreet conversations about a client's affairs, even with the paralegal's spouse or family,
- shunning any gossip about a client's affairs, even though the client is not named or otherwise identified,
- not repeating any gossip or information about a client's business or affairs that is overheard or recounted to the paralegal, and
- avoiding indiscreet shop-talk between colleagues that may be overheard by third parties.

Office Procedures

RULE REFERENCE: RULE 3.03(1) & (3)
RULE 8.01(1)

15. A paralegal should establish office procedures to ensure that the confidentiality of client information is protected. These procedures could include the following:

- recording the identity and particulars of every client or potential client,
- screening for conflicts of interest when a potential client first contacts the firm, and prior to his or her disclosure of confidential information to the paralegal,
- establishing a communication policy with each client outlining how communications between the client and firm will be conducted,
- keeping file cabinets away from the reception area, placing computer screens so they cannot be viewed by people not in the firm, keeping client files out of sight, locking file cabinets when no one is in the office, limiting access to client files only to staff who work on the matter, shredding confidential information before discarding, ensuring appropriate security for off-site storage of files,

- taking steps to protect confidential information obtained and sent in an electronic form,
- ensuring that all staff understand their obligations with respect to confidentiality and,
- limiting access to confidential information by outside service providers.

GUIDELINE 9: CONFLICTS OF INTEREST

GENERAL

Definition

RULE REFERENCE: RULE 3.04(1)

1. Conflicts of interest are defined in Rule 3.04(1).

DUTY TO AVOID CONFLICTS OF INTEREST

The Duty

RULE REFERENCE: RULE 3.04(2) & (3)

2. The duty to avoid conflicts of interest is found in Rule 3.04(2) and (3).

To Whom Is the Duty Owed—Current Clients and Prospective Clients

RULE REFERENCE: RULE 3.04(1) & (3)

3. A paralegal owes the duty of avoiding conflicts of interest to all clients, including prospective clients. A paralegal should identify potential conflicts of interest at the first contact with a prospective client. A *prospective client* can be described as one who has consulted with a paralegal or paralegal firm to see if the firm will take on his or her matter or to see if he or she would like to hire the paralegal or firm.

4. Conflicts of interest may arise at any time. A paralegal should use a conflicts checking system to assist in managing conflicts of interest. The paralegal should examine whether a conflict of interest exists not only at the outset, but throughout the duration of a retainer because new circumstances or information may establish or reveal a conflict of interest.

5. At the time that a paralegal becomes aware of a conflict, or potential conflict, the paralegal should consider whether to accept the retainer, or to continue to act. This applies even where the client consents or where the retainer would not, in the paralegal's opinion, breach the *Rules*. The paralegal should consider the delay, expense and inconvenience that would arise for the client and/or the paralegal, should the paralegal be required to withdraw from the matter at a later stage in the proceedings.

To Whom Is the Duty Owed— The Firm's Clients

RULE REFERENCE: RULE 1.02 DEFINITION OF "CLIENT"

6. Since every client of a paralegal firm is also the client of every other paralegal employed at the firm, if one paralegal in the firm has a conflict of interest in a matter, then all paralegals in the firm have a conflict in that matter. As a result, when checking for conflicts, the paralegal should review the names of all current and former clients of the firm and not just the clients personally served by the individual paralegal.

To Whom Is the Duty Owed—Persons Involved or Associated with Clients

RULE REFERENCE: RULE 3.04(4)

7. Sometimes there will be others who are involved or associated with the client in the client's matter. Persons *involved or associated with clients* may include the client's spouse, family members, business associates or employees of any related companies. The duty to avoid conflicts of interest may require a paralegal to avoid acting against those individuals as well.

DEALING WITH A CONFLICT OF INTEREST

Disclosing All Information

RULE REFERENCE: RULE 3.04(3)

8. The client needs to know of anything that may influence the paralegal's judgment or loyalty. Once the paralegal has provided the client with all the details, the paralegal must allow the client time to consider them or to ask for further clarification.

9. There may be situations where it is impossible for a paralegal to give a client or prospective client all necessary information. This may happen when the details about the conflict involve another client or a former client. Since a paralegal cannot reveal confidential information regarding another client, the paralegal may only say that there is a conflict and that he or she cannot continue with or accept the retainer.

Obtaining Consent

RULE REFERENCE: RULE 1.02 DEFINITION OF "CONSENT"
RULE 3.04(3)

10. The client may only consent after being given all information required to make an informed decision. This is called *informed consent.*

11. Where any other relevant persons must consent, the paralegal must make sure that their consent is also informed consent.

Independent Legal Advice/Legal Representation

RULE REFERENCE: RULES 3.04(9), 3.06(1)(B) AND 3.06(5)(B), 3.06(7)(C)

12. There are situations where the client's informed and written consent is not enough to allow the paralegal to accept or continue with a matter. In some circumstances, the client must receive advice from an independent legal advisor regarding the matter or transaction before the paralegal may taken any further steps in the client's matter.

13. An independent legal advisor is another paralegal or lawyer, who can provide the client with *independent legal advice.* This advisor is unrelated to the client's matter, associated parties or the paralegal. He or she is unbiased and objective and does not have a conflict of interest.

14. In circumstances where the paralegal is prohibited from acting for a client or prospective client, the paralegal must suggest that the individual obtain his or her own independent legal representation. *Independent legal representation* means that the individual has retained a legal representative, either a paralegal or lawyer, to act as his or her own representative in the matter. This retained representative is objective and does not have any conflicting interest with regards to the matter.

Refusal to Act, Withdrawal of Services

RULE REFERENCE: RULES 3.04(2) AND 3.08

15. In some cases, the only way to deal with the conflict is to refuse to act. The paralegal may have to decline the retainer at the outset or may have to terminate the retainer and withdraw from representing the client at a later time. A paralegal may need to take this step even where the client wants the paralegal to accept the retainer, or to continue to act.

JOINT CLIENTS

General

RULE REFERENCE: RULE 3.04(8)–(14)

16. A paralegal may be asked to represent more than one client in a matter or transaction. This is referred to as a *joint retainer.*

17. Acting in a joint retainer places the paralegal in a potential conflict of interest. A paralegal has an obligation to all clients and in a joint retainer, the paralegal must remain loyal and devoted to all clients equally—the paralegal cannot choose to serve one client more carefully or resolutely than any other. If the interests of one client change during the course of the retainer, the paralegal may be in a conflict of interest.

Before Accepting the Joint Retainer

RULE REFERENCE: RULE 3.04(8)–(11)
RULE 3.02(7) & (8)

18. In cases where one of the joint clients is not sophisticated or is vulnerable, the paralegal should consider the provisions of Rule 3.02(7) & (8) regarding clients under a disability. The paralegal may want to recommend that the client obtain independent legal advice prior to agreeing to the joint retainer. This will ensure that the client's consent to the joint retainer is informed, genuine and uncoerced.

If a Conflict Develops Between Joint Clients

RULE REFERENCE: RULE 3.04(12)–(14)

19. Subrules 3.04(12)–(14) set out the steps a paralegal must take in the event that a conflict develops between joint clients.

ACTING AGAINST CLIENTS

Acting Against Clients or Former Clients in the Same or Related Matters

RULE REFERENCE: RULE 3.04(2), (3), (4)(A) & (B)

20. A paralegal is not permitted to act against clients or former clients in the same or related matters, except in accordance with subrules 3.04(2), (3), (4)(a) and (b).

Acting Against Clients or Former Clients in New Matters

RULE REFERENCE: RULE 3.04(3), (4)(C), (5), (6) & (7)

21. A paralegal is permitted to act against a client or former client in a fresh, independent and unrelated matter, in certain circumstances.

22. Even where the *Rules* do not prohibit a paralegal from acting against a client or former client, the paralegal should consider whether to accept the retainer (or continue acting). To act against a client or former client may damage the paralegal-client relationship, may result in court proceedings or a complaint to the Law Society.

PARALEGAL TRANSFER BETWEEN FIRMS

General

RULE REFERENCE: RULE 3.05

23. Problems concerning confidential information may arise when a paralegal changes firms and both firms act for opposing clients in the same or a related matter. The potential risk is that confidential information about the client from the paralegal's former office may be revealed to the members of the new firm and used

against that client. A paralegal should carefully review the *Rules* when transferring to a new office or when a new paralegal is about to join the paralegal firm.

DEALING WITH UNREPRESENTED PERSONS

General

RULE REFERENCE: RULE 4.05
RULE 3.04(2), (8)–(14)

24. In the course of providing legal services, a paralegal may have to deal with opposite parties or other individuals with an interest in the matter who are not represented by a paralegal or a lawyer. The potential danger to the paralegal in this situation is that the unrepresented person may think that the paralegal is looking after his or her interests.

25. If an unrepresented person who is the opposite party requests the paralegal to advise or act in the matter, the paralegal is not permitted to accept the retainer. If the unrepresented party otherwise has an interest in the matter, such as a co-accused, the paralegal may be permitted to act, but should be governed by the considerations outlined in Rule 3.04(8)–(14) about joint retainers.

FINANCIAL INTERESTS

Doing Business With a Client

RULE REFERENCE: RULE 3.06(1)–(4)

26. A paralegal should be cautious about entering into a business arrangement with his or her client(s) that is unrelated to the provision of paralegal services. Since the paralegal is or was the client's advisor, the paralegal may have a conflict of interest. The paralegal may unknowingly influence the client to agree to an arrangement that may be unfair or unreasonable to the client. This danger is present when the client wants to invest with the paralegal.

Borrowing From Clients

RULE REFERENCE: RULE 3.06(5)

27. A paralegal must not borrow from clients except in accordance with Rule 3.06(5).

Guaranteeing Client Debts

RULE REFERENCE: RULE 3.06(6)–(7)

28. A paralegal must not guarantee client debts except in accordance with Rule 3.06(6).

PERSONAL INTERESTS

Conflicts of Interest Arising From Personal Relationships

RULE REFERENCE: RULE 3.04(1)

29. The *Rules* do not prohibit a paralegal from providing legal services to friends or family members, but they do require the paralegal to avoid existing or potential conflicts of interest.

30. A conflict of interest may arise when a paralegal provides legal services to a friend or family member, or when the client and the paralegal have a sexual or intimate personal relationship. In these circumstances, the paralegal's personal feelings for the client may impede the paralegal's ability to provide objective, disinterested professional advice to the client. Before accepting a retainer from or continuing a retainer with a person with whom the paralegal has a sexual or intimate personal relationship, a paralegal should consider the following factors:

- The vulnerability of the client, both emotional and economic;
- The fact that the paralegal and client relationship may create a power imbalance in favour of the paralegal or, in some circumstances, in favour of the client;
- Whether the sexual or intimate personal relationship may jeopardize the client's right to have all information concerning the client's business and affairs held in strict confidence. For example, the existence of the personal relationship may obscure whether certain information was acquired by the paralegal in the course of the paralegal and client relationship;
- Whether such a relationship may require the paralegal to act as a witness in the proceedings;
- Whether such a relationship may interfere with the paralegal's fiduciary obligations to the client, including his or her ability to exercise independent professional judgment and his or her ability to fulfill obligations owed as an officer of the court and to the administration of justice.

31. Generally speaking, there is no conflict of interest if another paralegal or lawyer at the firm who does not have a sexual or intimate personal relationship with the client, handles the client's matter.

Conflicts of Interest Arising From a Paralegal's Outside Interests

RULE REFERENCE: RULE 3.04(1)
RULE 2.01(4) & (5)

32. A conflict of interest may arise from the paralegal's outside interests. Outside interests covers the widest possible range of activities and includes those that may overlap with the business of providing legal services, as well as activities that have no connection to the law or working as a paralegal. If a paralegal has other

businesses or interests separate from his or her paralegal firm, those interests may influence the way the paralegal serves clients. Whatever the outside interest, a paralegal must guard against allowing those outside interests to interfere or conflict with his or her duties to clients. (Also refer to Guideline 2: Outside Interests.)

33. If a paralegal is in public office while still providing legal services to clients, the paralegal must not allow his or her duties as a public official to conflict with his or her duties as a paralegal. If there is a possibility of a conflict of interest, the paralegal should avoid it either by removing himself or herself from the discussion and voting in the public capacity or by withdrawing from representation of the client.

MULTI-DISCIPLINE PRACTICE

Conflicts of Interest Arising From Multi-discipline Practice

RULE REFERENCE: 3.04(15) BY-LAW 7

34. A paralegal should be alert to conflicts of interest arising from a multi-discipline practice, as he or she is subject to the requirements of Rule 3.04(15).

AFFILIATIONS

Conflicts of Interest Arising From Paralegals and Affiliated Entities

RULE REFERENCE: RULE 3.04(1), (16), (17) & (18)
BY-LAW 7

35. A conflict of interest may arise from a paralegal's, or his or her associate's, interest in an affiliated firm of non-licensees where that interest conflicts with the paralegal's duties to a client. Rule 3.04(16) and (17) impose disclosure and consent requirements on a paralegal in an affiliation.

36. Conflicts of interest arising out of a proposed retainer by a client should be addressed as if the paralegal's practice and the practice of the affiliated entity were one where the paralegal accepts a retainer to provide legal services to that client jointly with non-legal services of the affiliated entity.

37. The affiliation is subject to the same conflict of interest rules as apply to paralegals.

GUIDELINE 11: WITHDRAWAL FROM REPRESENTATION

General

RULE REFERENCE: RULE 3.08

1. A client may end the paralegal-client relationship at any time and for any reason. A paralegal is subject to certain restrictions in ending the paralegal-client

relationship. Whether the paralegal has good cause for withdrawal will depend on many factors, including

- the nature and stage of the matter,
- the relationship with the client,
- the paralegal's expertise and experience, and
- any harm or prejudice to the client that may result from the withdrawal.

2. Rule 3.08 specifies a paralegal's obligations when withdrawing legal services. It sets out situations in which the paralegal

- may choose to withdraw (*optional withdrawal*),
- must withdraw (*mandatory withdrawal*), and
- must comply with special rules (*withdrawal from quasi-criminal and criminal cases*).

3. To avoid misunderstandings, it will be helpful for the paralegal to explain to the client, at the beginning of the relationship

- that all documents to which the client is entitled be provided will be returned to the client when their relationship ends or the matter concludes, and
- which documents in the file will belong to the paralegal, so that they will be kept by the paralegal when their relationship ends or the matter is finished.

4. To ensure that the client understands these details, the paralegal should consider including them in his or her engagement letter or retainer agreement.

5. When the paralegal withdraws, he or she is subject to restrictions relating to the disclosure of client information. This would restrict the paralegal from revealing the reason for withdrawing to a *successor* (a paralegal or lawyer who accepts the client's matter after the original paralegal has withdrawn). Refer to Guideline 8: Confidentiality for further information on this subject.

Optional Withdrawal

RULE REFERENCE: RULE 3.08(2), (3), (4), (6), (7), (8) & (9)

6. During a retainer, a situation may arise that will allow the paralegal to withdraw from representing the client.

7. A *serious loss of confidence* means that the paralegal and the client can no longer trust and rely on each other, making it impossible to have a normal paralegal-client relationship. An example would be where the client deceives or lies to the paralegal. Another example would be where the client refuses unreasonably to accept and act on the paralegal's advice on an important point.

8. If the retainer relates to a criminal or quasi-criminal matter, the paralegal must ensure that he or she complies with the special rules relating to withdrawal in those types of cases (refer to section entitled "Withdrawal From Quasi-Criminal and Criminal Cases" at (iv)).

Mandatory Withdrawal

RULE REFERENCE: RULE 3.08(5), (7), (8) & (9)

9. In certain situations, a paralegal is required to withdraw from representing a client, even if the paralegal or the client wishes to continue with the retainer.

Withdrawal From Criminal or Quasi-Criminal Matters

RULE REFERENCE: RULE 3.08(7), (8) & (9)

10. Whether a paralegal may withdraw in these types of matters, has to do with the amount of time between *the withdrawal* (the date and time the paralegal intends to stop representing the client) and *the trial* (the date and time the client's trial begins).

11. Generally, the amount of time between the withdrawal and trial must be sufficient to allow the client to hire another representative and the new representative to prepare properly for trial.

12. While the *Rules* do not require the paralegal to make an application to the court to be removed as the client's representative, most rules of court do. Therefore, the paralegal should consult the rules of the court to determine what process is to be followed. The paralegal must not tell the court or the prosecutor the reasons for withdrawal, unless disclosure is justified in accordance with the *Rules.*

13. The paralegal may seek to adjourn the trial to give the client or the new representative more time to prepare, as long as the adjournment does not prejudice the client.

Manner of Withdrawal

RULE REFERENCE: RULES 3.08 (10) AND (11)

14. Where a paralegal withdraws from representation of a client, the required manner of withdrawal is set out in subrules 3.08(10) and (11).

Duties of the Successor Paralegal

RULE REFERENCE: RULE 3.08(12)

15. If a client who was represented by another paralegal or a lawyer contacts a paralegal, that paralegal has obligations as the *successor paralegal.*

Written Confirmation

16. If a paralegal's services are terminated while the client's matter is ongoing and the client requests that the matter be transferred to a new paralegal or lawyer, the paralegal should confirm, in writing, the termination of the retainer. The paralegal should also obtain a *direction*, signed by the client, for release of the client's file to a successor paralegal or lawyer. A *direction* is a written document instructing the paralegal to release the file to the successor paralegal or lawyer. If the file will be

collected by the client personally, the paralegal should obtain a written acknowledgement signed by the client, confirming that the client has received the file.

GUIDELINE 16: DUTY TO THE ADMINISTRATION OF JUSTICE

General

RULE REFERENCE: RULE 6.01(1)
RULE 7.01(4)

1. An important part of a paralegal's duty to act with integrity is his or her obligation to the administration of justice detailed in Rule 6. The obligation includes a paralegal's duty to assist in maintaining the security of court facilities, to refrain from inappropriate public statements, and the obligation to prevent unauthorized practice.

Security of Court Facilities

RULE REFERENCE: RULE 6.01(3)
RULE 3.03

2. An aspect of supporting the justice system is ensuring that its facilities remain safe. Where appropriate, a paralegal in the situation covered by Rule 6.01(3) should consider requesting additional security at the facility and notifying other paralegals or lawyers who may be affected. In considering what, if any, action to take with respect to this obligation, the paralegal must consider his or her obligations under Rule 3.03.

Public Appearances and Statements

RULE REFERENCE: RULE 6.01(1), (2), (4) & (4.1)
RULE 3.03, 3.04
RULE 4.01(1)
RULE 7.01(4)

3. When making statements to the media with, or on behalf of, a client, a paralegal must be mindful of his or her obligations to act in the client's best interests and within the scope of his or her instructions from the client. It is also important that a person's, particularly an accused person's, right to a fair trial or hearing not be impaired by inappropriate public statements made before a case has concluded.

Provision of Legal Services Without a Licence/Practice of Law Without a Licence

RULE REFERENCE: RULE 6.01(5) & (6)

4. The obligations found in subrules 6.01(5) & (6) stem from a paralegal's obligation to the administration of justice and from the regulatory scheme for paralegals and lawyers set out in the *Act* and discussed below.

5. Under the *Act*, anyone who provides legal services or practices law must be licensed by the Law Society, unless they are exempt from this requirement, or deemed not to be providing legal services or practicing law. A person who is not a lawyer or a licensed paralegal is subject neither to a professional code of conduct nor the Law Society's jurisdiction, which exist to protect the public. Only clients of regulated service providers have important protections, such as the following:

- adherence to a mandatory code of professional conduct,
- maintenance and operation of a trust account in accordance with strict mandatory guidelines,
- mandatory professional liability insurance coverage, and
- the Law Society's Compensation Funds.

GUIDELINE 17: DUTY TO PARALEGALS, LAWYERS AND OTHERS

General

RULE REFERENCE: RULE 2.01(3)
RULE 7.01

1. Discourteous and uncivil behaviour between paralegals or between a paralegal and a lawyer will lessen the public's respect for the administration of justice and may harm the clients' interests. Any ill feeling that may exist between parties, particularly during adversarial proceedings, should never be allowed to influence paralegals or lawyers in their conduct and demeanour toward each other or the parties. Hostility or conflict between representatives may impair their ability to focus on their respective clients' interests and to have matters resolved without undue delay or cost.

Prohibited Conduct

RULE REFERENCE: RULE 7.01

2. The presence of personal animosity between paralegals or between a paralegal and a lawyer involved in a matter may cause their judgment to be clouded by emotional factors and hinder the proper resolution of the matter. To that end, Rule 7.01 outlines various types of conduct that are specifically prohibited.

3. One of the prohibitions in Rule 7.01(1) refers to sharp practice. Sharp practice occurs when a paralegal obtains, or tries to obtain, an advantage for the para-

legal or client(s), by using dishonourable means. This would include, for example, lying to another paralegal or a lawyer, trying to trick another paralegal or a lawyer into doing something or making an oral promise to another paralegal or lawyer with the intention of reneging on the promise later. As another example, if an opposing paralegal were under a mistaken belief about the date of an upcoming trial, a paralegal would be obligated to tell the opposing representative about the error, rather than ignoring the matter in the hope the opposing representative would not appear at the trial.

Source: Paralegal Professional Conduct Guidelines, Law Society of Upper Canada, www.lsuc.on.ca/media/paralegal_prof_conduct_guidelines.pdf.

APPENDIX E

Provincial Offences Act: Part IV

R.S.O. 1990, c. P.33

PART IV TRIAL AND SENTENCING

Trial

APPLICATION OF PART

28. This Part applies to a proceeding commenced under this Act.

TERRITORIAL JURISDICTION

29(1) Subject to subsection (2), a proceeding in respect of an offence shall be heard and determined by the Ontario Court of Justice sitting in the county or district in which the offence occurred.

IDEM

(2) A proceeding in respect of an offence may be heard and determined in a county or district that adjoins that in which the offence occurred if,

(a) the court holds sittings in a place reasonably proximate to the place where the offence occurred; and

(b) the place of sitting referred to in clause (a) is named in the summons or offence notice.

TRANSFER TO PROPER COUNTY

(3) Where a proceeding is taken in a county or district other than one referred to in subsection (1) or (2), the court shall order that the proceeding be transferred to the proper county or district and may where the defendant appears award costs under section 60.

CHANGE OF VENUE

(4) Where, on the motion of a defendant or prosecutor made to the court at the location named in the information or certificate, it appears to the court that,

(a) it would be appropriate in the interests of justice to do so; or

(b) both the defendant and prosecutor consent thereto,

the court may order that the proceeding be heard and determined at another location in Ontario.

CONDITIONS

(5) The court may, in an order made on a motion by the prosecutor under subsection (3) or (4), prescribe conditions that it thinks proper with respect to the payment of additional expenses caused to the defendant as a result of the change of venue.

TIME OF ORDER FOR CHANGE OF VENUE

(6) An order under subsection (3) or (4) may be made even if a motion preliminary to trial has been disposed of or the plea has been taken and it may be made at any time before evidence has been heard.

PRELIMINARY MOTIONS

(7) The court at a location to which a proceeding is transferred under this section may receive and determine any motion preliminary to trial although the same matter was determined by the court at the location from which the proceeding was transferred.

DELIVERY OF PAPERS

(8) Where an order is made under subsection (3) or (4), the clerk of the court at the location where the trial was to be held before the order was made shall deliver any material in his or her possession in connection with the proceeding forthwith to the clerk of the court at the location where the trial is ordered to be held.

JUSTICE PRESIDING AT TRIAL

30(1) The justice presiding when evidence is first taken at the trial shall preside over the whole of the trial.

WHEN PRESIDING JUSTICE UNABLE TO ACT BEFORE ADJUDICATION

(2) Where evidence has been taken at a trial and, before making his or her adjudication, the presiding justice dies or in his or her opinion or the opinion of the Chief Justice of the Ontario Court of Justice is for any reason unable to continue, another justice shall conduct the hearing again as a new trial.

WHEN PRESIDING JUSTICE UNABLE TO ACT AFTER ADJUDICATION

(3) Where evidence has been taken at a trial and, after making his or her adjudication but before making his or her order or imposing sentence, the presiding justice dies or in his or her opinion or the opinion of the Chief Justice of the Ontario Court of Justice is for any reason unable to continue, another justice may make the order or impose the sentence that is authorized by law.

CONSENT TO CHANGE PRESIDING JUSTICE

(4) A justice presiding at a trial may, at any stage of the trial and upon the consent of the prosecutor and defendant, order that the trial be conducted by another

justice and, upon the order being given, subsection (2) applies as if the justice were unable to act.

RETENTION OF JURISDICTION

31. The court retains jurisdiction over the information or certificate even if the court fails to exercise its jurisdiction at any particular time or the provisions of this Act respecting adjournments are not complied with.

STAY OF PROCEEDING

32(1) In addition to his or her right to withdraw a charge, the Attorney General or his or her agent may stay a proceeding at any time before judgment by direction in court to the clerk of the court and thereupon any recognizance relating to the proceeding is vacated.

RECOMMENCEMENT

(2) A proceeding stayed under subsection (1) may be recommenced by direction of the Attorney General, the Deputy Attorney General or a Crown Attorney to the clerk of the court but a proceeding that is stayed shall not be recommenced,

(a) later than one year after the stay; or

(b) after the expiration of any limitation period applicable, which shall run as if the proceeding had not been commenced until the recommencement,

whichever is the earlier.

DIVIDING COUNTS

33(1) A defendant may at any stage of the proceeding make a motion to the court to amend or to divide a count that,

(a) charges in the alternative different matters, acts or omissions that are stated in the alternative in the enactment that creates or describes the offence; or

(b) is double or multifarious,

on the ground that, as framed, it prejudices the defendant in the defendant's defence.

IDEM

(2) Upon a motion under subsection (1), where the court is satisfied that the ends of justice so require, it may order that a count be amended or divided into two or more counts, and thereupon a formal commencement may be inserted before each of the counts into which it is divided.

AMENDMENT OF INFORMATION OR CERTIFICATE

34(1) The court may, at any stage of the proceeding, amend the information or certificate as may be necessary if it appears that the information or certificate,

(a) fails to state or states defectively anything that is requisite to charge the offence;

(b) does not negative an exception that should be negatived; or

(c) is in any way defective in substance or in form.

IDEM

(2) The court may, during the trial, amend the information or certificate as may be necessary if the matters to be alleged in the proposed amendment are disclosed by the evidence taken at the trial.

VARIANCES BETWEEN CHARGE AND EVIDENCE

(3) A variance between the information or certificate and the evidence taken on the trial is not material with respect to,

(a) the time when the offence is alleged to have been committed, if it is proved that the information was laid or certificate issued within the prescribed period of limitation; or

(b) the place where the subject-matter of the proceeding is alleged to have arisen, except in an issue as to the jurisdiction of the court.

CONSIDERATIONS ON AMENDMENT

(4) The court shall, in considering whether or not an amendment should be made, consider,

(a) the evidence taken on the trial, if any;

(b) the circumstances of the case;

(c) whether the defendant has been misled or prejudiced in the defendant's defence by a variance, error or omission; and

(d) whether, having regard to the merits of the case, the proposed amendment can be made without injustice being done.

AMENDMENT, QUESTION OF LAW

(5) The question whether an order to amend an information or certificate should be granted or refused is a question of law.

ENDORSEMENT OF ORDER TO AMEND

(6) An order to amend an information or certificate shall be endorsed on the information or certificate as part of the record and the trial shall proceed as if the information or certificate had been originally laid as amended.

PARTICULARS

35. The court may, before or during trial, if it is satisfied that it is necessary for a fair trial, order that a particular, further describing any matter relevant to the proceeding, be furnished to the defendant.

MOTION TO QUASH INFORMATION OR CERTIFICATE

36(1) An objection to an information or certificate for a defect apparent on its face shall be taken by motion to quash the information or certificate before the defendant has pleaded, and thereafter only by leave of the court.

GROUNDS FOR QUASHING

(2) The court shall not quash an information or certificate unless an amendment or particulars under section 33, 34 or 35 would fail to satisfy the ends of justice.

COSTS ON AMENDMENT OR PARTICULARS

37. Where the information or certificate is amended or particulars are ordered and an adjournment is necessary as a result thereof, the court may make an order under section 60 for costs resulting from the adjournment.

JOINDER OF COUNTS OR DEFENDANTS

38(1) The court may, before trial, where it is satisfied that the ends of justice so require, direct that separate counts, informations or certificates be tried together or that persons who are charged separately be tried together.

SEPARATE TRIALS

(2) The court may, before or during the trial, where it is satisfied that the ends of justice so require, direct that separate counts, informations or certificates be tried separately or that persons who are charged jointly or being tried together be tried separately.

ISSUANCE OF SUMMONS

39(1) Where a justice is satisfied that a person is able to give material evidence in a proceeding under this Act, the justice may issue a summons requiring the person to attend to give evidence and bring with him or her any writings or things referred to in the summons.

SERVICE

(2) A summons shall be served and the service shall be proved in the same manner as a summons under section 26.

ATTENDANCE

(3) A person who is served with a summons shall attend at the time and place stated in the summons to give evidence and, if required by the summons, shall bring with him or her any writing or other thing that the person has in his or her possession or under his or her control relating to the subject-matter of the proceeding.

REMAINING IN ATTENDANCE

(4) A person who is served with a summons shall remain in attendance during the hearing and the hearing as resumed after adjournment from time to time unless the person is excused from attendance by the presiding justice.

ARREST OF WITNESS

40(1) Where a judge is satisfied upon evidence under oath or affirmation, that a person is able to give material evidence that is necessary in a proceeding under this Act and,

(a) will not attend if a summons is served; or

(b) attempts to serve a summons have been made and have failed because the person is evading service,

the judge may issue a warrant in the prescribed form for the arrest of the person.

IDEM

(2) Where a person who has been served with a summons to attend to give evidence in a proceeding does not attend or remain in attendance, the court may, if it is established,

(a) that the summons has been served; and

(b) that the person is able to give material evidence that is necessary,

issue or cause to be issued a warrant in the prescribed form for the arrest of the person.

BRINGING BEFORE JUSTICE

(3) The police officer who arrests a person under a warrant issued under subsection (1) or (2) shall immediately take the person before a justice.

RELEASE ON RECOGNIZANCE

(4) Unless the justice is satisfied that it is necessary to detain a person in custody to ensure his or her attendance to give evidence, the justice shall order the person released upon condition that the person enter into a recognizance in such amount and with such sureties, if any, as are reasonably necessary to ensure his or her attendance.

BRINGING BEFORE JUDGE

(5) Where a person is not released under subsection (4), the justice of the peace shall cause the person to be brought before a judge within two days of the justice's decision.

DETENTION

(6) Where the judge is satisfied that it is necessary to detain the person in custody to ensure his or her attendance to give evidence, the judge may order that the person be detained in custody to testify at the trial or to have his or her evidence taken by a commissioner under an order made under subsection (11).

RELEASE ON RECOGNIZANCE

(7) Where the judge does not make an order under subsection (6), he or she shall order that the person be released upon condition that the person enter into a recognizance in such amount and with such sureties, if any, as are reasonably necessary to ensure his or her attendance.

MAXIMUM IMPRISONMENT

(8) A person who is ordered to be detained in custody under subsection (6) or is not released in fact under subsection (7) shall not be detained in custody for a period longer than ten days.

RELEASE WHEN NO LONGER REQUIRED

(9) A judge, or the justice presiding at a trial, may at any time order the release of a person in custody under this section where he or she is satisfied that the detention is no longer justified.

ARREST ON BREACH OF RECOGNIZANCE

(10) Where a person who is bound by a recognizance to attend to give evidence in any proceeding does not attend or remain in attendance, the court may issue a warrant in the prescribed form for the arrest of that person and,

(a) where the person is brought directly before the court, subsections (6) and (7) apply; and

(b) where the person is not brought directly before the court, subsections (3) to (7) apply.

COMMISSION EVIDENCE OF WITNESS IN CUSTODY

(11) A judge or the justice presiding at the trial may order that the evidence of a person held in custody under this section be taken by a commissioner under section 43, which applies thereto in the same manner as to a witness who is unable to attend by reason of illness.

ORDER FOR PERSON IN A PRISON TO ATTEND

41(1) Where a person whose attendance is required in court to stand trial or to give evidence is confined in a prison, and a judge is satisfied, upon evidence under oath or affirmation orally or by affidavit, that the person's attendance is necessary to satisfy the ends of justice, the judge may issue an order in the prescribed form that the person be brought before the court, from day to day, as may be necessary.

IDEM

(2) An order under subsection (1) shall be addressed to the person who has custody of the prisoner and on receipt thereof that person shall,

(a) deliver the prisoner to the police officer or other person who is named in the order to receive the prisoner; or

(b) bring the prisoner before the court upon payment of the person's reasonable charges in respect thereof.

IDEM

(3) An order made under subsection (1) shall direct the manner in which the person shall be kept in custody and returned to the prison from which he or she is brought.

PENALTY FOR FAILURE TO ATTEND

42(1) Every person who, being required by law to attend or remain in attendance at a hearing, fails without lawful excuse to attend or remain in attendance accordingly is guilty of an offence and on conviction is liable to a fine of not more than $2,000, or to imprisonment for a term of not more than thirty days, or to both.

PROOF OF FAILURE TO ATTEND

(2) In a proceeding under subsection (1), a certificate of the clerk of the court or a justice stating that the defendant failed to attend is admissible in evidence as proof, in the absence of evidence to the contrary, of the fact without proof of the signature or office of the person appearing to have signed the certificate.

ORDER FOR EVIDENCE BY COMMISSION

43(1) Upon the motion of the defendant or prosecutor, a judge or, during trial, the court may by order appoint a commissioner to take the evidence of a witness who is out of Ontario or is not likely to be able to attend the trial by reason of illness or physical disability or for some other good and sufficient cause.

ADMISSION OF COMMISSION EVIDENCE

(2) Evidence taken by a commissioner appointed under subsection (1) may be read in evidence in the proceeding if,

(a) it is proved by oral evidence or by affidavit that the witness is unable to attend for a reason set out in subsection (1);

(b) the transcript of the evidence is signed by the commissioner by or before whom it purports to have been taken; and

(c) it is proved to the satisfaction of the court that reasonable notice of the time and place for taking the evidence was given to the other party, and the party had full opportunity to cross-examine the witness.

ATTENDANCE OF ACCUSED

(3) An order under subsection (1) may make provision to enable the defendant to be present or represented by representative when the evidence is taken, but failure of the defendant to be present or to be represented by representative in accordance with the order does not prevent the reading of the evidence in the proceeding if the evidence has otherwise been taken in accordance with the order and with this section.

APPLICATION OF RULES IN CIVIL CASES

(4) Except as otherwise provided by this section or by the rules of court, the practice and procedure in connection with the appointment of commissioners under this section, the taking of evidence by commissioners, the certifying and return thereof, and the use of the evidence in the proceeding shall, as far as possible, be the same as those that govern like matters in civil proceedings in the Superior Court of Justice.

TRIAL OF ISSUE AS TO CAPACITY TO CONDUCT DEFENCE

44(1) Where at any time before a defendant is sentenced a court has reason to believe, based on,

(a) the evidence of a legally qualified medical practitioner or, with the consent of the parties, a written report of a legally qualified medical practitioner; or

(b) the conduct of the defendant in the courtroom,

that the defendant suffers from mental disorder, the court may,

(c) where the justice presiding is a judge, by order suspend the proceeding and direct the trial of the issue as to whether the defendant is, because of mental disorder, unable to conduct his or her defence; or

(d) where the justice presiding is a justice of the peace, refer the matter to a judge who may make an order referred to in clause (c).

EXAMINATION

(2) For the purposes of subsection (1), the court may order the defendant to attend to be examined under subsection (5).

FINDING

(3) The trial of the issue shall be presided over by a judge and,

(a) where the judge finds that the defendant is, because of mental disorder, unable to conduct his or her defence, the judge shall order that the proceeding remain suspended;

(b) where the judge finds that the defendant is able to conduct his or her defence, the judge shall order that the suspended proceeding be continued.

APPLICATION FOR REHEARING AS TO CAPACITY

(4) At any time within one year after an order is made under subsection (3), either party may, upon seven days notice to the other, make a motion to a judge to rehear the trial of the issue and where upon the rehearing the judge finds that the defendant is able to conduct his or her defence, the judge may order that the suspended proceeding be continued.

ORDER FOR EXAMINATION

(5) For the purposes of subsection (1) or a hearing or rehearing under subsection (3) or (4), the court or judge may order the defendant to attend at such place or before such person and at or within such time as are specified in the order and submit to an examination for the purpose of determining whether the defendant is, because of mental disorder, unable to conduct his or her defence.

IDEM

(6) Where the defendant fails or refuses to comply with an order under subsection (5) without reasonable excuse or where the person conducting the examination satisfies a judge that it is necessary to do so, the judge may by warrant direct that the

defendant be taken into such custody as is necessary for the purpose of the examination and in any event for not longer than seven days and, where it is necessary to detain the defendant in a place, the place shall be, where practicable, a psychiatric facility.

LIMITATION ON SUSPENSION OF PROCEEDING

(7) Where an order is made under subsection (3) and one year has elapsed and no further order is made under subsection (4), no further proceeding shall be taken in respect of the charge or any other charge arising out of the same circumstance.

TAKING OF PLEA

45(1) After being informed of the substance of the information or certificate, the defendant shall be asked whether the defendant pleads guilty or not guilty of the offence charged therein.

CONVICTION ON PLEA OF GUILTY

(2) Where the defendant pleads guilty, the court may accept the plea and convict the defendant.

REFUSAL TO PLEAD

(3) Where the defendant refuses to plead or does not answer directly, the court shall enter a plea of not guilty.

PLEA OF GUILTY TO ANOTHER OFFENCE

(4) Where the defendant pleads not guilty of the offence charged but guilty of any other offence, whether or not it is an included offence, the court may, with the consent of the prosecutor, accept such plea of guilty and accordingly amend the information or substitute the offence to which the defendant pleads guilty.

TRIAL ON PLEA OF NOT GUILTY

46(1) Subject to section 6, where the defendant pleads not guilty, the court shall hold the trial.

RIGHT TO DEFEND

(2) The defendant is entitled to make full answer and defence.

RIGHT TO EXAMINE WITNESSES

(3) The prosecutor or defendant, as the case may be, may examine and cross-examine witnesses.

AGREED FACTS

(4) The court may receive and act upon any facts agreed upon by the defendant and prosecutor without proof or evidence.

DEFENDANT NOT COMPELLABLE

(5) Despite section 8 of the *Evidence Act*, the defendant is not a compellable witness for the prosecution.

EVIDENCE AND BURDEN OF PROOF

EVIDENCE TAKEN ON ANOTHER CHARGE

47(1) The court may receive and consider evidence taken before the same justice on a different charge against the same defendant, with the consent of the parties.

CERTIFICATE AS EVIDENCE

(2) Where a certificate as to the content of an official record is, by any Act, made admissible in evidence as proof, in the absence of evidence to the contrary, the court may, for the purpose of deciding whether the defendant is the person referred to in the certificate, receive and base its decision upon information it considers credible or trustworthy in the circumstances of each case.

BURDEN OF PROVING EXCEPTION, ETC.

(3) The burden of proving that an authorization, exception, exemption or qualification prescribed by law operates in favour of the defendant is on the defendant, and the prosecutor is not required, except by way of rebuttal, to prove that the authorization, exception, exemption or qualification does not operate in favour of the defendant, whether or not it is set out in the information.

EXHIBITS

48(1) The court may order that an exhibit be kept in such custody and place as, in the opinion of the court, is appropriate for its preservation.

RELEASE OF EXHIBITS

(2) Where any thing is filed as an exhibit in a proceeding, the clerk may release the exhibit upon the consent of the parties at any time after the trial or, in the absence of consent, may return the exhibit to the party tendering it after the disposition of any appeal in the proceeding or, where an appeal is not taken, after the expiration of the time for appeal.

CERTIFICATE EVIDENCE

48.1(1) The certified statements in a certificate of offence or certificate of parking infraction are admissible in evidence as proof, in the absence of evidence to the contrary, of the facts stated therein.

EXCEPTION

(2) Subsection (1) does not apply if the defendant has indicated under section 5.2, subsection 11(3), section 18.1.2 or subsection 19(3) that the defendant intends to challenge the evidence of the provincial offences officer who completed the certificate.

ADJOURNMENTS

49(1) The court may, from time to time, adjourn a trial or hearing but, where the defendant is in custody, an adjournment shall not be for a period longer than eight days without the consent of the defendant.

EARLY RESUMPTION

(2) A trial or hearing that is adjourned for a period may be resumed before the expiration of the period with the consent of the defendant and the prosecutor.

ADJOURNMENT

(3) Despite subsection (1), if the trial is being held in respect of a proceeding commenced under Part I or II, the court shall not adjourn the trial for the purpose of having the provincial offences officer who completed the certificate attend to give evidence unless the court is satisfied that the interests of justice require it.

APPEARANCE BY DEFENDANT

50(1) A defendant may appear and act personally or by representative.

APPEARANCE BY CORPORATION

(2) A defendant that is a corporation shall appear and act by representative.

EXCLUSION OF REPRESENTATIVES

(3) The court may bar any person, other than a person who is licensed under the *Law Society Act*, from appearing as a representative if the court finds that the person is not competent properly to represent or advise the person for whom he or she appears, or does not understand and comply with the duties and responsibilities of a representative.

COMPELLING ATTENDANCE OF DEFENDANT

51. Although a defendant appears by representative, the court may order the defendant to attend personally, and, where it appears to be necessary to do so, may issue a summons in the prescribed form.

RESTRICTIONS ON HEARING AND PUBLICATION

EXCLUDING DEFENDANT FROM HEARING

52(1) The court may cause the defendant to be removed and to be kept out of court,

(a) when the defendant misconducts himself or herself by interrupting the proceeding so that to continue in the presence of the defendant would not be feasible; or

(b) where, during the trial of an issue as to whether the defendant is, because of mental disorder, unable to conduct his or her defence, the court is satisfied that failure to do so might have an adverse effect on the mental health of the defendant.

EXCLUDING PUBLIC FROM HEARING

(2) The court may exclude the public or any member of the public from a hearing where, in the opinion of the court, it is necessary to do so,

(a) for the maintenance of order in the courtroom;

(b) to protect the reputation of a minor; or

(c) to remove an influence that might affect the testimony of a witness.

PROHIBITION OF PUBLICATION OF EVIDENCE

(3) Where the court considers it necessary to do so to protect the reputation of a minor, the court may make an order prohibiting the publication or broadcast of the identity of the minor or of the evidence or any part of the evidence taken at the hearing.

FAILURE OF PROSECUTOR TO APPEAR

53(1) Where the defendant appears for a hearing and the prosecutor, having had due notice, does not appear, the court may dismiss the charge or may adjourn the hearing to another time upon such terms as it considers proper.

IDEM

(2) Where the prosecutor does not appear at the time and place appointed for the resumption of an adjourned hearing under subsection (1), the court may dismiss the charge.

COSTS

(3) Where a hearing is adjourned under subsection (1) or a charge is dismissed under subsection (2), the court may make an order under section 60 for the payment of costs.

WRITTEN ORDER OF DISMISSAL

(4) Where a charge is dismissed under subsection (1) or (2), the court may, if requested by the defendant, draw up an order of dismissal stating the grounds therefor and shall give the defendant a certified copy of the order of dismissal which is, without further proof, a bar to any subsequent proceeding against the defendant in respect of the same cause.

CONVICTION IN THE ABSENCE OF THE DEFENDANT

54(1) Where a defendant does not appear at the time and place appointed for a hearing and it is proved by the prosecutor, having been given a reasonable opportunity to do so, that a summons was served, a notice of trial was given under Part I or II, an undertaking to appear was given or a recognizance to appear was entered into, as the case may be, or where the defendant does not appear upon the resumption of a hearing that has been adjourned, the court,

(a) may proceed to hear and determine the proceeding in the absence of the defendant;

(b) may, if it thinks fit, adjourn the hearing and issue a summons to appear or issue a warrant in the prescribed form for the arrest of the defendant; or

(c) may, where the defendant does not appear in response to the summons or warrant on the date to which the hearing is adjourned, proceed under clause (a) or (b).

PROCEEDING ARISING FROM FAILURE TO APPEAR

(2) Where the court proceeds under clause (1)(a), no proceeding arising out of the failure of the defendant to appear at the time and place appointed for the hearing or for the resumption of the hearing shall be instituted or if instituted shall be proceeded with, except with the consent of the Attorney General or his or her agent.

INCLUDED OFFENCES

55. Where the offence as charged includes another offence, the defendant may be convicted of an offence so included that is proved, although the whole offence charged is not proved.

Sentencing

PRE-SENTENCE REPORT

56(1) Where a defendant is convicted of an offence in a proceeding commenced by information, the court may direct a probation officer to prepare and file with the court a report in writing relating to the defendant for the purpose of assisting the court in imposing sentence.

SERVICE

(2) Where a report is filed with the court under subsection (1), the clerk of the court shall cause a copy of the report to be provided to the defendant or the defendant's representative and to the prosecutor.

OTHER INFORMATION RELEVANT TO SENTENCE

SUBMISSIONS AS TO SENTENCE

57(1) Where a defendant who appears is convicted of an offence, the court shall give the prosecutor and the defendant's representative an opportunity to make submissions as to sentence and, where the defendant has no representative, the court shall ask the defendant if he or she has anything to say before sentence is passed.

OMISSION TO COMPLY

(2) The omission to comply with subsection (1) does not affect the validity of the proceeding.

INQUIRIES BY COURT

(3) Where a defendant is convicted of an offence, the court may make such inquiries, on oath or otherwise, of and concerning the defendant as it considers

desirable, including the defendant's economic circumstances, but the defendant shall not be compelled to answer.

PROOF OF PREVIOUS CONVICTION

(4) A certificate setting out with reasonable particularity the finding of guilt or acquittal or conviction and sentence in Canada of a person signed by,

(a) the person who made the adjudication; or

(b) the clerk of the court where the adjudication was made,

is, upon the court being satisfied that the defendant is the person referred to in the certificate, admissible in evidence and is proof, in the absence of evidence to the contrary, of the facts stated therein without proof of the signature or the official character of the person appearing to have signed the certificate.

TIME SPENT IN CUSTODY CONSIDERED

58. In determining the sentence to be imposed on a person convicted of an offence, the justice may take into account any time spent in custody by the person as a result of the offence.

PROVISION FOR MINIMUM PENALTY

59(1) No penalty prescribed for an offence is a minimum penalty unless it is specifically declared to be a minimum.

RELIEF AGAINST MINIMUM FINE

(2) Although the provision that creates the penalty for an offence prescribes a minimum fine, where in the opinion of the court exceptional circumstances exist so that to impose the minimum fine would be unduly oppressive or otherwise not in the interests of justice, the court may impose a fine that is less than the minimum or suspend the sentence.

IDEM, RE IMPRISONMENT

(3) Where a minimum penalty is prescribed for an offence and the minimum penalty includes imprisonment, the court may, despite the prescribed penalty, impose a fine of not more than $5,000 in lieu of imprisonment.

COSTS

FIXED COSTS ON CONVICTION

60(1) Upon conviction, the defendant is liable to pay to the court an amount by way of costs that is fixed by the regulations.

COSTS RESPECTING WITNESSES

(2) The court may, in its discretion, order costs towards fees and expenses reasonably incurred by or on behalf of witnesses in amounts not exceeding the maximum fixed by the regulations, to be paid,

(a) to the court or prosecutor by the defendant; or

(b) to the defendant by the person who laid the information or issued the certificate, as the case may be,

but where the proceeding is commenced by means of a certificate, the total of such costs shall not exceed $100.

COSTS COLLECTABLE AS A FINE

(3) Costs payable under this section shall be deemed to be a fine for the purpose of enforcing payment.

SURCHARGE

60.1(1) If a person is convicted of an offence in a proceeding commenced under Part I or III and a fine is imposed in respect of that offence, a surcharge is payable by that person in the amount determined by regulations made under this Act.

COLLECTION

(2) The surcharge shall be deemed to be a fine for the purpose of enforcing payment.

PRIORITIES

(3) Any payments made by a defendant shall be credited towards payment of the fine until it is fully paid and then towards payment of the surcharge.

PART X AGREEMENTS

(3.1) When an agreement made under Part X applies to a fine, payments made by the defendant shall first be credited towards payment of the surcharge, not as described in subsection (3).

SPECIAL PURPOSE ACCOUNT

(4) Surcharges paid into the Consolidated Revenue Fund shall be credited to the victims' justice fund account and shall be deemed to be money received by the Crown for a special purpose.

SAME

(4.1) Subsection (4) also applies to payments received under clause 165(5)(a).

(5), (6) Repealed.

REGULATIONS

(7) The Lieutenant Governor in Council may make regulations,

(a) prescribing the amount of the surcharges or the method by which they are to be calculated;

(b) Repealed.

(c) exempting any offence or class of offence from the application of subsection (1).

(8) Repealed.

GENERAL PENALTY

61. Except where otherwise expressly provided by law, every person who is convicted of an offence is liable to a fine of not more than $5,000.

MINUTE OF CONVICTION

62. Where a court convicts a defendant or dismisses a charge, a minute of the dismissal or conviction and sentence shall be made by the court, and, upon request by the defendant or the prosecutor or by the Attorney General or his or her agent, the court shall cause a copy thereof certified by the clerk of the court to be delivered to the person making the request.

TIME WHEN IMPRISONMENT STARTS

63(1) The term of imprisonment imposed by sentence shall, unless otherwise directed in the sentence, commence on the day on which the convicted person is taken into custody thereunder, but no time during which the convicted person is imprisoned or out on bail before sentence shall be reckoned as part of the term of imprisonment to which he or she is sentenced.

IDEM

(2) Where the court imposes imprisonment, the court may order custody to commence on a day not later than thirty days after the day of sentencing.

SENTENCES CONSECUTIVE

64. Where a person is subject to more than one term of imprisonment at the same time, the terms shall be served consecutively except in so far as the court has ordered a term to be served concurrently with any other term of imprisonment.

WARRANT OF COMMITTAL

65(1) A warrant of committal is sufficient authority,

(a) for the conveyance of the prisoner in custody for the purpose of committal under the warrant; and

(b) for the reception and detention of the prisoner by keepers of prisons in accordance with the terms of the warrant.

CONVEYANCE OF PRISONER

(2) A person to whom a warrant of committal is directed shall convey the prisoner to the correctional institution named in the warrant.

PRISONER SUBJECT TO RULES OF INSTITUTION

(3) A sentence of imprisonment shall be served in accordance with the enactments and rules that govern the institution to which the prisoner is sentenced.

WHEN FINE DUE

66(1) A fine becomes due and payable fifteen days after its imposition.

EXTENSION OF TIME FOR PAYMENT OF A FINE

(2) Where the court imposes a fine, the court shall ask the defendant if the defendant wishes an extension of the time for payment of the fine.

INQUIRIES

(3) Where the defendant requests an extension of the time for payment of the fine, the court may make such inquiries, on oath or affirmation or otherwise, of and concerning the defendant as the court considers desirable, but the defendant shall not be compelled to answer.

GRANTING OF EXTENSION

(4) Unless the court finds that the request for extension of time is not made in good faith or that the extension would likely be used to evade payment, the court shall extend the time for payment by ordering periodic payments or otherwise.

NOTICE WHERE CONVICTED IN THE ABSENCE OF THE DEFENDANT

(5) Where a fine is imposed in the absence of the defendant, the clerk of the court shall give the defendant notice of the fine and its due date and of the defendant's right to make a motion for an extension of the time for payment under subsection (6).

FURTHER MOTION FOR EXTENSION

(6) The defendant may, at any time by motion in the prescribed form filed in the office of the court, request an extension or further extension of time for payment of a fine and the motion shall be determined by a justice and the justice has the same powers in respect of the motion as the court has under subsections (3) and (4).

DEFENDANT'S ADDRESS

66.1 If a court imposes a fine, grants an extension of time for payment of a fine or deals with a fine under section 69, and the defendant is before the court, the court shall require the defendant to provide the defendant's current address to the clerk of the court.

FEE FOR REFUSED CHEQUE COLLECTABLE AS A FINE

66.2 When a person purports to pay a fine by a cheque that the drawee of the cheque refuses to cash and thereby becomes liable to pay a fee in the amount prescribed for the purpose of section 8.1 of the *Financial Administration Act*, the fee shall be deemed to be a fine for the purpose of enforcing payment.

REGULATION FOR WORK CREDITS FOR FINES

67. The Lieutenant Governor in Council may make regulations establishing a program to permit the payment of fines by means of credits for work performed, and, for the purpose and without restricting the generality of the foregoing may,

(a) prescribe classes of work and the conditions under which they are to be performed;

(b) prescribe a system of credits;

(c) provide for any matter necessary for the effective administration of the program,

and any regulation may limit its application to any part or parts of Ontario.

CIVIL ENFORCEMENT OF FINES

68(1) When the payment of a fine is in default, the clerk of the court may complete a certificate in the prescribed form as to the imposition of the fine and the amount remaining unpaid and file the certificate in a court of competent jurisdiction and upon filing, the certificate shall be deemed to be an order or judgment of that court for the purposes of enforcement.

LIMITATION

(2) A certificate shall not be filed under subsection (1) after two years after the default in respect of which it is issued.

CERTIFICATE OF DISCHARGE

(3) Where a certificate has been filed under subsection (1) and the fine is fully paid, the clerk shall file a certificate of payment upon which the certificate of default is discharged and, where a writ of execution has been filed with the sheriff, the clerk shall file a certificate of payment with the sheriff, upon which the writ is cancelled.

COSTS OF ENFORCEMENT

(4) Costs incurred in enforcing the deemed court order or judgment shall be added to the order or judgment and form part of it.

MORE THAN ONE FINE

(5) The clerk may complete and file one certificate under this section in respect of two or more fines imposed on the same person.

DEFAULT

69(1) The payment of a fine is in default if any part of it is due and unpaid for fifteen days or more.

ORDER ON DEFAULT

(2) A justice of the peace who is satisfied that payment of a fine is in default,

(a) shall order that any permit, licence, registration or privilege in respect of which a suspension is authorized under any Act because of non-payment of the fine be suspended until the fine is paid;

(b) shall order that any permit, licence, registration or privilege in respect of which any Act authorizes a refusal to renew, validate or issue the permit, licence, registration or privilege because of non-payment of the fine not be renewed, validated or issued until the fine is paid; and

(c) may direct the clerk of the court to proceed with civil enforcement under section 68.

HIGHWAY TRAFFIC ACT PERMITS

(3) If section 7 of the *Highway Traffic Act* authorizes an order or direction under this section that any permit under that Act not be validated or issued because payment of a fine is in default, a person designated by the regulations who is satisfied that payment of a fine is in default shall direct that until the fine is paid,

(a) validation of any permit held by the person who has defaulted be refused; and

(b) issuance of any permit to the person who has defaulted be refused.

RESTRICTION

(4) If a person holds more than one permit and a direction in respect of that person is made under clause (3)(a), the direction shall not apply so as to prevent validation of any permit in respect of which the numbered plate evidencing validation of the permit had not been displayed on the vehicle involved in the infraction.

HIGHWAY TRAFFIC ACT LICENCES

(5) If section 46 of the *Highway Traffic Act* authorizes an order or direction under this section that any licence under that Act be suspended or not be issued because payment of a fine is in default, a person designated by the regulations who is satisfied that payment of a fine is in default shall direct that until the fine is paid,

(a) if the person who has defaulted holds a licence, the licence be suspended; or

(b) if the person who has defaulted does not hold a licence, no licence be issued to him or her.

OBTAINING CONVICTED PERSON'S ATTENDANCE

(6) A justice may issue a warrant requiring that a person who has defaulted be arrested and brought before a justice as soon as possible if other reasonable methods of collecting the fine have been tried and have failed, or would not appear to be likely to result in payment within a reasonable period of time.

ALTERNATIVE SUMMONS PROCEDURE

(7) The clerk of the court that imposed the fine that is in default may issue a summons requiring the person who has defaulted to appear before a justice if the conditions described in subsection (6) exist.

SERVICE OF SUMMONS

(8) The summons referred to in subsection (7) may be served by regular prepaid mail.

HEARING

(9) If a person who has defaulted in paying a fine is brought before a justice as a result of a warrant issued under subsection (6) or such a person appears before a justice as a result of a summons issued under subsection (7), the justice shall hold

a hearing to determine whether the person is unable to pay the fine within a reasonable period of time.

ONUS

(10) In a hearing under subsection (9), the onus of proving that the person is unable to pay the fine within a reasonable period of time is on the person who has defaulted.

ADJOURNMENT

(11) The justice may adjourn the hearing from time to time at the request of the person who has defaulted.

WARNING

(12) When an adjournment is granted, the justice shall warn the person who has defaulted that if the person fails to appear for the resumption of the hearing, the hearing may proceed in the person's absence.

FAILURE TO WARN

(13) If a hearing was adjourned and the person who has defaulted does not appear when it is resumed, the hearing may proceed in the person's absence even if the warning required by subsection (12) was not given.

WARRANT OF COMMITTAL

(14) If the justice is not satisfied that the person who has defaulted is unable to pay the fine within a reasonable period of time and that incarceration of the person would not be contrary to the public interest, the justice may issue a warrant for the person's committal or may order that such other steps be taken to enforce the fine as appear to him or her to be appropriate.

INABILITY TO PAY FINE

(15) If the justice is satisfied that the person who has defaulted is unable to pay the fine within a reasonable period of time, the justice may,

(a) grant an extension of the time allowed for payment of the fine;

(b) require the person to pay the fine according to a schedule of payments established by the justice;

(c) in exceptional circumstances, reduce the amount of the fine or order that the fine does not have to be paid.

TERM OF IMPRISONMENT

(16) Subject to subsection (17), the term of imprisonment under a warrant issued under subsection (14) shall be for three days, plus,

(a) if the amount that has not been paid is not greater than $50, one day; or

(b) if the amount that has not been paid is greater than $50, a number of days equal to the sum of one plus the number obtained when the unpaid amount is divided by $50, rounded down to the nearest whole number.

LIMIT

(17) The term of imprisonment shall not exceed the greater of,

(a) ninety days; and

(b) half of the maximum number of days of imprisonment that may be imposed on conviction of the offence that the person who has defaulted was convicted of.

EFFECT OF PAYMENTS

(18) Subject to subsection (19), a payment in respect of the fine in default that is made after a warrant is issued under subsection (14) shall result in a reduction of the term of imprisonment by the number of days that is in the same proportion to the term as the payment is to the amount in default.

RESTRICTION

(19) A payment that is less than the amount outstanding on the fine shall not result in a reduction of the term of imprisonment unless it is an amount that would reduce the term by a number of days that is a whole number.

EXCEPTIONS

(20) Subsections (6) to (19) do not apply if,

(a) the person who has defaulted is less than eighteen years old; or

(b) the fine was imposed on conviction of an offence under subsection 31(2) or (4) of the *Liquor Licence Act.*

EXCEPTIONAL CIRCUMSTANCES

(21) In exceptional circumstances where, in the opinion of the court that imposed the fine, to proceed under subsections (6) to (14) would defeat the ends of justice, the court may order that no warrant be issued under subsection (6) and that no summons be issued under subsection (7).

REGULATIONS

(22) The Lieutenant Governor in Council may make regulations,

(a) designating a person or class of persons for purposes of subsections (3) and (5);

(b) prescribing criteria to be considered by a justice in determining whether a person is unable to pay a fine within a reasonable period of time.

DISCLOSURE TO CONSUMER REPORTING AGENCY

69.1(1) When a fine has been in default for at least 90 days, the Ministry of the Attorney General may disclose to a consumer reporting agency the name of the defaulter, the amount of the fine and the date the fine went into default.

SAME

(2) When a fine disclosed to a consumer reporting agency has been paid in full, the Ministry of the Attorney General shall inform the agency of this fact as soon as possible after payment.

FEE WHERE FINE IN DEFAULT

70(1) Where the payment of a fine is in default and the time for payment is not extended or further extended under subsection 66(6), the defendant shall pay the administrative fee prescribed by the regulations.

FEE COLLECTABLE AS A FINE

(2) For the purpose of making and enforcing payment, a fee payable under this section shall be deemed to be part of the fine that is in default.

SUSPENSION OF FINE ON CONDITIONS

71. Where an Act provides that a fine may be suspended subject to the performance of a condition,

(a) the period of suspension shall be fixed by the court and shall be for not more than one year;

(b) the court shall provide in its order of suspension the method of proving the performance of the condition;

(c) the suspension is in addition to and not in lieu of any other power of the court in respect of the fine; and

(d) the fine is not in default until fifteen days have elapsed after notice that the period of suspension has expired is given to the defendant.

PROBATION ORDER

72(1) Where a defendant is convicted of an offence in a proceeding commenced by information, the court may, having regard to the age, character and background of the defendant, the nature of the offence and the circumstances surrounding its commission,

(a) suspend the passing of sentence and direct that the defendant comply with the conditions prescribed in a probation order;

(b) in addition to fining the defendant or sentencing the defendant to imprisonment, whether in default of payment of a fine or otherwise, direct that the defendant comply with the conditions prescribed in a probation order; or

(c) where it imposes a sentence of imprisonment on the defendant, whether in default of payment of a fine or otherwise, that does not exceed ninety days, order that the sentence be served intermittently at such times as are specified in the order and direct that the defendant, at all times when he or she is not in confinement pursuant to such order, comply with the conditions prescribed in a probation order.

STATUTORY CONDITIONS OF ORDER

(2) A probation order shall be deemed to contain the conditions that,

(a) the defendant not commit the same or any related or similar offence, or any offence under a statute of Canada or Ontario or any other province of Canada that is punishable by imprisonment;

(b) the defendant appear before the court as and when required; and

(c) the defendant notify the court of any change in the defendant's address.

CONDITIONS IMPOSED BY COURT

(3) In addition to the conditions set out in subsection (2), the court may prescribe as a condition in a probation order,

(a) that the defendant satisfy any compensation or restitution that is required or authorized by an Act;

(b) with the consent of the defendant and where the conviction is of an offence that is punishable by imprisonment, that the defendant perform a community service as set out in the order;

(c) where the conviction is of an offence punishable by imprisonment, such other conditions relating to the circumstances of the offence and of the defendant that contributed to the commission of the offence as the court considers appropriate to prevent similar unlawful conduct or to contribute to the rehabilitation of the defendant; or

(d) where considered necessary for the purpose of implementing the conditions of the probation order, that the defendant report to a responsible person designated by the court and, in addition, where the circumstances warrant it, that the defendant be under the supervision of the person to whom he or she is required to report.

FORM OF ORDER

(4) A probation order shall be in the prescribed form and the court shall specify therein the period for which it is to remain in force, which shall not be for more than two years from the date when the order takes effect.

NOTICE OF ORDER

(5) Where the court makes a probation order, it shall cause a copy of the order and a copy of section 75 to be given to the defendant.

REGULATIONS FOR COMMUNITY SERVICE ORDERS

(6) The Lieutenant Governor in Council may make regulations governing restitution, compensation and community service orders, including their terms and conditions.

EXCEPTION

(7) The court shall not make a probation order when an individual has been convicted of an absolute liability offence, unless the order is made in addition to

a sentence of imprisonment imposed under section 69 in default of payment of a fine.

WHEN ORDER COMES INTO FORCE

73(1) A probation order comes into force,

(a) on the date on which the order is made; or

(b) where the defendant is sentenced to imprisonment other than a sentence to be served intermittently, upon the expiration of that sentence.

CONTINUATION IN FORCE

(2) Subject to section 75, where a defendant who is bound by a probation order is convicted of an offence or is imprisoned in default of payment of a fine, the order continues in force except in so far as the sentence or imprisonment renders it impossible for the defendant to comply for the time being with the order.

VARIATION OF PROBATION ORDER

74. The court may, at any time upon the application of the defendant or prosecutor with notice to the other, after a hearing or, with the consent of the parties, without a hearing,

(a) make any changes in or additions to the conditions prescribed in the order that in the opinion of the court are rendered desirable by a change in circumstances;

(b) relieve the defendant, either absolutely or upon such terms or for such period as the court considers desirable, of compliance with any condition described in any of the clauses in subsection 72(3) that is prescribed in the order; or

(c) terminate the order or decrease the period for which the probation order is to remain in force,

and the court shall thereupon endorse the probation order accordingly and, if it changes or adds to the conditions prescribed in the order, inform the defendant of its action and give the defendant a copy of the order so endorsed.

BREACH OF PROBATION ORDER

75. Where a defendant who is bound by a probation order is convicted of an offence constituting a breach of condition of the order and,

(a) the time within which the defendant may appeal or make a motion for leave to appeal against that conviction has expired and the defendant has not taken an appeal or made a motion for leave to appeal;

(b) the defendant has taken an appeal or made a motion for leave to appeal against the conviction and the appeal or motion for leave has been dismissed or abandoned; or

(c) the defendant has given written notice to the court that convicted the defendant that the defendant elects not to appeal,

or where the defendant otherwise wilfully fails or refuses to comply with the order, the defendant is guilty of an offence and upon conviction the court may,

(d) impose a fine of not more than $1,000 or imprisonment for a term of not more than thirty days, or both, and in lieu of or in addition to the penalty, continue the probation order with such changes or additions and for such extended term, not exceeding an additional year, as the court considers reasonable; or

(e) where the justice presiding is the justice who made the original order, in lieu of imposing the penalty under clause (d), revoke the probation order and impose the sentence the passing of which was suspended upon the making of the probation order.

Source: *Provincial Offences Act*, R.S.O. 1990, c. P.33, www.canlii.org/on/laws/sta/p-33/20080821/whole.html.

APPENDIX F

Landlord and Tenant Board Resources

Landlord and Tenant Board Rules (Excerpts)

RULE 23: REQUIRING A WITNESS TO ATTEND A HEARING

Legislation:

Section 12 of the *Statutory Powers Procedure Act* (the "SPPA")
Section 12 of the SPPA permits the Board to issue a summons to require a witness to attend a hearing and give sworn or unsworn evidence and to produce documents, records, and things which are relevant and admissible.

23.1 ANY MEMBER MAY SIGN A SUMMONS TO A WITNESS.

This Rule clarifies that the Chair is not required to sign a summons, nor will it always be the Member who eventually hears the case. Since the RTA does not address who may issue a summons, clause 12(2)(b) of the SPPA provides the Chair will do so. The Rule allows any Member to sign the summons.

23.2 AN APPLICANT WHO REQUESTS THE ISSUANCE OF A SUMMONS TO A WITNESS SHALL PROVIDE A WRITTEN REQUEST TO THE BOARD, STATING THE NECESSITY AND RELEVANCE OF THE SUMMONS. THIS REQUEST SHALL BE MADE PROMPTLY AFTER THE APPLICANT BECOMES AWARE OF THE NEED FOR THE SUMMONS.

If a Member is satisfied by the written request that the evidence sought will be relevant and will likely be admissible, the Member will issue a summons. It is preferable that the summons be issued as soon before the hearing as possible so that it can be served on the witness in time to allow them to arrange to attend the hearing. The written request should set out the following:

- the name of the witness and their address for service;
- a summary of the evidence to be given by the witness;

- an explanation of why the evidence of the witness would be relevant and necessary; and
- details of any documents or things which the witness should be required to bring to the hearing.

If the party requesting the summons is represented by a lawyer or paid agent, the request should be accompanied by a drafted summons, ready to be signed by a Member.

23.3 A RESPONDENT WHO REQUESTS THE ISSUANCE OF A SUMMONS TO A WITNESS SHALL PROVIDE A WRITTEN REQUEST, STATING THE NECESSITY AND RELEVANCE OF THE SUMMONS, PROMPTLY AFTER BEING SERVED WITH THE NOTICE OF HEARING.

The timing of making the request (same contents as listed under Rule 23.2) is different for a respondent since they do not become aware of the application until the notice of hearing is served on them by the applicant. Again, it is preferable to file the request as early as possible so that the summons may be served by the respondent on the witness as much before the hearing as possible.

23.4 THE ISSUANCE OR REFUSAL TO ISSUE A SUMMONS MAY BE REVIEWED BY THE MEMBER PRESIDING AT THE HEARING.

In some cases, the Board may choose not to decide whether to issue a summons until the start of the hearing, after hearing the requesting party's explanation, and asking any questions. In other cases, where a summons has been issued before the hearing, the Member conducting the hearing may decide that the summons should be cancelled or amended, or if the witness is present, they may be excused from remaining. For example, the Member may decide that some of the documents which the witness was required to bring to the hearing will have no relevance to the facts in issue, and excuse that some were not produced.

23.5 THE PARTY WHO REQUESTED THE SUMMONS SHALL BE RESPONSIBLE FOR SERVING THE SUMMONS ON THE WITNESS, PAYING ANY ASSOCIATED EXPENSES AND FEES, AND ENFORCING THE SUMMONS.

Subsection 12(3) of the SPPA requires that the summons be "served personally" on the witness, which means handing it to the person. The rules for serving by mail or leaving it with another person, etc. do not apply. Where a person fails to appear at a hearing pursuant to a summons, a party may seek to have the summons enforced pursuant to section 12 of the SPPA. Section 12 provides that a judge of the Superior Court of Justice may issue a warrant against a person if the judge is satisfied that the person was served with a summons, the person failed to participate, attend or to remain in attendance in accordance with the summons, and the person's attendance or participation is material to the ends of justice. A party seeking to enforce a summons is encouraged to seek legal advice.

23.6 IF THE WITNESS APPEARS AT THE HEARING, THE PARTY WHO REQUESTED THE SUMMONS SHALL PAY TO THE WITNESS THE FEES AND ALLOWANCES SET OUT IN THE TARIFF WHICH IS APPENDIX "B" OF THESE RULES BEFORE THE WITNESS TESTIFIES.

Under subsection 12(3.1) of the SPPA, a witness need not be paid until they attend the hearing.

23.7 A PERSON EFFECTING PERSONAL SERVICE OF A SUMMONS NEED NOT PRODUCE THE ORIGINAL SIGNED DOCUMENT OR HAVE IT IN THEIR POSSESSION.

Although there are many permitted methods of serving an application and notice of hearing, there is only one way to serve a summons. "Personal service" means handing the document to the potential witness (a specific individual, never a company, partnership, etc.), or at least approaching the individual and offering it to them. This Rule makes it clear that the person will be serving a copy of the summons and does not even need to take the signed original with them. This Rule is based on R.16.02(2) of the Rules of Civil Procedure for the Courts.

Amended July 5, 2007

RULE 27: ORDERING COSTS TO A PARTY OR BOARD COSTS

Legislation:

Sections 74, 78, 182, 206 and subsections 204(2) to (4) of the *Residential Tenancies Act, 2006* ("the RTA")

Interpretation Guideline:

Guideline #3—Costs

Subsection 204(2) of the RTA gives the Board the discretion to order one party to pay another party's "costs" of the application. Subsection 204(3) allows the Board to order that its costs of an application be paid by a party or a paid agent or counsel to a party. The amount of an order for costs shall, according to subsection 204(4), be set in these Rules.

The Interpretation Guideline on Costs sets out the usual approach of the Board to ordering costs against a party or representative of a party. These Rules complement the approach suggested in the Guideline.

Allowing Application Fee as "Costs"

27.1 IF THE APPLICANT IS SUCCESSFUL, THE BOARD MAY ORDER THE RESPONDENT TO PAY THE APPLICATION FEE TO THE APPLICANT AS "COSTS."

This Rule will generally allow a successful applicant to obtain an order for recovery of the application fee they have paid. See Guideline # 3—Costs regarding when an applicant should be considered to have been "successful." Note that there are some sections of the RTA that explicitly authorize or require the Board to issue an order for the payment of the application fee, or other fees, as costs. For example: sections 74, 78, 182 and 206.

27.2 WHERE THE BOARD ORDERS A PARTY TO AN APPLICATION TO PAY THE COSTS OF ANOTHER PARTY UNDER SUBSECTION 204(2) OF THE RTA, REPRESENTATION FEES SHALL NOT EXCEED $75 PER HOUR FOR THE SERVICES OF A LAWYER OR PAID AGENT.

This Rule sets the maximum amount which may be allowed if a Member decides it is appropriate to order one party to pay another party's "costs." The Guideline on costs suggests this is appropriate only where a party has been responsible for unreasonable conduct. It also suggests situations in which a party is not entitled to costs even if there has been unreasonable conduct by another party.

Although it may be difficult to estimate, the intention is to allow the representation fees only for the portion of the hearing that was affected by the unreasonable conduct. For example, if the Member warned the respondent's representative that an issue they raised did not seem relevant to the application, and yet they continued to pursue the issue for an hour, the Member could order the respondent to pay the applicant $75 as costs.

27.3 IF THE MEMBER DECIDES TO ALLOW COSTS RELATED TO THE REPRESENTATIVE'S PREPARATION TIME, FEES MAY BE ALLOWED NOT EXCEEDING $75 PER HOUR FOR THE TIME SPENT.

The Guideline on costs suggests that preparation fees are only to be allowed in the most serious cases of unreasonable conduct. For example, if the applicant raises a totally irrelevant issue in their application, the respondent's representative may be allowed a preparation fee of up to $75 per hour for reviewing the RTA, Guidelines and any past significant decisions related to that issue.

27.4 EXPENSES OF THE BOARD WHICH A PARTY OR REPRESENTATIVE MAY BE ORDERED TO PAY SHALL NOT EXCEED $75 PER HOUR FOR THE HEARING OR $500 IN TOTAL IN RESPECT OF THE PROCEEDINGS AS A WHOLE.

This Rule recognizes unreasonable conduct in any stage of the proceedings will be relevant in considering the Board's costs, not just unreasonable conduct at the hearing.

There are two limits on the amount ordered. First, if the unreasonable conduct affects only part of the hearing, the order shall not exceed $75 per hour. (However, there may be an order for Board costs even where the unreasonable conduct did not affect the hearing.) Second, the amount allowed in total for the proceedings cannot exceed $500, including any amount ordered for the hearing.

Amended July 5, 2007

Source: Ontario Landlord and Tenant Board website, www.ltb.gov.on.ca/en/Law/STEL02_111324.html.

Landlord and Tenant Board Interpretation Guidelines (Excerpts)

GUIDELINE 1: ADJOURNING AND RESCHEDULING HEARINGS

Interpretation Guidelines are intended to assist the parties in understanding the Board's usual interpretation of the law, to provide guidance to Members and promote consistency in decision-making. However, a Member is not required to follow a Guideline and may make a different decision depending on the facts of the case.

Section 184 of the *Residential Tenancies Act, 2006* (the RTA) provides that the Statutory Powers Procedure Act applies to all proceedings before the Board; and the authority to adjourn hearings is found in section 21 of the *Statutory Powers Procedure Act* which provides that:

> A hearing may be adjourned from time to time by a tribunal of its own motion or where it is shown to the satisfaction of the tribunal that the adjournment is required to permit an adequate hearing to be held.

This guideline identifies situations that may warrant the rescheduling or adjournment of a Board hearing.

Rescheduling and adjourning can be defined in the following way:

> Rescheduling involves staff setting a new date for the hearing in advance of the date originally set for it, usually confirmed by a new Notice of Hearing;
>
> Adjourning involves a Member's decision regarding when the hearing of an application will proceed and/or be completed.

GENERAL APPROACH OF THE BOARD

Section 183 of the RTA directs the Board to "adopt the most expeditious method of determining the questions arising in a proceeding that affords to all persons directly affected by the proceeding an adequate opportunity to know the issues and to be heard on the matter."

Parties should assume that all of their evidence and submissions will usually be heard on the date stated in the Notice of Hearing. This means that the parties should be prepared to present their evidence, call and question witnesses and make their submissions. The Board's decision will generally be made shortly afterwards.

RISKS OF FAILING TO ATTEND THE HEARING OR PREPARE FOR IT

Parties failing to appear at the hearing specified on the Notice take considerable risks. Section 7 of the *Statutory Powers Procedure Act* provides that a tribunal may proceed with a hearing in the absence of any party. In exceptional circumstances, a

Member may exercise the jurisdiction to adjourn a case on the Board's motion in order to determine whether the party who did not appear will do so on a later date. However, parties should not expect such a decision.

Where an applicant fails to appear, the Member will normally proceed with the hearing, which means the applicant's case will be dismissed as abandoned, whether or not the respondent has attended.

Where the respondent fails to appear, the Member will normally proceed with the hearing, and may make a decision based on the evidence of the applicant.

Not preparing for a hearing based on the expectation that it will be postponed, even though the other party prefers to proceed, has substantial risks. If the Member decides to proceed with the hearing on the date set, the evidence presented will be considered, even if additional evidence should rightfully have been presented. Being unprepared strongly increases the risk of failure to prove one's case.

Finally, the only remedies for an incorrect order may be "review of the order" (reconsideration), judicial review or appeal; however, appeal is limited to questions of law, and both appeal and judicial review can be very expensive court procedures. It is highly advisable to deal with the application promptly at the start, rather than count on someone interceding later to reverse an order already issued.

Rescheduling Hearings

If a party realizes it will be difficult to attend a hearing or that they will not be prepared in time for a hearing, they may seek the rescheduling of the hearing date set out in the Notice of Hearing. They should request rescheduling as soon as possible after they realize it is necessary.

The Board will generally only reschedule a hearing if the party seeking the delay is able to obtain the agreement of the other party or parties (see Rule 12).

If a tenant requests rescheduling, they should deal with the landlord's representative, if there is one, or with the landlord directly. If there are multiple landlords, the agreement of each must be obtained.

When a landlord requests rescheduling, they should deal with the tenant's representative, if one exists, or with the tenant directly. If there is more than one tenant, the agreement of each must be obtained.

It is important that parties respond reasonably to requests from another party to reschedule. Although there are always a number of factors to take into account, if parties are unreasonable in their responses to requests to rescheduling, a Member may find that since rescheduling caused no prejudice to either party, the party who refused the request may be ordered to pay costs.

The party seeking the hearing's rescheduling should send or fax to the Board a written request for rescheduling indicating:

- confirmation that the other party or parties have agreed to the rescheduling;
- what dates the party requesting the rescheduling will be available (subject to the availability of a Member); and
- what dates, if any, the other party(ies) indicated they preferred for the rescheduled hearing.

This written request must be received by the Board no later than the morning of the day before the hearing and a copy should be sent to the other party(ies).

All parties should phone the Board no later than the afternoon of the day before the hearing to ensure that the written request was received, and that the hearing has in fact been rescheduled, and to what date, time and place.

In some cases, exceptional circumstances arise at the last moment (such as the death of a close family member) which prevent the party from meeting the procedures set out above. In such circumstances, the party should notify the Board by telephone as soon as they become aware of this, and inform the other party or their agent, as well. The case will remain on the list of hearings for the scheduled time, but the Member will be apprised of the telephone message and, if convinced that the circumstances are indeed exceptional, may adjourn the hearing without the party being present.

It may be necessary from time to time for the Board to reschedule a hearing on its own initiative. In such cases, the parties and their representatives will be notified.

WHEN PARTIAL MEDIATION IS ACHIEVED

When a Board Mediator assists the parties in mediation and a partial settlement is reached by the parties, an interim agreement may be signed by the parties. The parties to the interim agreement may agree to reschedule the hearing to a later date for a Member to determine the unresolved issues (see Rule 13.12).

Adjournments

PROCEDURAL ISSUES

If a party is unable to obtain consent to a rescheduling from the other parties in advance of the hearing date, the party or their agent must attend on the hearing date to request an adjournment from the Member. A request for an adjournment will normally be heard at the outset of the session for which the hearing is scheduled.

An adjournment is a procedural decision. If the request is made at the start of the hearing, the Member is not "seized" with the case, thus the same Member is not required to conduct the hearing on the adjourned date. However, if the request is made part way through a hearing, the Member will likely be seized with the case because they heard evidence. For instance, an applicant may discover that the respondent's case involves facts that they did not realize were going to be raised, and that evidence from a witness who is not present is necessary to counter the respondent's defence. In such a situation, the hearing must be adjourned to a time when the same Member can continue the hearing.

BALANCING RIGHTS BETWEEN THE PARTIES

Section 183 of the RTA states that the Board should be expeditious, but should ensure that the parties are given "an adequate opportunity to know the issues and to be heard on the matter." The key question becomes how to balance the rights of the parties to ensure that matters are resolved quickly while not sacrificing their rights to a fair hearing. The determining factors a Member will weigh are very different depending on whether the parties agree to adjourn, or one party's request to adjourn is contested by one or more other parties.

AGREEMENT TO ADJOURN

If the parties agree to adjourn the hearing, the Board will not interfere with this agreement in most circumstances. The hearing will be adjourned to a date set by the Board, although the parties may have an opportunity to offer some preferred dates.

However, sometimes the Member may decide it would not be in the public interest to proceed as the parties have arranged. Although the Member will not normally force the parties into a hearing immediately, the parties may be required to proceed on an earlier date than what was agreed upon.

CONSIDERATIONS WHERE THERE IS NO AGREEMENT

Parties are generally required to make themselves available to attend scheduled hearings by making whatever arrangements are necessary. The granting of adjournments is in the discretion of the Member hearing the application. However, if the parties cannot attend the scheduled hearing and are not able to reach an agreement regarding one party's wish to adjourn the hearing, the Member should weigh the prejudice that might be suffered by each party. The Member will consider the prejudice to a party having to appear repeatedly, without a good reason for having to do so. As discussed below, if a Member grants an adjournment, certain conditions may be imposed upon either party in order to alleviate the prejudice the other party may experience as a result of the adjournment.

Therefore, when appearing before the Member the parties should present specific reasons why they would be significantly prejudiced by an adjournment. For example, a delay may economically prejudice a party or may mean a lost opportunity. There may also be aggravating circumstances, such as an urgent need for certain repairs or the continued tenancy will be a threat to other tenants' safety.

The Member is also entitled to consider the conduct of the party opposing the adjournment. For example, if that party is the applicant, and they delayed serving the application until the last day permitted by the Rules, thus giving the respondent the minimum time contemplated, the request is more likely to be granted. Also, if the party opposing the request has shown bad faith or refused to provide information about their case to the respondent which would allow them to prepare quickly for the hearing, this should weigh in favour of an adjournment.

The Member must take into account the public interest in resolving the case as soon as possible. However, the public interest in an expeditious result is greater in some types of applications than in others. A claim for eviction because the tenant threatens the safety of the landlord or other tenants should be dealt with as swiftly as possible, as should a case in which the tenant claims there is ongoing harassment by the landlord or their staff.

ADJOURNMENT TO ALLOW REPRESENTATION

Section 10 of the *Statutory Powers Procedure Act* allows parties the right to be represented by a lawyer or agent at the hearing. However, the right to representation does not automatically guarantee an adjournment. Therefore, the onus is on a party notified of a hearing and wishing to be represented and to make all reasonable efforts to find a lawyer or agent able to represent them on the date on their Notice of Hearing. Nevertheless, a short adjournment may be allowed where a representative has been retained, but is unavailable on the date set for the hearing, or where the party can demonstrate that they have made reasonable efforts to retain a lawyer or agent before the hearing but have yet been unable to do so.

ADJOURNMENT TO PERMIT ANOTHER APPLICATION

A respondent may also request an adjournment because they have filed or will be filing an application against the applicant. This should merit an adjournment only if the respondent's application will affect the outcome of the application being considered.

ADJOURNMENT REQUESTS RESPECTING COURT PROCEEDINGS

Some parties seek adjournments on the basis that a Court will rule on a similar issue between other parties in the future. This would generally be an invalid reason for permitting a case to remain undecided for a long period: it would be preferable to proceed with the hearing.

ADJOURNMENT ON CONSENT FOR MEDIATION

A party sometimes hopes that a case may be settled, and that they need more time to resolve the issues with the other party. Although the Board encourages this, and in many cases offers mediation services, a hearing should not be delayed for this purpose, unless both parties agree.

ADJOURNMENT TO PREPARE CASE

A respondent may request an adjournment because they may not know the case they must answer. If the respondent demonstrates that the information about the applicant's claims is unclear or not detailed enough to allow them to know what evidence they must present at the hearing, this may justify an adjournment. In deciding whether the claim is sufficiently complete and clear, the Member should evaluate the application, documents filed with it and any information the respondent already had.

A party may request an adjournment to acquire evidence required to prove the facts of the case. It may be a respondent who makes this request because they have received the application too close to the hearing date (though technically "on time" according to the rules for giving applications). Also, any party who has become aware of the other party's intended evidence, and wishes to review or obtain their own evidence to refute their position may request an adjournment.

ADJOURNMENT TO PREPARE FOR SECTION 82

In an application by a landlord for rent arrears (section 87 of the RTA) or for termination of the tenancy for rent arrears (section 59 of RTA), section 82 permits tenants to raise any issue that could be raised in a tenant application under the RTA. Where the tenant raises issues under section 82 that the landlord could not reasonably have anticipated and cannot address at the hearing with a short recess, the landlord may request an adjournment to another date for the purpose of investigating the tenant's allegations and obtaining relevant evidence.

CONDITIONS FOR AN ADJOURNMENT

The Member may decide that a condition should be attached to the granting of an adjournment. Examples of some conditions that may be included:

- an adjournment may be given on the condition that the party requesting it will disclose to the other party(ies) some further information about their position or a copy of evidence that the party will present to the Board when the hearing resumes;
- in a case involving a claim for the payment of money, the Member may decide that a respondent requesting an adjournment should pay the amount claimed by the applicant, or a lesser sum, into the Board as security for the payment of any order which may result from the application, or may come due before the next hearing date (see section 195 of the RTA and Guideline 3, entitled "Costs");
- the adjournment will be granted on a "peremptory" basis, which means that no further adjournment requests will be granted to the party that requested the adjournment, except in the most exceptional circumstances or where the other party consents to the subsequent adjournment request;
- a party opposing the adjournment may ask for costs incurred resulting from the adjournment and any such costs will be considered pursuant to Guideline 3 (also see subsection 204(2) of the RTA).

Released Date: January 31, 2007

GUIDELINE 3: COSTS

Interpretation Guidelines are intended to assist the parties in understanding the Board's usual interpretation of the law, to provide guidance to Members and promote consistency in decision-making. However, a Member is not required to follow a Guideline and may make a different decision depending on the facts of the case.

Generally, when someone takes another person to court, they hope that they will collect from the other party some part of their expenses of the lawsuit. The Board has a discretionary power similar to that of the Courts to order "costs." The Board may order one of the parties to pay costs to another party or may order that the Board's costs be paid by a party, a paid agent or counsel to a party. However, the Board does not want to use its power to award costs in a way which would discourage landlords and tenants from exercising their statutory rights.

Subsections 2, 3 and 4 of section 204 of the *Residential Tenancies Act, 2006* (the "RTA") provide that:

(2) The Board may order a party to an application to pay the costs of another party.

(3) The Board may order that its costs of a proceeding be paid by a party or a paid agent or counsel to a party.

(4) The amount of an order for costs shall be determined in accordance with the Rules.

This Guideline sets out the Board's position on when it may be appropriate to order costs. Generally costs may be ordered where a party's conduct in the proceeding was unreasonable. Costs should not be confused with an administrative fine. An administrative fine is a remedy to be used by the Board to encourage compliance with the RTA and to deter landlords from engaging in similar activity in the future. For further information on administrative fines, see Guideline 16.

Submissions on Representation Costs and Board Costs

Before ordering a party to pay representation costs of another party or before ordering a party, agent or lawyer to pay the costs of the Board, a Member should ensure that the person who will be affected by the order for costs has an opportunity to make submissions on the matter.

However, if a party has received notice of a hearing and does not attend or if an agent or lawyer is on the record as representing a party and does not attend a hearing, a Member may proceed to make an order for costs without notifying the person affected of the intention to do so, provided that the failure to attend the hearing delayed the process unnecessarily or caused unnecessary expense to the other party.

Ordering Costs Against a Party or a Paid Representative

COSTS ORDERED IN MOST CASES

In most cases, the only costs allowed will be the application fee. This should be ordered if the applicant is successful in obtaining an order which allows the relief they asked for in the application, or substantially all of that relief. This includes cases which are resolved by an order based on an application for which no notice is required (section 77 of the RTA). Where appropriate, this cost will be ordered regardless of whether or not the applicant seeks such a remedy.

It is anticipated that return of the application fee will not usually be ordered in the situations listed below:

1. Applications to increase rents above the guideline; such applications involve many respondents and it would be impractical to order costs in these cases.
2. Applications to evict tenants based on their own notice or agreement to terminate where the application is made before the date of termination.
3. Applications to evict a tenant based on a no-fault ground (e.g., a landlord application for termination of the tenancy for the landlord's own use).

OTHER COSTS

A party who wants to claim costs in addition to the application fee should be prepared to speak to the matter and to provide support for the claim. The other party will also be allowed to make submissions on the issue.

In most cases, costs should not be allowed for the other expenses incurred by the successful party such as travel, expert reports, etc. Neither the fees of a representative for preparation time, nor hearing time, should be allowed except in the circumstances set out below.

FURTHER COSTS WHERE A PARTY'S CONDUCT IS UNREASONABLE

A Member has the discretion to require a party to pay, as costs, any representation or preparation expenses of another party where the conduct of the party was unreasonable. Conduct is unreasonable if it causes undue expense or delay and includes the following:

1. Bringing a frivolous or vexatious application or motion
2. Initiating an application or any procedure in bad faith
3. Taking unnecessary steps in a proceeding
4. Failing to take necessary steps, such as those required by the RTA or Rules
5. Any misconduct at the hearing or in the proceeding
6. Raising an issue which is irrelevant to the proceedings and continuing to pursue that issue after the Member has pointed out that it is irrelevant
7. Asking for adjournments or delays without justification
8. Failing to prepare adequately for the hearing
9. Acting contemptuously toward the Member or showing a lack of respect for the process or the Board
10. Failing to follow the directions of the Member or upsetting the orderly conduct of the hearing
11. Unreasonably maligning another party or slurring the character of the other party

Examples of failing to comply with the RTA or Rules would include the following situations:

- Failing to follow a procedural order or direction such as an order to serve another party with a document
- Serving another party in a way which was not appropriate
- Delaying the hearing by not taking actions required in the Rules

The amount ordered by a Member will usually be less than the actual cost since the Rules will set out maximum amounts for the Member to consider.

Generally, only fees for a representative's time spent at the hearing will be allowed. However, in some cases, a further amount for preparation time may be allowed if the unreasonable conduct led to the need for the representative to spend additional time preparing for the hearing.

Representation fees should not be allowed if the representative did not conduct themselves in a professional manner.

Generally speaking, the Member may refuse to allow representation fees if the conduct of the representative does not demonstrate an understanding of the following:

- Legislation, Regulations, Rules and Guidelines
- The position of their client
- The role of an agent appearing before a quasi-judicial Board
- Standards of proper behaviour and conduct in a hearing

FURTHER COSTS WHERE THE CONDUCT OF THE PAID REPRESENTATIVE OF A PARTY IS UNREASONABLE

A Member has the discretion to order a party to pay costs to another party where the conduct of the party's representative was unreasonable. Conduct is unreasonable if it causes undue expense or delay and includes situations listed above under the heading "Further Costs Where a Party's Conduct is Unreasonable." Unreasonable conduct may also include displaying an inadequate knowledge of the RTA and other relevant legislation.

In addition to making an award of costs, the Board may exclude from a hearing any person, other than a lawyer qualified to practice in Ontario, appearing as an agent on behalf of a party if it is found that the agent is not competent to properly represent or advise the party or does not understand and comply at the hearing with the duties and responsibilities of an advocate and adviser.

CASES WHERE COSTS SHOULD NOT BE ALLOWED

As a general principle, a Member should not order costs of any kind in favour of a party if the conduct of that party was not proper. For example, if the applicant was responsible for an adjournment because they were not prepared, the Member might decide that they should not be awarded any costs. If both parties were responsible for unreasonable conduct, neither should be ordered to pay the costs to the other, although one or both may be ordered to pay the Board costs.

AMOUNT OF COSTS

Rule 27 of the Board's Rules of Practice sets out the criteria for Members to consider when determining the amount of costs to order.

ORDERING THE BOARD'S COSTS

The Board expects parties and their paid representatives to act reasonably in pursuing their applications or defending their positions. This includes bringing applications only when there are substantial grounds. It also includes taking all required procedural steps, not taking unnecessary ones and acting in a courteous and orderly way at a hearing.

When a party or a paid representative acts improperly or unreasonably in a proceeding, the Board may order the party or their paid representative to pay to the Board an amount that will partly cover the expenses that the Board has incurred as a result of that conduct. If the unreasonable conduct was the fault of the party's representative, the Board will normally order that the paid representative pay the Board's costs.

Pursuant to section 196 and Rule 9, failure to pay costs ordered may result in the Board refusing to allow the filing of an application; a stay in proceedings; a delay in the issuance of an order; and/or a discontinuance of the proceeding. See Rule 9 "Refusing to Accept or Proceed with an Application" for further details.

GENERAL APPROACH

A Member has the discretion to order a party or a paid representative to pay the costs of the Board. This power, however, should be used sparingly. It was not the intent of the Legislature that this power should ever be used to obtain cost recovery for salaries, administration or other expenses of the Board.

In those rare situations in which a party or their representative is responsible for unreasonable conduct, this power allows the Board to accomplish two objectives:

1. Recover some of the taxpayers' monies which funded the proceedings, and,
2. Discourage inappropriate practices and conduct by parties and their representatives.

An award of Board costs is appropriate in cases in which the adjudicative costs to the public have been unjustifiably increased by the unreasonable conduct or omission of a party or their agent or lawyer.

Unreasonable conduct would include the situations listed above under the headings "Further Costs Where a Party's Conduct is Unreasonable" and "Further Costs Where the Conduct of the Paid Representative of a Party is Unreasonable."

Ordering Board costs is not related to which party is successful. Since the reason such costs are awarded is to encourage proper conduct, it is conceivable that a successful party who adds unnecessary steps to the proceeding or behaves inappropriately at a hearing, may have to pay the Board's expenses for part of the proceeding.

The discretion for a Member to order Board costs to be paid by an agent or lawyer would only be used where, on the balance of probabilities, it is the behaviour of the agent or lawyer and not the client which is in issue.

ORDERING PARTY COSTS AND BOARD COSTS

An order for a party to pay both the representation/preparation fees of another party and to pay the Board's costs in the same case would only be made in exceptional circumstances.

This would usually include the following:

- A case in which a party clearly and knowingly misled the Board, such as filing an inflated claim for arrears, a false certificate of service, or an altered invoice
- A case where a party was reckless or indifferent about the truthfulness of their evidence, such as stating that the other party did not serve a document which they know they received
- Situations in which the party failed to comply with directions from the Member about the orderly conduct of the hearing

- Evidence of harassment of the other party to prevent the application or defence of the application

Generally, if the party who would pay the costs has been unsuccessful, it is more appropriate to order them to pay costs to the successful party. If the party whose conduct was unreasonable was the successful party, they should be ordered to pay Board costs.

Released Date: January 31, 2007

Source: Ontario Landlord and Tenant Board website, www.ltb.gov.on.ca/en/Law/STEL02_111691.html.

Selected Landlord and Tenant Board Brochures

IMPORTANT INFORMATION ABOUT YOUR HEARING

THE LANDLORD AND TENANT BOARD

The *Residential Tenancies Act* has rules for landlords and tenants to follow. If one side thinks the other side has not followed these rules, they can file an application with the **Landlord and Tenant Board**.

WHY A HEARING IS HELD

When an application is filed, the Board will schedule a hearing. The Board holds a hearing to consider the application made by a landlord or tenant.

The person who made the application will try to show why the application should be granted, and the other persons who are affected by the application can respond and try to show why it should not be granted.

The person in charge of the hearing is called a Member of the Board. The Member will listen to what each person has to say and then make a decision about the application.

PEOPLE AT THE HEARING

A Board **Member** will be at your hearing. The Member is in charge of the hearing.

The person who filed the application is called the **applicant**. The applicant or their representative must come to the hearing. If they do not, their application may be dismissed.

The other person named in the application is called the **respondent**. They are also given notice to come to the hearing. If the respondent, or their representative, do not come, a decision can be made without them.

The applicant and the respondent are called **parties** to the application. In most cases, this is the landlord and tenant. In some cases, there may be more than one landlord or more than one tenant.

If a party has a **witness or witnesses** who can tell the Member something about the situation, then they will also be in the hearing room for some or all of the hearing.

TYPES OF HEARINGS

There are four different types of hearings:

- an **oral** hearing, where the applicant and respondent appear in person before a Member (this is the most common type of hearing),
- a **video conference** hearing, where the hearing takes place using a video link between the Member and the parties,

- a **telephone** hearing, where the hearing takes place using a telephone link between the Member and the parties, or
- a **written** hearing, where the parties file written documents, instead of appearing in person.

The Board will decide which type of hearing you will have.

HEARING DATE AND TIME

When an application is filed, the Board will give the applicant a copy of the Notice of Hearing.

The applicant must give a copy of the application and the Notice of Hearing to all of the other parties before the hearing date.

The Notice of Hearing tells you the time, date, and location of your hearing, or if a written hearing will be held, it tells you the deadlines for filing documents with the Board.

You should arrive at your hearing 30 minutes before the actual start time so that you have time to sign in, locate your hearing room and organize yourself for the hearing. If you are late, the Board can decide to hold the hearing or make a decision about the application without you.

LENGTH OF THE HEARING

Every hearing takes a different amount of time. The length of your hearing may depend on things like: who appears at the hearing, the issues that are being talked about, the evidence that is being presented, and so forth.

There are usually several hearings booked on the same day and time as yours. Everyone is asked to come at the same time. The Board Member will decide the order in which each application will be heard that day.

You should not be late to your hearing because if you are, the application may be heard without you. At the same time, you may have to wait several hours for your case to be called. You should plan to be at your hearing for the entire day, just in case your hearing is called later in the day.

What to Do Before the Hearing

DECIDE IF YOU WANT TO HAVE A REPRESENTATIVE AT THE HEARING

Parties can represent themselves at the hearing, or they can have someone else (called an **agent**) represent them. An agent can be a lawyer, a paralegal, a friend or a relative.

If you have anyone other than a lawyer represent you, you must give the Board your written permission to have that person represent you.

MAKE COPIES OF ANY EVIDENCE

If you want to give any evidence at the hearing, such as a document or a picture, you should bring three copies—one for the Member, one for the other side and one for you.

ARRANGE FOR ANY WITNESSES TO COME

If you have witnesses that you want at the hearing, you must arrange for them to come.

If you think your witness will come to the hearing if you ask them to, then ask them to come. Make sure they know when and where the hearing will take place.

If you are not sure if a witness will come if asked, you can ask the Board to issue a **summons**. A summons is a legal document that tells that person to go to the hearing.

If you think a summons may be needed, you should contact the Board well in advance of your hearing for more information.

The Board also has a **Summons** brochure that you should read. It tells you important information you will need to know.

IF YOU CANNOT COME TO THE HEARING

A hearing before the Board is an important legal matter. It is important that you attend.

If you know before your hearing date that you cannot come to the hearing:

You can ...	If you do, ...
Ask a person to go to the hearing and represent you.	▪ and that person is someone other than a lawyer, they must have your written permission to represent you. You must also give them all of the information they will need to go ahead with the hearing.
Ask all of the other parties *before* the hearing date if they will agree to set a new hearing date.	▪ and if they agree, you must file a letter with the Board no later than noon the day before your hearing. The letter must have the application file number and say that all of the parties agree that a new hearing date can be set. ▪ and all of the other parties do *not* agree, then you cannot do this.
You or your representative can attend the hearing and ask for the hearing to be adjourned.	▪ you or your representative must explain why you cannot go ahead with your hearing that day. Note: If the Member does not allow the adjournment request, the hearing will happen that day.

REQUEST FRENCH LANGUAGE SERVICES

The Board will have French language services at your hearing if:

- a party asks for it, or if the application is filed in French, *and*
- if the address of the rental unit, or the address of the party is located in an area designated by the *French Language Services Act.*

If you are in a designated area and need French language services at your hearing, you should tell the Board as soon as possible. The Board will provide a French interpreter at the hearing.

The Board will not translate or pay for the translation of documents that have been filed.

Note: The Board does not provide interpreters at the hearing for languages other than French. If you cannot communicate with the Member or other parties in English, or French in a designated area, it is your responsibility to bring someone to the hearing to be your interpreter.

REQUEST SIGN LANGUAGE AND OTHER SERVICES

The Board will arrange and pay for the services of a sign language interpreter for a party who has a hearing disability. If you need a sign language interpreter, you should make a written request to the Board as soon as possible.

If you have any other special needs, please contact the Board as quickly as possible to see if arrangements can be made to accommodate them.

On the Hearing Day

THE HEARING PROCESS

Note: *The following describes the standard process for an oral, video conference or telephone hearing. If you have a written hearing, you will be given instructions in the Notice of Hearing.*

First, the applicant tells their side:

At the hearing, the applicant tells why they made the application and gives any evidence they have to back up those reasons. He or she may give evidence, or call witnesses to give evidence. The applicant should give the Member and the respondent a copy of any documents they have brought to the hearing.

The respondent can ask them questions:

When the applicant and their witnesses have finished, the respondent can ask them questions. The reason for asking questions is to clarify something they said, to get more details, or to show that an error may have been made—it is not to argue with them.

Then, the respondent tells their side:

The respondent then tells their side and gives any evidence they have to back up what they have said. They can also call witnesses to give evidence. The respondent should give the Member and the applicant a copy of any documents they have brought to the hearing.

The applicant can ask them questions:

When the respondent and their witnesses have finished, the applicant can ask them questions.

The Member may also ask questions:

The Board Member can also ask questions of any party or their witnesses at any time during the hearing.

Then, each side sums up their case:

After both sides have finished, each side makes a final statement to sum up their evidence, and give their view of the other parties' evidence. Each party can tell the Member what decision they think should be made based on the evidence given during the hearing.

The Member decides:

The Member will make the final decision about the application.

In some cases, the Member will announce their decision at the end of the hearing. However, in most cases, the Member will need more time to make a decision. Either way, the Member's decision will always be put in writing (this written decision is called an **order**). A copy of the order will be mailed to all of the parties.

TENANT CAN RAISE OTHER ISSUES ON AN APPLICATION INVOLVING ARREARS OF RENT

If the landlord files either:

- an Application to Terminate the Tenancy for Non-Payment of Rent (Form L1), or
- an Application for Arrears of Rent (Form L9)

the tenant can raise issues at the hearing that they could have raised had they filed their own application—such as maintenance concerns, illegal charges, etc.

For more information on this topic, see the separate brochure on *Issues a Tenant Can Raise at a Hearing about a Landlord's Application for Non-payment of Rent (Form L1 or L9)*. A copy of this brochure is available from the Board.

MEDIATION SERVICES

Mediation is a service that is offered by the Board. In mediation, a Board Mediator talks to the parties to see if they can come to an agreement to settle some or all of the issues in the application. If all of the issues are settled, a hearing does not need to be held.

Mediation is voluntary, which means that all of the parties have to want to try it. Mediation is offered for most types of applications.

If you do try mediation and you do not settle the application, your hearing will take place as scheduled. At your hearing, you cannot talk about what was said in mediation, because mediation is confidential.

TENANT DUTY COUNSEL SERVICES

Tenant Duty Counsel is a service for tenants. This service is independent of the Landlord and Tenant Board.

Tenant Duty Counsel is a lawyer or other legal professional who helps tenants on the day of their hearing by providing them with basic legal advice and information.

Tenants do not need an appointment to speak with Tenant Duty Counsel and Tenant Duty Counsel do not make appointments to speak with tenants. Tenants should come to their hearing *before* the start time if they want to meet with Tenant Duty Counsel. Tenant Duty Counsel gives priority to tenants with eviction hearings.

If you are speaking with Tenant Duty Counsel when your hearing is scheduled to begin, you must go to the hearing room and tell the Member. If you do not, your hearing may proceed without you. Tenant Duty Counsel is *not* always available at all hearing locations on all hearing days.

For More Information

CONTACT THE BOARD

This brochure provides general information only. For more information, or to obtain copies of the Board's forms and publications, you may:

- visit the Board's website at www.LTB.gov.on.ca,
- call the Board at 416-645-8080 or toll-free at 1-888-332-3234, or
- visit your local Landlord and Tenant Board office. A list of Board office locations can be found on our website, or you may call us at the numbers listed above.

Release date: January 31, 2007

Source: Ontario Landlord and Tenant Board website, www.ltb.gov.on.ca/en/Key_Information/STEL02_111563.html.

RULES FOR REPRESENTATIVES INVOLVED IN BOARD APPLICATIONS

INTRODUCTION

For many years, lawyers in Ontario have had to be members of the Law Society of Upper Canada (the Law Society) to be allowed to represent parties and act on their behalf before Ontario's Courts.

As of May 1, 2008, the Law Society put rules in place for other types of representatives. These rules affect representatives, other than lawyers, who represent parties in applications made to Ontario's Courts, Tribunals and Boards—including the Landlord and Tenant Board (the Board).

The rules mean that most people acting as *paid* representatives before the Board will have to be licensed. However, the rules also allow some unlicensed people to be representatives before the Board.

People Who Don't Need a License

PARTIES CAN REPRESENT THEMSELVES

The Law Society's rules apply to *representatives*; they do *not* apply to the parties to a Board application. (Parties are usually landlords or tenants.) Parties can choose to represent themselves—they do *not* have to ask someone to be their representative for a Board application unless they want to. Parties who choose to represent themselves on a Board application do *not* need to be licensed.

FRIENDS AND FAMILY MEMBERS MAY BE REPRESENTATIVES

The Law Society's rules about representatives allow some people to be representatives even though they are *not* licensed. For example, if you are a party to a Board application and you want an unlicensed family member or a friend to act as your *unpaid* representative, this is all right—provided you give them written permission to be your representative.

OTHER PEOPLE WHO DON'T NEED A LICENSE

In addition to unpaid family and friends, the *Law Society Act* allows other people to act as representatives without having a license. Some of the people who do not need a license to be a representative are:

- articling students,
- employees of legal clinics, and
- people who work for only one employer and only provide legal services for or on behalf of that employer.

On their website, the Law Society has the complete list of the types of people who do *not* need a license to represent someone.

WRITTEN PERMISSION TO BE YOUR REPRESENTATIVE

If the representative you choose is *not* a licensed representative, you must give them written permission to be your representative and act on your behalf. This written permission, also known as an agency authorization, must be signed by you and it must be provided to the Board before, or at your hearing.

If the Board believes that an agency authorization is required and a representative doesn't have one, they may not be allowed to act on your behalf before the Board, and this could delay resolving the application.

People Who Must Be Licensed by the Law Society

PARALEGALS MUST BE LICENSED

As of May 1, 2008, representatives, unless otherwise exempt, who are hired and *paid* by landlords or tenants to act on their behalf in an application to the Board must be licensed. These representatives, known as paralegals, have written a test and have met other qualifications set out by the Law Society. They are now licensed by the Law Society—similar to the way lawyers are licensed in Ontario.

Status Under the Law Society Act

THE BOARD MAY ASK ABOUT A REPRESENTATIVE

Board Members and Mediators may ask about a representative's *status* under the *Law Society Act*—that is, whether or not the representative is licensed under the *Law Society Act.*

- If the representative says that they are licensed, they may be asked to provide their licensing number.
- If the representative says that they don't need a license, they may be asked to tell why they think that they don't need a license to represent a party before the Board.

For More Information

ABOUT THE LAW SOCIETY'S RULES

If you think you need to know more about the Law Society's rules such as the licensing requirements for paralegals, or about representatives who do not need a license, you should visit the Law Society's website at www.lsuc.on.ca/paralegals/ or call them toll-free at 1-800-668-7380, or at 416-947-3315 from the GTA calling area.

ABOUT THE LANDLORD AND TENANT BOARD

This brochure provides general information only. For more information or to obtain copies of the Board's forms and publications, you can:

- call the Board at 416-645-8080 or toll-free at 1-888-332-3234, or
- visit your local Landlord and Tenant Board office. For a list of Board office locations visit the Board's website, or call the numbers listed above.

Release date: July 25, 2008

Source: Ontario Landlord and Tenant Board website, www.ltb.gov.on.ca/en/Key_Information/249649.html.

Glossary

administrative tribunal: quasi-judicial body dealing with matters under a specific statute

advocacy: process of presenting a case or defence at a trial or hearing

advocate: person who pleads the cause of another before a court or tribunal

applicant: party who files an application with a tribunal

application: document filed by an applicant that starts a proceeding at a tribunal

book of authorities: book containing a copy of each case and statutory provision relied on for a trial or hearing

closing argument: summary of a party's case, including a discussion of the relevant law

corroborate: confirm or support with additional evidence

costs: monetary award made to the successful party for fees and expenses incurred in the conduct of a case

cross-examination: questioning of a witness by the advocate of the party who did not call the witness

defence: document filed in court setting out the nature of the defendant's position

defendant: person against whom relief is sought in an action

direct examination: questioning of a witness by the advocate of the party who called that witness

endorse: make a note of the decision

exhibit: object introduced as evidence at a trial or hearing

exhibit list: list setting out the number and a brief description of each exhibit as it is entered into evidence

expert witness: a person who, because of education, skill, or experience, has more knowledge than the average person about a particular subject matter

hearsay: evidence that repeats what the witness has heard others say

law of evidence: way in which the facts are to be proved, as required by substantive law

leading question: question that suggests a desired answer or that assumes a fact in dispute that has not yet been proven

notice of hearing: tribunal document served on a respondent along with an application

notice of intention to appear: form to be filed by the defendant with the provincial offences office notifying of the defendant's intention to dispute the charge

objection: statement directed to the decision-maker that a question asked, an answer given, or an object introduced by the opposing party is improper

offence notice: document that starts some types of provincial offence processes

plaintiff: person who brings a civil action against another

plaintiff's claim: document filed in court setting out the plaintiff's case against the defendant

plea bargain: negotiate a resolution to the matter

pleadings: court documents setting out the nature of the plaintiff's and defendant's cases

post-judgment interest: interest on the amount awarded calculated from the date of judgment to the date payment is made

pre-judgment interest: interest on the amount awarded calculated from the date the cause of action arose to the date of judgment

procedural law: law that deals with the way a dispute comes to a court or tribunal and then continues to its final resolution

provincial offences: quasi-criminal offences arising under provincial statutes

re-examination: questioning of a witness by the advocate of the party who called the witness after the opposing advocate has cross-examined

reply: plaintiff's opportunity to respond to new matters raised by the defendant

respondent: party against whom an applicant files an application with a tribunal

sentence: penalty imposed for an offence

serve: provide a copy of a party's court or tribunal documents to the opposite party

settlement conference: informal and confidential meeting during which the parties try to resolve or simplify issues in dispute

substantive law: legal rights and obligations

summons: document that initiates some types of provincial offence processes; demand issued by the court or tribunal compelling a witness's attendance

theme: brief theory of a case (one or two sentences)

trial or hearing notebook: notebook prepared and used by each party, containing all important information needed at the trial or hearing in a secure and organized format

Index